THE LEGAL SYSTEM OF ISRAEL

THE
LEGAL SYSTEM
OF ISRAEL

BY

HENRY E. BAKER

M.A., B.C.L. (Oxon.), LL.B. (Lond.)
President, District Court, Jerusalem
Research Fellow, Hebrew University, Jerusalem

ISRAEL UNIVERSITIES PRESS

JERUSALEM · LONDON · NEW YORK, 1968

ISRAEL UNIVERSITIES PRESS
is a publishing division of the
ISRAEL PROGRAM FOR SCIENTIFIC TRANSLATIONS
Kiryat Moshe, P. O. Box 7145, Jerusalem, Israel

IPST Cat. no. 2604

The present book is a completely revised and updated edition
of the first edition published in 1961, since out of print.

This book has been composed in Monophoto Bembo at IPST
printed by S. Monson and bound by Wiener Bindery Ltd.,
Jerusalem, Israel, 1968.

PREFACE

This book describes the legal system of Israel as it was in mid-December, 1967, six months after the cease fire in the Six Day War (June 5-10, 1967) and six months before the twentieth anniversary of the establishment of the State (May 15, 1968). The text is in a continuous narrative form without any footnotes to distract the attention of the reader and explains systematically and in detail the provisions of Israel law in all its important branches and describes what the Israel legislature, known as the Knesset, has done so far in order to replace the heterogeneous body of Israel law, derived from various systems of law written originally in four languages—Turkish, Arabic, French and English—by a homogeneous body of law written in one language—Hebrew, the language of the Bible and of a vast legal literature—and suited to the needs of a modern progressive state.

After the completion of the text of this book, the Knesset passed an amendment to the Chamber of Advocates Law (see pp. 232 — 3), which came into force on December 22, 1967, and provides, *inter alia*, that the seat of the Israel Chamber of Advocates shall be in Jerusalem, which is also, by law, the seat of the Knesset (see p. 27), the President of the State (see p. 13), and the Supreme Court of Israel (see p. 201), and it also passed the the Obsolete Enactments Repeal Law, which came into force on December 27, 1967 and repealed, *inter alia*, the Animal Tax Ordinance, 1944 (see p. 144) and the Trade Boards Ordinance, 1945 (see p. 132).

While this book is primarily intended for readers outside of Israel, both lawyers and laymen, it is hoped that it will be found useful and of interest to readers in Israel who wish to have a comprehensive and completely up to date survey of the legal system of Israel and at the same time, if necessary, to learn, or improve their knowledge of, legal English.

Henry E. Baker   Jerusalem January 1, 1968

CONTENTS

Declaration of the Establishment of the State (in Hebrew) kept in the State Archives in Jerusalem. An English translation follows on the next page.

DECLARATION OF THE ESTABLISHMENT
OF THE STATE OF ISRAEL

ERETZ-ISRAEL (Land of Israel) was the birthplace of the Jewish people. Here their spiritual, religious and political identity was shaped. Here they first attained statehood, created cultural values of national and universal significance and gave to the world the eternal Book of Books.

After being forcibly exiled from their land, the people kept faith with it throughout their Dispersion and never ceased to pray and hope for their return to it and for the restoration in it of their political freedom.

Impelled by this historic and traditional attachment, Jews strove in every successive generation to re-establish themselves in their ancient homeland. In recent decades they returned in their masses. Pioneers, immigrants and defenders, they made deserts bloom, revived the Hebrew language, built villages and towns, and created a thriving community, controlling its own economy and culture, loving peace but knowing how to defend itself, bringing the blessings of progress to all the country's inhabitants, and aspiring towards independent nationhood.

In the year 5657 (1897), at the summons of the spiritual father of the Jewish State, Theodor Herzl, the First Zionist Congress convened and proclaimed the right of the Jewish people to national rebirth in its own country.

This right was recognised in the Balfour Declaration of the 2nd November, 1917, and re-affirmed in the Mandate of the League of Nations which, in particular, gave international sanction to the historic connection between the Jewish people and Eretz-Israel and to the right of the Jewish people to rebuild its National Home.

The catastrophe which recently befell the Jewish people— the massacre of millions of Jews in Europe—was another clear demonstration of the urgency of solving the problem of its homelessness by re-establishing in Eretz Israel the Jewish State, which would open wide to every Jew the gates of the homeland and confer upon the Jewish people the status of a fully-privileged member of the family of nations.

Survivors of the Nazi holocaust in Europe, as well as Jews from other parts of the world, continued to immigrate to Israel, undaunted by difficulties, restrictions and dangers, and never ceased to assert their right to a life of dignity, freedom and honest toil in their national homeland.

In the Second World War, the Jewish community of this country contributed its full share to the struggle of freedom- and peace-loving nations against the forces of Nazi wickedness and, by the blood of its soldiers and its war effort, gained the right to be reckoned among the peoples who founded the United Nations.

On the 29th November, 1947, the United Nations General Assembly passed a resolution calling for the establishment of a Jewish State in Eretz-Israel; the General Assembly required the inhabitants of Eretz-Israel to take such steps as were necessary on their part for the implementation of that resolution. This recognition by the United Nations of the right of the Jewish people to establish their State is irrevocable.

This right is the natural right of the Jewish people to be masters of their own fate, like all other nations, in their own sovereign State.

ACCORDINGLY WE, MEMBERS OF THE PEOPLE'S COUNCIL, REPRE-SENTATIVES OF THE JEWISH COMMUNITY OF ERETZ-ISRAEL AND OF THE ZIONIST MOVEMENT, ARE HERE ASSEMBLED ON THE DAY OF THE TERMINATION OF THE BRITISH MANDATE OVER ERETZ-ISRAEL AND, BY VIRTUE OF OUR NATURAL AND HISTORIC RIGHT AND ON THE STRENGTH OF THE RESOLUTION OF THE UNITED NATIONS GENERAL ASSEMBLY, HEREBY DECLARE THE ESTABLISHMENT OF A JEWISH STATE IN ERETZ-ISRAEL, TO BE KNOWN AS THE STATE OF ISRAEL.

WE DECLARE that, with effect from the moment of the termination of the Mandate, being tonight, the eve of Sabbath, the 6th Iyar, 5708 (15th May, 1948), until the establishment of the elected, regular authorities of the State in accordance with the Constitution which shall be adopted by the Elected Constituent Assembly not later than the 1st October, 1948, the People's Council shall act as a Provisional Council of State, and its executive organ, the People's Administration, shall be the Provisional Government of the Jewish State, to be called 'Israel'.

THE STATE OF ISRAEL will be open for Jewish immigration and for the Ingathering of the Exiles; it will foster the development of the country for the benefit of all its inhabitants; it will be based on freedom, justice and peace as envisaged by the prophets of Israel; it will ensure complete equality of social and political rights to all its inhabitants irrespective of religion, race or sex; it will guarantee freedom of religion, conscience, language, education and culture; it will safeguard the Holy Places of all religions; and it will be faithful to the principles of the Charter of the United Nations.

THE STATE OF ISRAEL is prepared to cooperate with the agencies and representatives of the United Nations in implementing the resolution of the General Assembly of the 29th November, 1947, and will take steps to bring about the economic union of the whole of Eretz-Israel.

WE APPEAL to the United Nations to assist the Jewish people in the upbuilding of its State and to receive the State of Israel into the family of nations.

WE APPEAL—in the very midst of the onslaught launched against us now for months—to the Arab inhabitants of the State of Israel to preserve peace and participate in the upbuilding of the State on the basis of full and equal citizenship and due representation in all its provisional and permanent institutions.

WE EXTEND our hand to all neighbouring states and their peoples in an offer of peace and good neighbourliness, and appeal to them to establish bonds of cooperation and mutual help with the sovereign Jewish people settled in its own land. The State of Israel is prepared to do its share in a common effort for the advancement of the entire Middle East.

WE APPEAL to the Jewish people throughout the Diaspora to rally round the Jews of Eretz-Israel in the tasks of immigration and upbuilding and to stand by them in the great struggle for the realization of the age-old dream—the redemption of Israel

PLACING OUR TRUST IN THE ALMIGHTY, WE AFFIX OUR SIGNA-TURES TO THIS PROCLAMATION AT THIS SESSION OF THE PROVISIONAL COUNCIL OF STATE, ON THE SOIL OF THE HOMELAND, IN THE CITY OF TEL-AVIV, ON THIS SABBATH EVE, THE 5TH DAY OF IYAR, 5708 (14TH MAY, 1948).

David Ben-Gurion	Herzl Vardi	David Zvi Pinkas
Daniel Auster	Rachel Cohen	Aharon Zisling
Mordekhai Bentov	Rabbi Kalman Kahana	Moshe Kolodny
Yitzchak Ben Zvi	Saadia Kobashi	Eliezer Kaplan
Eliyahu Berligne	Rabbi Yitzchak Meir	Abraham Katznelson
Fritz Bernstein	Levin	Felix Rosenblueth
Rabbi Wolf Gold	Meir David Loewenstein	David Remez
Meir Grabovsky	Zvi Luria	Berl Repetur
Yitzchak Gruenbaum	Golda Myerson	Mordekhai Shattner
Dr. Abraham Granovsky	Nachum Nir	Ben Zion Sternberg
Eliyahu Dobkin	Zvi Segal	Behor Shitreet
Meir Wilner-Kovner	Rabbi Yehuda Leib	Moshe Shapira
Zerach Wahrhaftig	Hacohen Fishman	Moshe Shertok

REMEMBRANCE DAY

THE REMEMBRANCE Day for the Fallen of the War of Liberation and the Defence Army of Israel Law, 5723–1963, which came into force on the 5th April, 1963, proclaims the fourth day of Iyar as Remembrance Day, and provides that on that day a two minutes silence shall be observed throughout the country, memorial meetings shall be held and the broadcast programmes shall express the special purpose of the day, and the Minister of Defence is empowered, in consultation with the Public Advisory Council appointed for the purposes of the Military Cemeteries Law, 5710–1950, to give directions for the observance of the day in accordance with the Law.

ESTABLISHMENT OF THE STATE

The Proclamation

ON THE 14th May, 1948, when His Britannic Majesty relinquished the Mandate over Palestine, the Declaration of Independence, proclaiming the establishment of the State of Israel, was issued by a body of thirty-seven persons representative of the Yishuv (Jewish community in Palestine) and the Zionist movement. This body, which was known as 'Moetzet Ha-am' (National Council), declared that, on the termination of the Mandate and until elected and permanent authorities of the State had been set up in accordance with a constitution to be adopted by the elected Constituent Assembly not later than the 1st October, 1948, it would act as Provisional Council of State, and that its executive organ, known as 'Minhelet Ha-am' (National Executive), would constitute the Provisional Government of the newly created Jewish State of Israel.

On the same day the Provisional Council of State issued a Proclamation proclaiming itself to be the legislative authority, repealing the provisions of laws emanating from the British Government White Paper of 1939 and, in particular, the severe provisions regarding illegal immigration and restrictions on land transfers to Jews. The Proclamation also declared that as long as no laws were passed by, or with the authority of, the Provisional Council of State, the law in force in Palestine on the 14th May, 1948 should be in force in the State of Israel, in so far as was consistent with the provisions of the Proclamation, with any future laws, and with the modifications emanating from the establishment of the State and its authorities.

For nine months, from the 14th May, 1948 until the 14th February, 1949, when it was replaced by the First Knesset, the Provisional Council of State was the supreme legislature of the State of Israel.

LAW AND ADMINISTRATION ORDINANCE,

5708 — 1948

THE FIRST law to be enacted by the Provisional Council of State was the Law and Administration Ordinance, 5708—1948, which was passed on the 19th May, 1948, with retroactive effect from the 15th May, 1948.

Amplifying and interpreting the Proclamation of the 14th May, 1948, the Law and Administration Ordinance, 5708—1948, prescribed the composition and functions of the Provisional Council of State and of the Provisional Government and its Ministers, and declared that the municipal councils, local councils and the remaining local authorities should continue to function within the limits of their jurisdiction and the scope of their authority. It also declared that the law obtaining in Palestine on the 14th May, 1948, should continue in force, in so far as it was not in conflict with that Ordinance or any other law enacted by, or on behalf of, the Provisional Council of State, and with such modifications as emanated from the establishment of the State and its authorities, and that, so long as no new law was enacted concerning the Courts, the Courts in the territory of the State should continue to function within the scope of the powers conferred upon them by law.

The Law and Administration Ordinance Amendment Law (No. 11), 5727–1967, which came into force on the 27th June, 1967, adds a new section (section 11 B), to the Ordinance whereunder 'the law, jurisdiction and administration of the State shall apply in every area of Eretz Israel (Palestine) which the Government prescribes by order'.

On the 28th June, 1967 the Government made an order prescribing the area of the Old City of Jerusalem and certain neighbouring villages and areas specified in a Schedule to the order for the purposes of the said section 11 B.

The Ordinance also provided for emergency legislation. If the Provisional Council of State declared that a state of emergency existed in the State, the Provisional Government was authorised to empower the Head of the Government or any of the Ministers, to make Emergency Regulations to such an extent as he considered desirable for the defence of the State, public security and the maintenance of supplies and essential services. Such Emergency Regulations could amend any law, temporarily suspend its operation, or modify it, and were to cease to have effect at the expiration of three months from the date upon which they were made, unless before that date their period of validity was extended or they were repealed by the Minister who made them, or by an Ordinance of the Provisional Council of State. Immediately after passing the Ordinance, the Provisional Council of State issued a declaration that a state of emergency existed in Israel, and that declaration is still in force.

During the nine months of its existence as the legislature of Israel, the Provisional Council of State enacted 98 Ordinances, and the various Ministers made 34 sets of Emergency Regulations. Generally speaking, the Emergency Regulations were reenacted, with certain modifications, in the form of Ordinances by the Provisional Council of State.

On the 18th November, 1948, ten days after a census of the population had been taken, the Provisional Council of State passed an Ordinance providing for the holding of elections to the Constituent Assembly composed of 120 members.

TRANSITION LAW, 5709 — 1949

ON THE 14th February, 1949, the Constituent Assembly held its inaugural meeting, and two days later passed its first law, the Transition Law, 5709–1949, which laid the foundations of the permanent Government of Israel.

Since then that law has been amended nine times, the first amendment of the 7th February, 1951, and the fifth amendment of the 5th June, 1956, providing for the appointment of deputy ministers, (see p. 20) the second amendment, effected by the Presidency of the State Law, 5712–1951, of the 5th December, 1951, replacing the provisions relating to the election, declaration and term of office of the President, the third and fourth

amendments providing for changes in the composition of the
Government and the transfer of powers from one Minister to
another (see p. 21), the sixth and seventh amendments adding
detailed provisions regarding the responsibility of Ministers
towards the Government (see pp. 21-2), and the formation of the
Government (see pp. 23-4) respectively, the eighth amendment,
effected by the Basic Law: President of the State, replacing the
provisions relating to signature of laws by, and the functions of, the
President of the State (see pp. 14-5, 16) and the ninth amendment
which came into force on the 18th July, 1965, providing that
where a Minister who is a member of the Knesset resigns from the
Knesset his resignation is deemed to be a resignation from the
Government.

Under the Transition Law, 5709-1949, the legislature of
Israel was to be known as 'the Knesset' and the Constituent
Assembly as 'the First Knesset'. Thenceforth, the legislative
acts of the Israel legislature were to be known as 'Laws', and
not 'Ordinances'—the name used by the legislature of the
Palestine Mandatory Government and retained by the Provisional Council of State. Every Law is to be signed by the
Head of the Government and the Minister or Ministers charged
with its implementation, and also by the President of the State,
unless it is a law concerning the powers of the President, and
must be published in *Reshumot* (the Official Gazette) within
ten days of its being passed by the Knesset. Although there is
no express provision in any law to that effect, it is the accepted
view that every law comes into force upon the date of its publication in *Reshumot* unless it is otherwise expressly provided
therein, and that laws may be retroactive.

Until the coming into force of the Continuity of Consideration
of Draft Laws Law, 5725-1964 on the 19th November, 1964, if a
draft law was not enacted by an outgoing Knesset, the incoming
Knesset could only consider it if it was submitted to it as a new
draft law, so that in effect the work put into it by the outgoing
Knesset was wasted. The new law was designed to change that
situation. It provides that where a draft law has been referred by
an outgoing Knesset to one of its committees after the first

reading, the Government formed in the incoming Knesset may notify the Knesset in plenary session that it wishes the continuity provisions of the Law to apply to it, and if it does so each Parliamentary party may propose within two weeks that those continuity provisions shall not apply to that draft law, and when such a proposal is submitted one of the members of the Parliamentary party submitting it must give reasons for the proposal. If no such proposal is submitted, or if the proposal is rejected by the Knesset, then the incoming Knesset must continue the consideration of the draft law, in the competent committee and in plenary session, from the stage reached by the outgoing Knesset and it must treat the deliberations on the draft law of the outgoing Knesset as if they were its own deliberations.

BASIC LAWS

THERE ARE NO restrictions upon the legislative powers of the Knesset, for no written constitution has yet been adopted. During the term of the First Knesset there were long and recurrent discussions, both within the Knesset and among the general public in Israel, on the question whether there should be a written constitution or not. Those discussions were ended by a compromise resolution passed by the Knesset on the 13th June, 1950, in the following terms: 'The Knesset resolves to impose upon the Constitution, Law and Justice Committee the task of preparing a draft of a Constitution for the State. The Constitution will be built up chapter by chapter in such a way that each chapter will constitute by itself a fundamental law. The chapters will be brought before the Knesset to the extent to which the Committee completes its work, and the chapters will be incorporated in the Constitution of the State.'

So far four chapters have been prepared. The first three, entitled the Basic Law: the Knesset (see pp. 27-30), the Basic Law: Israel Lands (see pp. 143-4) and the Basic Law: President of the State (see pp. 12-20), were passed by the Knesset on the 12th February, 1958, the 10th July, 1960 and the 16th June, 1964 respectively, while the fourth, entitled the Basic Law: the Government, is still under consideration by the Knesset.

PRESIDENT OF THE STATE

THE TRANSITION LAW, 5709–1949 provided for the election of the first President of the State by the First Knesset by a secret ballot, and fixed as his term of office the period of the duration of the First Knesset and thereafter until the expiration of three months after the new Knesset had assembled. It also prescribed the functions of the President of the State, namely, to sign every law other than a law concerning his powers; after consultation with the representatives of the Parliamentary parties in the Knesset, to call upon one of the members of the Knesset to form the Government whenever a Government has to be formed; to sign treaties with foreign states which have been approved by the Knesset; to appoint, on the recommendation of the competent Minister (the Foreign Minister) the diplomatic representatives of the State of Israel; to receive the diplomatic representatives of foreign states sent to Israel, and to grant exequaturs to foreign consuls. He was also empowered to grant pardon to offenders and to commute sentences.

The Presidency of the State Law, 5712–1951, which came into force on the 15th December, 1951, contained much more comprehensive provisions relating to the Presidency of the State, and those provisions were declared to apply also to the President elected by the Second Knesset on the 19th November, 1951. It left in force the above-mentioned provisions of the Transition Law, 5709–1949 with regard to the functions and powers of the President of the State, but replaced the provisions of that law with regard to the term of office of the President of the State, prescribing that his term of office is to be five years from the date upon which he assumes his office, namely, the day upon which he makes the prescribed declaration upon the expiration of the term of office of his predecessor.

The provisions of the Presidency of the State Law, 5712–1951 as well as the provisions of the Transition Law, 5709–1949 with regard to the functions and powers of the President of the State, other than the provision that the President of the State, after consultation with the representatives of the Parliamentary parties in the Knesset, must call upon one of the members of the Knesset to form the Government whenever a Government has to be formed, were repealed and replaced by the provisions of the Basic Law: President of the State passed by the Knesset on the 16th June, 1964, and published in *Reshumot* on the 25th June, 1964.

The Basic Law does not differ substantially from the Presidency of the State Law, 5712–1951, but it contains a number of new provisions, namely, that the State is headed by a President, the seat of the President of the State is Jerusalem, and every Israel citizen who is a resident of Israel is qualified to be a candidate for election as President of the State, but a person who has held office as President of the State for two consecutive periods may not be a candidate in the elections for the next following period.

The President of the State is elected by the Knesset for five years. His election must take place not earlier than ninety days, and not later than thirty days, before the expiration of the term of office of the officiating President. If the office of the President of the State becomes vacant before the expiration of the term of his office, the election must be held within forty five days from the date when the vacancy occurred. The Speaker of the Knesset, in consultation with his Deputies, must fix the date for the election and give notice thereof in writing to all the members of the Knesset at least twenty days in advance. Should the date of the election not fall at the time of one of the sessions of the Knesset, the Speaker must convene the Knesset for the election of the President of the State.

When a date for the election has been fixed, ten at least of the members of the Knesset may propose a candidate. The proposal must be in writing and be delivered to the Speaker of the Knesset together with the consent of the candidate in writing or by telegram, not later than ten days before the date of the election. A member of the Knesset may not participate in more than one proposal for a candidate. The Speaker of the Knesset must notify in writing all the members of the Knesset, not later than seven days before the date of the election, of every candidate who has been proposed and the names of the members of the Knesset who proposed him, and he must announce who are the candidates at the opening of the meeting for the election.

The election of the President of the State will be by secret ballot at a meeting of the Knesset convened for that purpose only.

The candidate who receives the votes of the majority of the members of the Knesset will be elected. If no candidate receives such a majority there will be a second vote. If there is no such majority at the second vote, another vote must be taken. At the third vote and every additional vote, the person who obtained the smallest number of votes at the previous vote will not be put up for election. The candidate who received at the third vote, or at one of the additional votes, a majority of the votes of the members of the Knesset participating in the voting and voting for one of the candidates will be elected. If two candidates receive an equal number of votes, another vote must be taken.

The President who is elected must make and sign before the Knesset the following declaration of allegiance:

'I undertake to preserve allegiance to the State of Israel and its laws and to perform faithfully my functions as President of the State.'

The elected President must make the declaration of allegiance and begin to officiate at the expiration of the term of office of the preceding President of the State. If the office of the preceding President of the State became vacant before the expiration of his term of office, the elected President must make his declaration as soon as possible after his election and he will begin to officiate upon making the declaration of allegiance.

The functions of the President of the State are enumerated in section 11 of the Basic Law. They are: (1) to sign every law other than laws concerning his powers; (2) to act for the formation of the Government and to receive the resignation of the Government in accordance with law; (3) to receive from the Government a report of its meetings; (4) to accredit the diplomatic representatives of the State, to receive the accreditation of diplomatic representatives of foreign states sent to Israel, to authorise the consular representatives of the State and to grant exequaturs to consular representatives which foreign states have sent to Israel; (5) to sign treaties with foreign states which have been approved by the Knesset; (6) to perform any function assigned to him by law in connection with the appointment of Judges and other office-holders and to dismiss them from office.

That section also provides that the President of the State is empowered to pardon offenders and to mitigate their sentences by reducing them or altering them, and that the President of the State must perform every other function, and may exercise every other power, assigned to him by law.

Under the State Comptroller Law, 5709–1949, of the 24th May, 1949, (see pp. 37-8) the President appoints the State Comptroller upon the recommendation of the House Committee of the Knesset; under the Red Shield of David Law, 5710–1950, of the 21st July, 1950, he appoints the President of the Red Shield of David Society established by that law; under the Bank of Israel Law, 5714–1954, of the 3rd September, 1954, (see p. 116), he appoints the Governor of the Bank of Israel upon the recommendation of the Government, while under the Judges Law, 5713–1953, (see pp. 204-7) the Dayanim Law, 5715–1955, (see p. 208) the Qadis Law, 5721–1961 (see p. 208), and the Druze Religious Courts Law, 5723–1962 (see p. 209) he appoints the members of the Civil Judiciary and the Judges of the Religious Courts respectively upon the recommendation of the competent Nominations Committee; under the Military Justice Law, 5715–1955, (see p. 52) upon the recommendation of the Chief of the General Staff, submitted by the Minister of Defence, he appoints an officer as President of the Military Court of Appeal; under the Defence Levy Law, 5716–1956, (see pp. 146, 149-50) upon the recommendation of the Government, he appointed a Defence Levy Council; under the Council for Higher Learning Law, 5718–1958, of the 14th August, 1958, he appoints the members of the Council for Higher Learning, upon the recommendation of the Government, and under the Israel Centre for the Advancement of Human Culture Law, 5719–1958, of the 31st December, 1958, he appointed the first members of the Israel Centre for the Advancement of Human Culture, upon the recommendation of the Board of Trustees of the Van Leer Institute for the Advancement of Human Culture and with the consent of the Government.

The signature of the President of the State on an official document requires the confirmatory signature of the Head of the Government, or of some other Minister decided upon by the Government, unless the document is connected with the formation of the Government.

As regards the immunities of the President of the State, the Basic Law provides that he shall not be tried by any Court or tribunal for any matter connected with his functions or powers, and he will have immunity from any legal act for any such matter. He will not be obliged to state in evidence anything which became known to him in the performance of his function as President of the State. His said immunities will be available to him also after he has ceased to be President of the State. The President of the State may not be brought before a criminal Court. The period during which he cannot be tried for an offence as a result of that provision will not be taken into account in calculating the period of limitation for that offence.

Where the President of the State is required to give evidence his evidence will be taken at the place and time fixed with his consent.

The Basic Law reenacts the provisions of the Law for Fixing the Salaries of the President of the State, Members of the Government and the Chief Rabbis of Israel Law, 5711–1950, whereunder the salary of the President of the State and the other payments to be paid to him during his term of office or thereafter, including those to be paid to his survivors, shall be fixed by a resolution of the Knesset, which may authorise the Finance Committee in that behalf, and such resolution must be published in *Reshumot*. Section 9 (1) of the Income Tax Ordinance, as enacted on the 9th March, 1967, exempts from income tax the salary payable to the President of the State and the benefits payable to him or his survivors under the Basic Law.

The President of the State may not officiate in any office or perform any function other than the office and function of the President of the State save with the consent of the House Committee of the Knesset. He is exempt from all compulsory service and may not go beyond the borders of the State save with the consent of the Government.

The President of the State may resign from his office by submitting his resignation in writing to the Speaker of the Knesset. His letter of resignation does not require any confirmatory signature. There will be a vacancy in the office of the President of the State at the expiration of forty-eight hours after the letter of resignation has reached the Speaker of the Knesset.

The Basic Law reproduces without any substantial change the provisions of the Presidency of the State Law, 5712–1951 with regard to the removal from office of the President of the State by the Knesset, save that under the Basic Law the initiating complaint which is to be brought before the House Committee of the Knesset, must be submitted by at least twenty members of the Knesset, which is double the number required by the previous law.

The Knesset may, by resolution, remove the President of the State from his office if it has determined that he is not fit for his office by reason of behaviour which is not befitting the status of the President of the State. The Knesset may only remove the President of the State from his office pursuant to a complaint brought before the House Committee by at least twenty members of the Knesset and in accordance with a proposal of that Committee accepted by a majority of three quarters of the members of the Committee. A resolution of the Knesset for the removal of the President from his office also requires a majority of three quarters of its members.

The House Committee of the Knesset may not propose the removal of the President from his office save after an opportunity has been given to him to refute the complaint in accordance with the procedure fixed by the Committee with the approval of the Knesset, and the Knesset may only resolve to remove the President of the State from his office after an opportunity has been given to him to state his case in accordance with the procedure fixed by the House Committee of the Knesset with the approval of the Knesset.

The President of the State may be represented before the House Committee and before the Knesset by his representative, save that a member of the Knesset shall not serve as the representative of the President. The House Committee and the Knesset may invite the President to be present at the time of the deliberations described above regarding his removal.

The deliberations of the Knesset must take place at a meeting convened for this purpose only, or at meetings soon after each other, convened therefor. They must be begun not later than twenty days after the resolution of the House Committee, and the Speaker of the Knesset must give written notice of the date of the commencement of the deliberations to all the members of the Knesset at least ten days in advance. Should the date for the commencement of the deliberations not fall at a time of one of the sessions of the Knesset, the Speaker must convene the Knesset for the holding of the deliberations.

The Knesset may also, by a resolution passed by a majority of its members, determine that, for health reasons, the President of the State is unable, permanently, to perform his function. The Knesset may pass such a resolution only in accordance with a proposal of the House Committee which has been passed by a majority of two thirds of its members on the strength of a medical opinion given in accordance with rules prescribed by the Committee. If the Knesset passes such a resolution then the office of the President of the State will be vacant as from the day of the resolution.

The President of the State will temporarily cease to perform his function and exercise his powers: (1) if he goes beyond the borders of the State—from the time of his departure until his return; (2) if he has notified the House Committee that for health reasons he cannot, temporarily, perform his function, and the House Committee has approved the notice by a majority of votes—from the approval of the notice until the expiration of the period which the Committee has fixed in its resolution or until the President of the State has notified the House Committee that he is no longer unable to perform his function, whichever is the earlier; (3) if the House Committee has resolved by a majority of two thirds of its members on the strength of a medical opinion given in accordance with rules prescribed by the Committee that for health reasons the President of the State is unable, temporarily, to perform his function—from the passing of the resolution or until it has resolved that the President is no longer unable to perform his function.

The House Committee may not fix for the above purposes a period exceeding three months, but it may extend it, without a break, for a further three months. A longer extension requires a resolution of the Knesset passed by a majority of the members of the Knesset in accordance with a proposal of the House Committee.

Where there is a vacancy in the office of the President of the State and so long as the new President of the State has not commenced to officiate, the Speaker of the Knesset will officiate as Acting President of the State.

During the period when the President of the State has temporarily ceased to perform his function and exercise his powers, the Speaker of the Knesset will officiate instead of the President of the State.

When officiating as Acting President of the State or instead of the President of the State, the Speaker of the Knesset must perform the functions imposed upon the President of the State by law and may exercise the powers conferred upon the President of the State by law.

The Speaker of the Knesset is required to give notice in *Reshumot* of: (1) the commencement of the officiation of the President of the State; (2) a vacancy in the office of the President of the State; (3) the commencement of the officiation of the Speaker of the Knesset instead of the President of the State and the termination thereof. The Head of the Government must give notice in *Reshumot* of the departure of the President of the State beyond the borders of the State and of his return.

It is expressly provided in the Basic Law that, notwithstanding anything contained in any other law, Emergency Regulations may not change the Basic Law, suspend its operation temporarily, or modify it.

The Basic Law also provides that the President elected by the Knesset on the 21st May, 1963 shall be deemed to have been elected thereunder and that he shall officiate in accordance therewith.

THE GOVERNMENT

THE TRANSITION LAW, 5709–1949 also contains provisions regarding the Government. Under it, the Provisional Government had to tender its resignation to the President immediately after he was elected, but had to continue to act until a new Government was set up.

After consultation with the representatives of the Parliamentary parties in the Knesset, the President is to call upon one of the members of the Knesset to form the Government, which will be composed of a Head of the Government and a number of Ministers from among the members of the Knesset, or persons who are not members of the Knesset. In addition, under the Transition (Amendment) Law, 5711–1951, and the Transition (Amendment) Law, 5716–1956, a member of the Government who is in charge of a Ministry may, with the approval of the Government, appoint one or two members of the Knesset as Deputy Minister or Deputy Ministers for his Ministry. Such a Deputy Minister will act in the Ministry and in the Knesset in the name of the member of the Government who appointed him in such matters, and with such powers, as the member of the Government appointing him may determine. The appointment of a Deputy Minister will not derogate from the responsibility of the member of the Government for the acts of his Ministry, or from his share in the collective responsibility of the Government. The Government is required to notify the Knesset of every appointment and termination of appointment of a Deputy Minister.

As soon as the Government is constituted, it is to appear

before the Knesset and will begin to function after receiving a vote of confidence from it. The Government will be collectively responsible to the Knesset for its acts, will report to it thereon, and will act so long as it enjoys the confidence of the Knesset. Should the Knesset pass a vote of non-confidence in the Government, or should the Government decide to resign, it must immediately tender its resignation to the President, but must continue to act until a new Government is set up.

The Transition (Amendment No. 2) Law, 5712–1952, of the 25th June, 1952, lays down the procedure for effecting changes in, or additions to, the membership of the Government, or in the functions of the Ministers, so that it will not be necessary for the Government to resign and for the reconstituted Government to obtain a vote of confidence from the Knesset, and provides that, if the Head of the Government notifies the Government of his resignation, his resignation will have the effect of a decision of the Government to resign, while the Transition (Amendment No. 3) Law, 5712–1952, of the 20th August, 1952, empowers the Government to transfer, in whole or in part, to another Minister, the powers conferred by law upon any particular Minister and provides that the resolution to effect such transfer must be published in *Reshumot* (the Official Gazette) and be notified to the Knesset by the Government.

Under the Law and Administration Ordinance, 5708–1948, all the powers which were conferred by law upon His Britannic Majesty or one of his Secretaries of State, upon the High Commissioner for Palestine, the High Commissioner in Council or the Government of Palestine, were conferred upon the Provisional Government, save in so far as any of such powers were conferred by Ordinance upon the Provisional Council of State. All those powers are now vested in the Government, as the Transition Law, 5709–1949 has conferred upon the Government all the powers which were previously vested in the Provisional Government.

The Transition (Amendment No. 6) Law, 5722–1962, which came into force on the 19th June, 1962, provides that a member of the Government is responsible to the Government for his vote in a plenary session of the Knesset and also for the vote in such a session of the party to which he belongs. Should a member of the Government vote in a plenary session of the Knesset against a proposal of the Government, or abstain from voting, without the prior consent of the Government, he will be deemed to have resigned from the Government as from the day upon which the Government gives notice thereof to the Knesset, provided that the notice is given within two weeks of the voting. Should the party to which a member of the Government belongs vote for a proposal to express non-confidence in the Government, or abstain from voting upon such a proposal, or vote in a plenary session of the Knesset against a proposal of the Government, or abstain from voting, without the prior consent of the Government, in one of the following matters, namely, the proposed State budget, or any part, or item, of that budget, proposed laws and provisions of laws reducing the revenues of the State or increasing its expenditure, either directly or indirectly, or proposed laws and provisions of laws and other proposals in security, political, or other, matters which the Government has decided in advance shall be matters to which the above provisions shall apply, and the Government decides, within a week of the voting, that it shall constitute a breach of responsibility under the above provisions, then such member of the Government will be deemed to have resigned from the Government as from the date upon which the Government notifies the Knesset thereof within two weeks of the decision of the Government. The above provisions, however, will not apply to those matters in respect of which the Government decides that there shall be freedom of voting or abstention, subject to such reservations as the Government may prescribe.

Under the Transition Law, 5709–1949, it is the duty of the President of the State, after consultation with the representatives of the parties in the Knesset, to impose upon one of the members of the Knesset the task of forming the Government. As a result of the experience gained from the various occasions upon which it was necessary for the President of the State to carry out his duty under that provision, it was found necessary to add many detailed provisions to the Law, and they are laid down by the Transition (Amendment No. 7) Law, 5722–1962, which came into force on the 8th August 1962. Under those provisions, where a member of the Knesset has notified the President of the State, within three days of the task of forming a Government being imposed upon him, that he is not prepared to accept it, the President of the State must impose the task upon another member of the Knesset, and he must so act whenever a member of the Knesset upon whom the task of forming a Government has been imposed informs him that he does not accept it. Should a member of the Knesset upon whom the task of forming a Government has been imposed not so inform the President of the State, then he must complete his task within 28 days, although the President of the State may extend that period for an additional period not exceeding 14 days and then extend it again for a further period not exceeding 7 days, if he considers it justifiable to do so upon a report submitted to him by that member of the Knesset before the expiration of each of those periods. Should the member of the Knesset not inform the President of the State by the end of the said periods that the Government has been formed, or should he inform him before that time that he is unable to form a Government, the President of the State must impose the task upon another member of the Knesset in accordance with the above provisions and such member must complete his task within 28 days. Should such member not inform the President of the State within 28 days that the Government has been formed, or should he inform him before then that he is unable to form a Government, the President of the State may, after consultation with the representatives of the parties in the Knesset, impose the task upon one of the members of the Knesset who has informed him that he is prepared to accept the task. Such member must complete his task within 21 days. Should the President of the State not impose the task upon such a member, or should he impose it upon him and should that member not inform him that the Government has been formed, and the representatives of the parties in the Knesset the members of which constitute the majority of the members of the Knesset recommend to the President of the State that he impose the task on a particular member of the Knesset, then the President of the State must impose it upon such member, but if the recommendation is made to the President of the State when the task has been imposed upon a member who has to complete his task within 21 days in accordance with the above provisions, then the President of the State must impose the task in accordance with the recommendation only after the expiration of 7 days from the date when the task was imposed upon a member who has to complete it within 21 days, unless such member has informed the President of the State before then that the Government has been formed or that he is unable to form a Government. The member of the Knesset upon whom the task of forming a Government is imposed in accordance with the said recommendation must complete his task within 21 days.

When the President of the State imposes upon a member of the Knesset the task of forming a Government he must forthwith so inform the Speaker of the Knesset and the latter must notify the members of the Knesset. When a member of the Knesset has formed a Government he must forthwith so inform the President of the State and the Speaker of the Knesset.

THE PARLIAMENT

BY THE Transition to the Constituent Assembly Ordinance, 5709–1949, all the powers conferred by law upon the Provisional Council of State were vested in the Constituent Assembly so long as the Constituent Assembly did not resolve otherwise; and by the Transition to the Second Knesset Law, 5711–1951, of the 12th April, 1951, all the powers, rights and obligations conferred, or imposed, by law upon the First Knesset and its members were conferred, or imposed, upon the Second Knesset and its members; and it is provided that the Second Knesset is to act in accordance with the rules of procedure, resolutions, precedents and practice, according to which the

First Knesset acted, *mutatis mutandis*, so long as it does not resolve to act otherwise.

Unlike the Transition Law, 5708–1949, which did not prescribe the term of the First Knesset, the Transition to the Second Knesset Law, 5711–1951 provides that the term of the Second Knesset shall be four years from the date of its assembly.

The Transition to the Second Knesset Law, 5711–1951 is expressly declared to apply, *mutatis mutandis*, also to the transition to the Third Knesset and every subsequent Knesset, so long as the Knesset does not pass any other law relating to the matters dealt with in that law.

The Term of the Third Knesset and its Members Law, 5718–1958 provides that the term of the Third Knesset shall be until the month of Heshvan, 5720 (1959), and that officiating rabbis and priests of other faiths and senior State officials and senior Army Officers will not be disqualified from being members of the Third Knesset.

Elections

The Elections to the Second Knesset Law, 5711–1951, of the 19th April, 1951, provided that the Second Knesset, like the First Knesset, should be composed of 120 members, elected by general, direct, equal, secret and proportional elections, in the manner prescribed by the law. Every person born in or before 1932 and registered on 1st March, 1951, as a resident under the Inhabitants Registration Ordinance, 5709–1949, was entitled to vote, unless he entered Israel illegally. A person born in or before 1929, and registered on the date for the submission of the lists of candidates as a resident under that law, was eligible for election to the Second Knesset unless he entered Israel illegally. Judges could not be candidates for election, and Government officials (other than teachers) and members of the Defence Army of Israel in regular or permanent service, who had been nominated for election ceased to serve as such from the date of the submission of the lists of candidates until the date of the elections and, if elected, until they ceased to be members of the Knesset.

The Knesset Elections Law, 5715–1955, of the 3rd February, 1955, makes certain amendments to the Elections to the Second Knesset Law, 5711–1951, and provides that that Law as so amended shall apply to the elections to the Third Knesset and every subsequent Knesset. The most important amendment is the requirement that all voters and candidates shall be Israel citizens.

The Knesset Elections (Amendment) Law, 5719–1959, of the 5th March, 1959, made a number of changes in the provisions of the Elections to the Second Knesset Law, 5711–1951, and the Knesset Elections Law, 5715–1955, and empowered the Minister of Justice to publish in *Reshumot*, a Knesset Elections Law, 5719–1959, which would be a consolidated version of those two laws, excluding those provisions relating solely to the Third Knesset, and upon the publication of that consolidated version on the 19th April, 1959, those two laws were deemed to be repealed. Among the provisions of the Knesset Elections (Amendment) Law, 5719–1959, mention should be made of those relating to candidates for election to the Knesset. It provides, in implementation of the Basic Law: the Knesset, that the following persons may not be candidates: (1) State employees of Grade 5 and upwards of the General Administrative grading; (2) State employees of a professional grade the commencing basic salary of which is not lower than that of Grade 5 of the General Administrative grading (known as 'the corresponding grade'); (3) State employees of a grade lower than Grade 5 of the General Administrative grading or the corresponding grade, if for their post there is a fixed range of grades including Grade 5 or a corresponding grade; (4) Army officers of any rank in the permanent service of the Defence Army of Israel, unless they cease to be such State employees or Army officers at least 100 days before the election day. Furthermore, where the name of a State employee, other than a teacher, a soldier, other than an officer in the permanent service of the Defence Army of Israel or a soldier in regular service under the Security Service Law, 5709–1949, is included in any of the lists of candidates, his service will be suspended from the date of the submission of the list which included his name until the election day, and, if he is elected as a member of the Knesset, so long as he is a member of the Knesset.

The Knesset Voters Register Law, 5719–1958, which came into force on the 30th December, 1958, provides for the preparation of a Knesset voters register every year, and the establishment, for the purposes of the Law, of a Voters Register Committee composed of representatives of the various parties in the Knesset and presided over by a Justice of the Supreme Court chosen by the members of that Court. No person will have a right to vote in any Knesset election in any particular year unless he is registered in the voters register for that year. The Law lays down in detail the procedure and time table for the preparation of the register.

Basic Law: The Knesset

The Basic Law: the Knesset, passed by the Knesset on the 12th February, 1958, and published in *Reshumot* on the 20th February, 1958, provides that the Knesset is the Parliament of the State, composed of 120 members, and shall have its seat in Jerusalem. Section 4 provides that the Knesset is to be elected in general, national, direct, equal, secret and proportional elections according to the Knesset Elections Law and that that section may not be altered save by a majority of members of the Knesset. Every Israel citizen of eighteen years of age and upwards has a right to vote for the Knesset, if a Court has not deprived him of such right under any law. The Knesset Elections Law is to fix the date when a person is deemed to be eighteen years of age for the purpose of the exercise of his right to vote for the Knesset. Every Israel citizen who on the date of the submission of the list of candidates in which his name is included, is twenty-one years and upwards, is eligible for elections to the Knesset, if a Court has not deprived him of such right under any law.

The Law extends considerably the number of persons who may not be candidates for election to the Knesset. They are the President of the State, the two Chief Rabbis, a Judge, so long as he is acting as such, a Judge of a Religious Court, so long as he is acting as such, the State Comptroller, the Chief of the General Staff, Defence Army of Israel, rabbis and priests of other faiths, so long as they are acting as such for remuneration, senior State officials and senior army officers of such ranks as may be prescribed by law.

The term of the Knesset will be four years from the date of its election. Elections to the Knesset will be held on the third Tuesday of the month of Heshvan (November) in the year in which the term of the outgoing Knesset terminates, unless the preceding year was a leap year, in which case the elections will be held on the first Tuesday of that month.

Under the Basic Law: the Knesset (Amendment No. 4), which came into force on the 23rd March, 1967, provisions are added to the Basic Law: the Knesset regarding a Substitute Speaker and an Acting Speaker which were discovered to be necessary when, during the absence abroad of the Speaker, the President of the State had also to go abroad, for there was no provision in the Basic Law to deal with such a situation and the Speaker had to return from abroad before the departure of the President in order to perform the functions of the President. The amending Law provides that where the Speaker of the Knesset has gone beyond the borders of the State a Deputy Speaker will take his place until his return. It is also provided that where the Speaker notifies the House Committee, or the House Committee has determined, that for reasons of health the Speaker is temporarily unable to perform his functions, a Deputy Speaker will take his place until the Speaker notifies the House Committee, or until the House Committee determines, that he is no longer unable to perform his functions. Where the office of the Speaker falls vacant, either because he has resigned, or died, or the House Committee has determined that for reasons of health he is permanently unable to perform his functions, a Deputy Speaker will act as Acting Speaker until a new Speaker is elected. The Deputy Speaker who will act as Substitute Speaker or Acting Speaker is the Deputy Speaker elected in that behalf by the House Committee.

When acting as Substitute Speaker or Acting Speaker the

Deputy Speaker will serve in every capacity in which the Speaker can act according to law, and will perform every function imposed upon the Speaker according to law and will exercise every power conferred upon the Speaker according to law.

The above provisions will apply, *mutatis mutandis*, also if the circumstances described above as respects the Speaker obtain as respects a person acting as Substitute Speaker or Acting Speaker.

The Knesset will elect from among its members a Speaker and Deputy Speakers, and also permanent committees, and it may also elect from among its members committees for particular matters. The functions, powers and procedure of such committees, in so far as they are not prescribed by the Law, will be prescribed by the Standing Rules of the Knesset. The Knesset may also appoint inquiry committees.

A member of the Government who is not a member of the Knesset will be treated as a member of the Government who is a member of the Knesset for all purposes, save that he has no right to vote.

The Knesset may deliberate and resolve with any number of members. Its resolutions will be passed by a majority of votes of those participating in the voting, those abstaining from voting not being counted as participating in the voting. The meetings of the Knesset are to be held in public unless it has been resolved to hold them in camera upon such conditions and in such manner as is prescribed by the Standing Rules.

No restrictions are imposed upon the publication of the proceedings of any open meeting of the Knesset or of what is said in such a meeting, and no criminal or civil responsibility will result from such publication, but the person presiding at such a meeting may, in the manner prescribed by the Standing Rules, prohibit the publication of anything the publication of which is likely, in his opinion, to affect the security of the State.

On the other hand, publication of proceedings at any closed meeting or what is said in such a meeting is forbidden, save to the extent to which it may be permitted in the manner prescribed by the Standing Rules.

Two sessions of the Knesset are to be held in each year, one of which is to begin within four weeks after the Feast of Tabernacles and the other within four weeks after Independence Day. The duration of the two sessions together is to be at least eight months. In addition, upon the requisition of thirty members of the Knesset or of the Government, the Speaker must call a meeting of the Knesset.

The Knesset may not resolve upon its dissolution before the termination of its term, save by passing a law in that behalf, and such law must include a provision fixing a date for the election of the next succeeding Knesset.

Every outgoing Knesset will continue to function until the incoming Knesset assembles.

A member of the Knesset may resign. His resignation will be effected by his personally submitting to the Speaker a written letter of resignation or, if he is unable to submit it personally, by his sending it in such manner as is prescribed by the Standing Rules. The letter of resignation must be signed on the date of its submission or dispatch. When a member of the Knesset has submitted his resignation, his membership will cease upon the expiration of forty eight hours after his letter of resignation has reached the Speaker, unless he has previously withdrawn his resignation.

When a member of the Knesset is elected or appointed to one of the offices the holders whereof are disqualified as candidates for election to the Knesset, his membership of the Knesset will terminate upon his election or appointment.

When a member of the Knesset ceases to be a member, he will be replaced, from the list of candidates which included his name, by the candidate whose name comes first after the name of the last candidate to be elected.

Finally, section 44 of the Law provides that, notwithstanding anything contained in any other law, Emergency Regulations may not amend or modify the Law or suspend its operation temporarily, and under section 45 of the Law such provision may not be altered save by a majority of eighty members of the Knesset.

Section 46 of the Law, which was added by the Basic Law:

the Knesset (Amendment No. 3) on the 16th August, 1959, provides that the majority required by the Law for amendments of sections 4, 44 or 45 of the Law will be necessary for resolutions of a plenary meeting of the Knesset at every stage of the legislation other than the debate upon a motion for the agenda of the Knesset, and, for the purpose of the sections, an amendment may be either express or implied.

Election Propaganda

The Elections (Propaganda Methods) Law, 5719–1959, which came into force upon being passed by the Knesset on the 6th July, 1959, imposes prohibitions and restrictions with regard to election propaganda during a period of 150 days preceding the day on which elections to the Knesset and local authorities are held and on the day of the elections. The law forbids election propaganda by the use of aircraft or watercraft or by means of a loud speaker other than a loud speaker used to amplify the voice of a speaker at a lawfully held meeting, or by means of showing on a screen at a cinema, while during a period of 30 days preceding the election day events in which the candidates for election to the Knesset take part may not be shown on the screen of a cinema. It also forbids election propaganda by means of lights or illuminated signs or notices other than the lighting of the letter of the alphabet and the designation lawfully approved for a list of candidates, while, save during the period of 60 days preceding the election day, there may be no propaganda by means of the use of the letter of the alphabet indicating a list of candidates. Election propaganda may not be accompanied by programmes of entertainment, including appearances of artists, music, singing, film shows and torch carrying, nor may it be connected with the giving of prizes, nor, save for receptions in private houses, may it be connected with the serving of food or drink. With the exception of printed notices stuck in a place intended for the sticking of public notices and which comply with certain conditions specified in the Law, there may be no election propaganda by means of sticking, affixing, writing, painting or floodlighting on buildings, fences or vehicles, or on roads, pavements or other areas in which it is intended that the public should walk or ride, save that on the day of the elections the prohibition will not apply to a vehicle at the disposal of a list of candidates on that day. The Law also provides that election propaganda on behalf of, or in support of, a party or a list of candidates shall not be in a form or in a manner which constitutes an unfair interference with the election propaganda of another political party or list of candidates. The Chairman of the Central Committee for Elections to the Knesset is empowered, after consultation with his deputies on that committee, to require the owner or occupier of a hall or open public place which is ordinarily available for hiring, to hire it out to a particular list of candidates on a specified date within 60 days preceding the date of the elections to the Knesset, if the Chairman is satisfied that it is necessary to do so in order to enable that list of candidates to deliver its message in that place. The Law also imposes certain obligations upon the Chairman. After consultation with the Committee, he must prescribe the times to be allotted to each of the political parties and lists of candidates for broadcasting election speeches before the day for the elections to the Knesset; each party and list is to be given 25 minutes, and every party represented in the outgoing Knesset is to be given an extra 4 minutes in respect of each member of the party in the Knesset. The Chairman is also required, on the 14th day, the 7th day, and on each of the two days, preceding the day of the elections, to publish in all the daily newspapers appearing in Israel, in the news broadcasts of 'the Voice of Israel' (the State broadcasting service) and in any other manner fixed after consultation with the Committee, a notice which will make clear to the electors their right to vote freely in accordance with their conscience and give particulars of the provisions of the law ensuring freedom of elections, their secrecy and purity. In addition to those persons who are empowered to institute criminal proceedings for an offence under the general law, members of the Central Committee for Elections to the Knesset and representatives of lists of candidates for the Knesset are empowered to institute criminal proceedings for an offence under the

Law, and if one of them exercises that right the Attorney General may not order a stay of proceedings. The maximum penalty for an offence under the Law is six months' imprisonment or a fine of IL. 10,000, and proceedings for such an offence must be instituted within one year of the commission of the offence.

Two new sections were inserted in the Law by the Elections (Propaganda Methods) (Amendment) Law, 5721–1961, which came into force on the 21st June, 1961.

Under the first section, no use may be made, in connection with election propagands, of moneys of an inspected body, within the meaning of the State Comptroller Law, 5718–1958 (see pp. 37-8), or of a corporation in the management or capital of which the Government has a share, and no such use may be made of movable or immovable property actually in the possession of any such body or corporation, other than the letting of halls and public open spaces ordinarily available for letting, and the use of property placed by the State at the disposal of a Minister or Deputy Minister.

Under the other section, where an offence under any of the provisions of the Law has been committed, there will also be guilty thereof, without prejudice to the criminal responsibility of others, the person who had possession of the moneys or property in respect of which the offence was committed, or who was in charge of the possession or safeguarding thereof, unless he proves that the offence was committed without his knowledge or that he took reasonable steps to prevent it.

Remuneration and Benefits

The Knesset Members Remuneration Law, 5709–1949, of the 7th June, 1949, as amended, provides that the State Treasury shall pay to members of the Knesset the salary, allowances, grants and other payments provided for by the Law. The salary is a monthly salary which is to be fixed as a percentage of the basic salary of members of the Government and linked to that salary by that percentage and the percentage is to be fixed by a resolution of the House Committee, which may fix different percentages for the salary of the Speaker of the Knesset, Deputy

Speakers, Deputy Ministers and other members of the Knesset, and the Chairman of the Committee is required to inform the Knesset of the resolutions of the Committee, which are also to be published in *Reshumot*. In addition, there is payable a family allowance of Il. 15 a month for a spouse, or child under 20 years of age, and IL. 5 a month for each child or additional child under that age, a cost of living allowance varying with the cost-of-living index, and also grants and payments for expenses free of income tax as fixed by the House Committee of the Knesset. Every member of the Knesset is required by the law to receive the salary, allowance and grants other than those for expenses, to which he is entitled, and no member is entitled to receive a salary from any other source in any manner whatsoever. In addition, the Benefits for Knesset Members Law, 5718–1958, which came into force on the 1st June, 1958, provides for payment upon certain conditions of a monthly pension, or a non-recurrent grant, to persons ceasing to be members of the Knesset, or to their survivors in the event of their death.

The Law does not apply to members of the Knesset who serve as members of the Government. Their salaries are fixed by the Finance Committee of the Knesset, in accordance with the law of the 7th December, 1950.

Under the Ministers' Benefits Law, 5717–1957, which is deemed to have come into force on the 15th May, 1948, monthly pensions not exceeding 70% of their salary, are payable to Ministers who have held office for at least two years, and to certain members of their family in the event of their decease. In calculating the period during which he has held office, four fifths of the period during which a Minister, immediately before becoming a Minister, held office as a member of the Executive of the Vaad Leumi, or the World Zionist Organisation, prior to the establishment of the State, will be taken into account.

Immunity, Rights and Duties

On the 3rd July, 1951, the Immunity, Rights and Duties of Members of the Knesset Law, 5711–1951, passed by the

First Knesset on the 25th June, 1951, was published. Under that law, no member of the Knesset is civilly or criminally responsible or liable to legal proceedings in respect of any vote cast, opinion expressed or any act done, in or out of the Knesset, in the fulfilment of his duty as a member of the Knesset, nor is he obliged to state in evidence anything known to him in the fulfilment of his duty as a member of the Knesset. Such immunity will continue even after he has ceased to be a member of the Knesset (Section 1).

Members of the Knesset are immune from searches of their dwelling houses, and also of their person and property, save by Customs authorities. Papers of a member of the Knesset, including postal packets sent by or to him in accordance with a special arrangement by the House Committee of the Knesset, are immune from search, opening and confiscation, save that for the purpose of currency and foreign exchange control, a member's papers may be opened in his presence, but may not be read unless they are currency notes, cheques, orders or valuable securities.

Members of the Knesset are immune from arrest unless they are caught in the act of committing a crime involving use of force or disturbance of the peace or treason, and then the arresting authority must notify the Speaker of the Knesset of the arrest; and the period of arrest may not exceed ten days unless the member loses his immunity in respect of the offence before the ten days have expired.

Furthermore, no member of the Knesset may be brought to trial for any offence committed while he is a member of the Knesset or before he became a member, unless he loses his immunity in respect of the offence.

Every member of the Knesset is exempt from regular service under the Security Service Law, 5719–1959 (Consolidated Version) and from all compulsory service under any other law, unless the Knesset resolves otherwise in time of war. He is not, however, exempt from service with the Reserves under the Security Service Law, 5719–1959, (Consolidated Version) but the arrangements with regard to the time of his service are to be determined by the House Committee of the Knesset in consultation with the Defence Minister or his representative. No restriction or prohibition of access to any place, other than private property, will apply to a member of the Knesset unless it was imposed on the ground of security of the State or military secrecy.

Members of the Knesset will not be required to obtain a permit to go abroad save in time of war, and when they go abroad they are entitled to a service passport.

They are also entitled to travel free of charge within the country on the railway and on omnibuses in the public service, to a telephone in their dwelling-house, which is to be installed free of charge, in priority to others, to a number of free calls fixed by the House Committee, and to priority for their trunk calls. Every letter sent by a member of the Knesset from the Knesset building to any place in Israel is exempt from postage. Furthermore, every member is entitled to receive all Government publications free of charge.

A member of the Knesset may be deprived of his immunity in respect of an offence if the Knesset so resolves upon a proposal by the House Committee at the request of the Attorney General; while he may be deprived of any other immunity or right other than his immunity for what he does in the fulfilment of his duty as a member of the Knesset, if the Knesset so resolves upon a proposal of the House Committee at the request of the Government or any member of the Knesset. No member, however, may be deprived of any immunity or right unless he has been given an opportunity of stating his case, and every member of the Knesset has been given at least twenty-four hours' notice of the proceedings and vote.

Finally, the law imposes a number of prohibitions upon members of the Knesset, ministers and deputy ministers. No member, minister or deputy minister may use the title of his office in any transaction concerned with his business or profession. A former member, minister or deputy minister may not, after he has vacated his office, draw attention in writing in any matter connected with his business or profession to the fact that he was a member of the Knesset, a minister or a deputy minister.

A former minister may not, for three years after the expiration of his term of office as minister, be a member of the board of directors of any company or association which received a concession from the State during his term of office. A former deputy minister may not, for three years after the expiration of his term of office as deputy minister, be a member of the board of directors of any company or association which received a concession from the State through the ministry in which he served as deputy minister. Persons acting contrary to those provisions are liable to two years' imprisonment or a fine of three thousand Pounds or to both those penalties.

The law applies to ministers who are not members of the Knesset as it applies to ministers who are members of the Knesset.

The Immunity of the Knesset Buildings Law, 5712–1952, of the 3rd April, 1952, provides for the preservation of order in and around the Knesset buildings and confers powers upon the Speaker to this end. An amendment of the Law passed by the Knesset on the 9th August, 1966 after it had moved into its permanent building redefined the expression 'Knesset buildings' and 'Knesset open space', appearing in the Law by reference to a map in the Schedule added to the Law.

OTHER CONSTITUTIONAL LAWS

State Comptroller

THE STATE COMPTROLLER Law, 5718–1958(Consolidated Version) of the 17th March, 1958, provides for the appointment of a State Comptroller by the President upon the recommendation of the House Committee of the Knesset. Originally in 1949 it was provided that he holds office for the term of the Knesset in which he is appointed until the expiration of four months from the assembly of the new Knesset, but, by an amendment of the 5th August, 1952, it was provided that he holds office for five years from the date of his appointment and that is still the law. In the exercise of his functions he is responsible only to the

Knesset and is independent of the Government. He acts in liaison with the Finance Committee of the Knesset and must report to it whenever he or it thinks it desirable that he should do so.

During his term of office the State Comptroller may not take any active part in political life, nor may he be a member of the Knesset, or the Council of any local authority, or the board of directors of any company or society carrying on any business for profit, nor may he hold any other office directly or indirectly, or carry on any business or exercise any profession. Furthermore, he may not take part, either directly or indirectly, in any undertaking, institution, fund or other body which holds a concession from, or is supported by, the Government or in the management of which the Government has a share, or which is subject to control of the Government or the State Comptroller. He may not enjoy, either directly or indirectly, any income therefrom. Finally, he may not acquire, use, or occupy, any State property, or receive any concession or grant in addition to his salary, save that he may receive land or a loan for settlement or housing.

The functions of the State Comptroller are stated generally to be examination of the finances of the State and their administration, of the economic enterprises of the State and its property, and the carrying out of the various other duties specified in the law.

The salary of the State Comptroller and other payments payable to him during his period in office and thereafter, including those payable to his dependants after his death will be fixed by a resolution of the Knesset which may authorise the Finance Committee in that behalf. Such resolutions of the Knesset must be published in *Reshumot*.

Flag and Emblem

The Flag and Emblem Law, 5709–1949, of the 24th May, 1949, imposes prohibitions upon the use of the flag and the use and manufacture of the emblem proclaimed by the Provisional Council of State to be the flag and emblem of the State on the 28th October, 1948, and the 10th February, 1949, respectively.

The Minister of the Interior is authorised to grant permits for their use and manufacture.

State Seal

The State Seal Law, 5710–1949, of the 7th December, 1949, prescribes the design of the State Seal, and provides that the Minister of Justice shall be in charge of it. The seal may not be placed upon any document save in accordance with the directions of the Government or the provisions of any law. A penalty of seven years' imprisonment may be imposed for forgery of the seal. There are also penalties for unlawful use or manufacture of the seal.

Territorial Waters

The Territorial Waters Law, 5717–1956, of the 2nd November, 1956, amends the definition of 'territorial waters' in the Interpretation Ordinance by substituting six nautical miles for three nautical miles, so that the expression now means any part of the open sea within six nautical miles of the coast of Israel measured from low water mark.

Law of the Return

The Law of the Return, 5710–1950, of the 7th July, 1950, provides that every Jew has the right to come to Israel as an immigrant. Immigration is by immigrant's visa, which is to be granted to every Jew who expresses his desire to settle in Israel, unless the Minister of the Interior is satisfied that the applicant is acting against the Jewish people or is likely to endanger public health or the security of the State, or has a criminal past which is likely to endanger the public peace. A Jew who comes to Israel and subsequent to his arrival expresses his desire to settle in Israel is entitled, while in Israel, to receive an immigrant's certificate. The same restrictions as those which apply to an immigrant's visa apply to an immigrant's certificate, save that a person is not to be considered to be endangering public health on account of an illness contracted after his arrival in Israel. Every Jew who came to the country, before the coming into force of the Law, and every Jew born in the country, whether before or after the coming into force of the Law, has the same status as a person coming to the country as an immigrant under the Law.

State Property

The State Property Law, 5711–1951, of the 15th February, 1951, provides that property of the Palestine Government situated in Israel is property of the State of Israel since the 15th May, 1948, as is any ownerless property from the date upon which it became ownerless or the 15th May, 1948, whichever is the later date.

The law empowers the Government to acquire property for the State, whether it is situated in Israel or abroad, and prescribes the manner in which State property may be acquired and disposed of.

The Minister of Finance is charged with the implementation of the Law.

State Service

The State Service (Appointments) Law, 5719–1959, which came into force on the 15th July, 1959, prescribes the conditions for appointment to an office in the State service. It does not apply to the acceptance of any person for any of the following offices: any office in respect of which the remuneration of the holder is fixed by law, or in accordance with the law, by resolution of the Knesset or one of its committees, any office of a member of a Moslem or Christian Religious Court, a soldier within the meaning of the Military Justice Law, 5715–1955, a member of the Police Force or the Prison Service, an employee in the service of the Defence Army of Israel, any office in any undertaking serving the security system if the conditions of work of the employee are prescribed by a collective agreement which applies only to such undertakings, an employee on a daily wage engaged in work which by its nature is not permanent.

The Law empowers the Government, by a notice published

in *Reshumot*, to direct that all or any of the provisions of the Law shall apply, *mutatis mutandis*, to a local authority, and after consultation with the Labour Affairs Committee of the Knesset, by notice in *Reshumot*, to prescribe the services, undertakings and units to the employees or classes of employees whereof all or any of the provisions of the Law shall not apply.

The Government is required to appoint a State Service Commissioner and a Service Committee, composed of that Commissioner, as chairman, and six other members, three of whom shall be a Director-General of a Ministry and three members of the public who are not State employees. The decisions of the Service Committee are to be submitted to the Government and they are subject to variation or revocation by the Government within 60 days of their submission.

The Government is empowered to prescribe the manner and conditions of appointment of the Attorney General and, in so far as it has not done so, the provisions of the Law will apply to his appointment. The Government is to appoint a Director-General for every Ministry, subject to the provisions of the Law, and upon such conditions as it may prescribe, upon recommendation of the Minister in charge of the Ministry, and it will not be necessary to make any public announcement of the vacancy. The Law provides that there is to be an establishment for each Ministry proposed by the Minister and approved by the State Service Commissioner. If the Commissioner does not approve it, the Service Committee will decide, and if it decides not to approve, then the Minister may lodge an objection to the Government.

No person may be appointed as a State employee save to a vacant office on the establishment and after the State Service Commissioner has, upon the request of the Director-General, made a public announcement that the office is vacant or likely to become vacant. Furthermore, every State employee must be an Israel citizen. The Government is empowered, upon a recommendation of the Service Committee and by notice in *Reshumot*, to prescribe offices to which the provisions of the Law as to public announcements shall not apply, while such provisions will not apply to offices to which a person is appointed through a Labour Exchange under the Employment Service Law, 5719–1959 (see pp. 194–7).

Save with the approval of the Government, and upon such conditions as it may prescribe, no person may be appointed to any of the following offices: Government Adviser, Secretary to the Government, State Attorney, Accountant General, Commissioner of Budgets, District Representative, Director of Water Affairs, Commissioner of Information Administration, Ambassador, Minister, Consul-General, any office the holder of which is, under any enactment, to be appointed by the Government so long as the power to make the appointment has not been transferred to any other person under any law, and any other office which the Government may add to the list.

Provisions are made for qualifying examinations for candidates for appointments, and it is provided that no person may be appointed a State employee unless he has been passed as medically fit for the appointment, with the exception of disabled persons to whom any law applies.

Every person before he is appointed a State employee must make the prescribed declaration of loyalty to the State and its laws, and every State employee must make a declaration of the property and debts of himself, his spouse and children living with him, and of the sources of their income in the past in so far as they are likely to be sources of income also in the future. Such declaration is to be kept secret and any unauthorised person violating its secrecy will be liable to one year's imprisonment.

Special provisions are laid down for the employment of temporary employees and persons on special contract.

The Law requires the Service Committee and the State Service Commissioner to consult the workers' organisation, which represents the largest number of workers in the State, and the representatives of the State employees in every matter under the Law in which they were required or accustomed to consult them before the commencement of the Law.

The State Service (Classification of Political Party Activity and Fund Raising) Law, 5719–1959, which came into force on the 14th August, 1959, imposes upon the Government the task of prescribing, in consultation with the Labour Affairs Committee of the Knesset and by notice published in *Reshumot*, the classes of State employees or holders of offices in the State service, to whom the prohibitions specified in the Law shall apply, either generally or for the period fixed by the Government. Those prohibitions are: being members of the active administration of a political party or a political body, organising a public meeting of a political character, sitting at the table of the persons presiding at such a meeting and making a speech at such a meeting, participating in a demonstration or procession of a political character, participating in written or verbal public propaganda for elections to the Knesset or to the council of a local authority, or for elections to which the Elections to Public Bodies Law, 5714–1954 applies, criticising the policies of their Ministries, or of other Ministries of the Government, at press conferences, interviews with journalists, in a speech in a public place, in a radio broadcast, a newspaper or a book. The Government is empowered to determine whether any particular body is a political party or a political body within the meaning of the Law, and if any doubt arises whether any particular employee is an employee of the class of employees prescribed by the Government for the purposes of the Law, the question shall be decided by the Service Committee established for the purposes of the State Service (Appointments) Law, 5719–1959.

The Law also forbids a State employee to organise any demonstration or procession of a political nature, or to get persons to contribute any money, or to collect or receive any money contributed for any purpose save for the State Treasury and in the performance of his duty, although the prohibition will not prevent deductions from the salary of a State employee which are permitted by the Wage Protection Law, 5718–1958 (see pp. 185–7), while the Government may permit a State employee to get persons to contribute, or to collect, or receive, money for a public purpose, either generally or in a particular case, and such permit must be published in *Reshumot*. If a State employee contravenes the provisions of the Law, he will be subject to disciplinary action.

The State Service (Discipline) Law, 5723–1963, which was published in *Reshumot* on the 8th March, 1963, and came into force upon the expiration of six months thereafter, consists of six parts, dealing with interpretation, appointment of a Disciplinary Tribunal, Prosecutor and Investigator, disciplinary offences, trial and punishment, suspension, re-trial and general provisions respectively.

The Law establishes a Disciplinary Tribunal to try disciplinary offences committed by State employees under the Law or any other law. The members of the Tribunal are State employees appointed for five years by the Minister of Justice in consultation with the Minister of Finance from among three panels of State employees. The first panel consists of persons qualified for appointment as a Magistrate submitted by the Minister of Justice. The second panel is submitted by the State Service Commissioner, and the third panel is submitted by the organisation of State employees representing the largest number of State employees, and in the event of its not being submitted within two months of the request for its submission, it will consist of persons from among the general body of State employees.

The Chairman of the Tribunal and his Deputy will be appointed by the Minister of Justice, in consultation with the Minister of Finance, from among the members of the panel submitted by the State Service Commissioner.

The appointments of the members of the Tribunal, the Chairman and Deputy Chairman must be published in *Reshumot*, and the rules of procedure of the Tribunal will be prescribed by regulations made by the Minister of Justice. No member of the Tribunal is subject in matters of adjudication to any authority other than the law. The Prosecutor before the Tribunal will be the State Attorney or a person authorised in that behalf by the State Attorney, or by the State Service Commissioner. The State Service Commissioner appoints investigators for the purposes of the Law and they will act in accordance with the instructions of the State Attorney. Should the State Attorney not give an investigator any instructions in any particular matter the State Service Commissioner may do so.

The second chapter of the Law also contains provisions with regard to the powers of the Tribunal as respects the taking of evidence and the summoning of witnesses, and it is expressly provided that the Tribunal may admit any written or oral evidence even if it is not admissible in a civil or criminal case.

Proceedings before the Tribunal are instituted by the filing of an action by the Prosecutor upon the basis of a complaint of the commission of a disciplinary offence by a State employee. Such a complaint may be submitted to the Prosecutor, by a Minister, the State Service Commissioner or the Attorney General, either upon his own initiative or upon the basis of a complaint lodged with him.

Unless the Tribunal otherwise orders, proceedings before it will be conducted in camera. The accused State employee is entitled to be heard at the proceedings, to adduce his evidence and to examine every witness appearing before the Tribunal, and he is also entitled to be represented by an advocate.

The Minister of Justice is empowered to appoint for every Ministry a Disciplinary Committee composed of three State employees to try State employees of the Ministry for disciplinary offences specified in Regulations made by the Minister of Finance, who is the Minister charged with the implementation of the Law. Proceedings before such a Disciplinary Committee are instituted by the filing by the State Service Commissioner, or a person appointed by the competent Minister in that behalf, of a complaint of the commission of a disciplinary offence within its jurisdiction. Where proceedings have been commenced in a Disciplinary Committee they will be stayed upon reasoned notice from the State Service Commissioner, upon the filing in the Tribunal of an action in the same matter, and upon a decision of the Disciplinary Committee that the gravity of the offence necessitates the transfer of the complaint to the Tribunal.

The State Service Commissioner is empowered to request

the Tribunal to set aside the disciplinary measures decided upon by a Disciplinary Committee or to appeal to the Tribunal against an acquittal or conviction of a State employee by a Disciplinary Committee or against the leniency of the disciplinary measure. A State employee who is aggrieved by the disciplinary measures decided upon by a Disciplinary Committee may appeal to the Tribunal against his conviction or the severity of the disciplinary measures.

The Law prescribes the disciplinary measures which a Disciplinary Committee and the Tribunal may decide upon. Both of them may issue a warning or a reprimand and decide upon the forfeiture of part of the State employee's salary or his transfer to another post, while the Tribunal may, in addition, decide upon deprivation of seniority rights, demotion, disqualification for holding certain posts, dismissal with compensation or without compensation, disqualification for State service permanently or for a specified period, and publication of the decision of the Tribunal. If the Tribunal decides upon dismissal or disqualification for State service permanently or for a specified period, and publication of the decision, the employee may appeal to a Justice of the Supreme Court, while if the Tribunal decides upon his transfer to another post or his disqualification for certain posts he may appeal to a Justice of the Supreme Court with leave of the Tribunal.

A State employee will be guilty of a disciplinary offence if, in Israel or abroad, he does an act, or conducts himself, in a manner which affects discipline in the State service, or does not carry out any obligation imposed upon him as a State employee, whether by custom, law, or regulation, or a general, or particular, instruction lawfully given to him, or he is negligent in carrying out such an obligation, or conducts himself in an improper manner in the performance of his duty, or in connection therewith, or he has been convicted of an offence involving moral turpitude.

The fourth chapter of the Law contains detailed provisions regarding the temporary suspension of State employees suspected of the commission of a disciplinary offence in various circumstances, for the payment of their salary and their engagement in other work during the period of suspension.

The fifth chapter contains provisions for re-trial similar to those applicable in the ordinary criminal courts.

The sixth chapter of the Law contains a number of general provisions, including one empowering the Government, with the authorisation of the Labour Affairs Committee of the Knesset, by notice in *Reshumot*, to direct that all, or any, of the provisions of the Law shall apply to employees of certain local authorities, or of an inspected body within the meaning of the State Comptroller Law, 5718–1958, (Consolidated Version) with such modifications as the Government considers necessary for the adaptation of those provisions to such local authorities or inspected bodies.

The Law expressly provides that the responsibility of a State employee under the Law in respect of any particular disciplinary offence does not derogate from his criminal responsibility for the same act or omission, and that disciplinary measures may be taken against him under the Law even if he has been punished or acquitted by a Court in respect of the same act or omission. It also provides that, save in certain specified circumstances, disciplinary measures may not be taken against a State employee more than once in respect of one disciplinary offence.

It is also provided that the retirement of a State employee from State service will not put a stop to proceedings commenced against him before the Tribunal, and that the Tribunal may continue such proceedings if it considers it necessary to do so. It is also provided that proceedings may be commenced before the Tribunal even after the State employee has retired from State service, provided that the action has been instituted within one year of his retirement, upon instructions from the Attorney General or the State Service Commissioner, or upon the request of the State employee.

Where there has been publication of information regarding a State employee imputing to him the commission of a disciplinary offence and the manner and extent of the publication are such as to harm him, the State employee may request the

State Service Commissioner to order an inquiry into the offence. Should the State Service Commissioner see from the results of the inquiry that there is no truth in the information, he must so notify the State employee in writing, and the State employee may publish the notice in such manner as he thinks fit, while should he see that there is a foundation for the information he must instruct the Prosecutor to institute an action.

The Law also provides that a State employee may not be dismissed by reason of a disciplinary offence save pursuant to a judgement of the Tribunal, unless the dismissal is during a period of probation when such a period is usual as respects the post in question, or as the result of a conviction for an offence involving moral turpitude.

The Law is expressly applied also to disciplinary offences committed before the Law came into force in respect of which the State employee had not been brought for a disciplinary trial under the rules in force at the time, but a State employee may not be brought for trial under that provision unless he could have been brought for a disciplinary trial before the Law came into force.

The Administrative Procedure Amendment (Reasons) Law, 5718–1958, which came into force on the 24th December, 1958, requires every public employee, that is, every State employee, local authority employee and every employee of any authority upon which any power is conferred under any law, to give the applicant written reasons for his refusal if he refuses any written application to him to exercise the power conferred upon him under any law, save in the following cases: (1) where in the law conferring the power upon him there is a provision that he may exercise the power in accordance with his discretion or without giving any reasons; (2) when the security of the State or of foreign relations requires that the reasons for the decision should not be disclosed; (3) when the application which he refused was for the appointment of the applicant to a particular office or to impose upon him a particular duty; (4) when the disclosure is, in the opinion of the public employee, likely unlawfully to affect the right of some person other than the applicant; (5) when the disclosure of the reasons would, in the opinion of the public employee, be a disclosure of a professional secret or secret information within the meaning of any law.

Should a public employee not inform the applicant of his reasons for refusing his application, he must inform the applicant by notice in writing which of the above grounds was his ground for refusing to inform the applicant of his reasons for refusing the application, and the applicant may lodge an objection within thirty days of the receipt of the notice. If the public employee is a State employee, the objection is to be made to the Minister to whom he is subordinate, while, in other cases, it is to be made to the Minister charged with the implementation of the law conferring the power upon the public employee concerned. Where the decision of the public employee is subject to an objection or an appeal under any enactment, the public employee must inform in writing the person entitled to lodge the objection or appeal of his right to object or appeal and of the procedure and time for exercising his right in so far as they are prescribed by the enactment. No decision or act of a public employee will be invalid by reason only of his not complying with the above provisions, but in every proceeding before an Objection Committee or Appeals Committee or before any Court, the public employee will be required to prove that the decision or act in respect of which notice was not given as above, was a lawful one, but that will not derogate from the disciplinary responsibility of the public employee for non-fulfilment of his duty under the Law. The provisions of the Law will not derogate from the provisions of any other law dealing with the giving of reasons for decisions of administrative authorities.

World Zionist Organisation

In the World Zionist Organisation—Jewish Agency (Status) Law, 5713–1952, which came into force on the 2nd December, 1952, it is recited that the State of Israel regards itself as the creation of the entire Jewish people, and that its gates are open, in accordance with its laws, to every Jew wishing to immigrate to it, that the World Zionist Organisation, from its foundation five decades ago, headed the movement and efforts of the Jewish people to realise the age-old vision of the return to its homeland and, with the assistance of other Jewish circles and bodies, carries the main responsibility for establishing the State of Israel, and that the World Zionist Organisation, which is also the Jewish Agency, takes care as before of immigration and directs absorption and settlement projects of the State, and the Law provides that the State of Israel recognises the World Zionist Organisation as the authorised agency which will continue to operate in the State of Israel for the development and settlement of the country, the absorption of immigrants from the Diaspora and the coordination of the activities in Israel of the Jewish institutions and organisations active in those fields. The Law also recites that the mission of gathering in the exiles, which is the central task of the State of Israel and the Zionist Movement in our days, requires constant effort by the Jewish people in the Diaspora, and therefore the State of Israel expects the cooperation of all Jews, both as individuals and groups, in building up the State and assisting the immigration to it of the masses of the people, and regards the unity of all sections of Jewry as necessary for this purpose, and that the State of Israel also expects efforts on the part of the World Zionist Organisation for achieving such unity, and that if, to that end, the World Zionist Organisation, with the consent of the Government and the approval of the Knesset, should decide to broaden its basis, the enlarged body will enjoy the status conferred upon the World Zionist Organisation in the State of Israel.

The Law then goes on to provide that details of the status of the World Zionist Organisation, represented by the Zionist Executive, known also as the Executive of the Jewish Agency, and the form of its cooperation with the Government shall be determined by a Covenant to be made in Israel between the Government and the Zionist Executive, and that the Covenant shall be based on the declaration of the 23rd Zionist Congress in Jerusalem that the practical work of the Zionist Organisation and the various bodies for the fulfilment of their historic tasks in Eretz Israel (the Land of Israel) requires full cooperation and coordination on its part with the State of Israel and its Government, in accordance with the laws of the State.

The Law also provides that there shall be set up a committee for the coordination of the activities of the Government and the Executive in the spheres in which the Executive will operate according to the Covenant, and that the tasks of the committee shall be determined by the Covenant.

The Covenant and any variations or amendments thereof made with the consent of the two parties were to be published in *Reshumot* and to come into force on the day of publication unless they provided for an earlier or later day for that purpose. On the 2nd December, 1954, it was published in *Reshumot* and it was expressly provided therein that it came into force upon the date of its signature (26th July, 1954).

' The Law also provides that the Executive is a juristic person and may enter into contracts, acquire, hold, and dispose of, property and be a party in any legal or other proceeding, and that it and its funds and other institutions shall be exempt from taxes and other compulsory Government charges, subject to such restrictions and conditions as may be laid down by the Covenant, and that the exemptions shall come into force upon the coming into force of the Covenant.

Defence Army of Israel

By the Law and Administration Ordinance, 5708–1948, the Provisional Government was empowered to raise armed forces on land, on the sea and in the air, which would have authority to do all lawful and necessary acts for the defence of the State. On the 31st May, 1948, there was published in the Official Gazette an Ordinance made by the Provisional Government on the 26th May, 1948, entitled the Defence Army of Israel Ordinance, 5708–1948. By that Ordinance there was established the Defence Army of Israel, consisting of land forces, a navy and an air force, and it was provided that in a state of emergency there should be compulsory enlistment for services of that army, the age of those liable to enlistment being as prescribed by the Provisional Government. Furthermore, it was forbidden to establish or maintain any armed forces other than the Defence Army of Israel. In addition, all orders, proclamations, regulations and other directions concerning matters of national service which were published by the Jewish Agency for Palestine, the General Council (Vaad Leumi) of the Jewish Community in Palestine, 'Minhelet Ha-am' (National Executive), the Provisional Government or any of their departments between the 16th Kislev, 5708 (29th November, 1947) and the date of the publication of the Ordinance (31st May, 1948) should remain in force so long as they were not varied, amended or revoked.

Military Justice

On the 8th September, 1948, the Minister of Defence promulgated Emergency Regulations giving legal effect to the Jurisdiction Code, 5708, which was a Code setting up a military legal administration, comprising military courts and counsel, for both the prosecution and the defence, and defining their powers, duties, and procedure, and also defining the various military offences and punishments for offenders.

That Code, as amended from time to time by laws passed by the Knesset, remained in force until the 31st December, 1955, when it was replaced by the comprehensive Military Justice Law, 5715–1955, passed by the Knesset on the 21st June, 1955. That Law comprises 546 sections and is divided into ten parts dealing with the following matters: general principles, offences and punishments, discipline, legal institutions, procedure, courts martial, rules of evidence, execution of judgments, special offences and miscellaneous provisions.

Security Service

The Security Service Law, 5709–1949, which came into force on the 1st October, 1949, provides for the calling up of permanent residents of Israel for military service in the regular and reserve forces of the Defence Army of Israel. Originally, males of the ages of 18 to 49, inclusive, and females of the ages of 18 to 34, inclusive were liable to be called up, but by an amendment of the 31st August, 1952, the age limit for women was increased to 38. Furthermore, while originally the maximum period of regular service for males was twenty-four months and that for females twelve months, by the amendment of the 31st August, 1952, the maximum periods were increased to thirty months and twenty-four months respectively. That amendment also makes special provisions for service by medical practitioners, both male and female, and permits the call-up of males of $17\frac{1}{2}$ years of age in certain cases at their request. At the time the Law came into force there was no law as to Israel nationality, so that it was impossible to make liability to military service dependent upon Israel nationality, and the test was therefore permanent residence in Israel. The Security Service (Amendment) Law, 5719–1959, of the 23rd January, 1959, adds Israel citizens to those who are liable to military service, but if an Israel citizen is also a national of the State in which he resides permanently, the Minister of Defence may exempt him, in whole or in part, from the duties imposed upon him by the Law.

A consolidated version of the Law, as amended from time to time, entitled the Security Service Law, 5719–1959 (Consolidated Version) was published in *Reshumot* on the 24th September, 1959.

National Service

The National Service Law, 5713–1953, of the 4th September, 1953, provides for the rendering of national service by women between the ages of 18 and 26 exempted from service under the Security Service Law, 5709–1949, by reason of their having declared that they are prevented from serving on grounds of conscience or religious conviction. Such women, other than married women (who are exempt), will be required to render 24 months' national service in agricultural settlements of a religious agricultural institution, in work for the Defence Army of Israel or for the security of the State, in an immigrants' camp, transit camp or an institution for education, social welfare or medical treatment, or in any other State institution determined by the Minister of Labour. Women exempted from security service on the ground of religion will be given the possibility of preserving their religious way of life while on national service.

Civil Defence

The Civil Defence Law, 5711–1951, of the 21st March, 1951, establishes a Civil Defence Service composed of males of the ages of 16 to 62, and females of the ages of 17 to 50, and prescribes which persons in addition to volunteers shall be members of the Service and which, such as members of the Police Force, may not be required to be members of the Service. It also provides for the construction and use of air raid shelters and lays down how the expenses for such shelters are to be met.

Police and Prison Service

The Police Force in Israel is a national force. Its organisation, discipline, powers and duties are regulated by the Police Ordinance (of 1926), the Criminal Procedure (Arrest and Searches) Ordinance (of 1924), and various other enactments. The 1924 Ordinance, based upon the corresponding provisions of English law, prescribes the conditions upon which offenders may be arrested, and searches of persons and property may be carried out.

Under the Police Ordinance, the Force, headed by an Inspector General of Police, is employed for the prevention, detection and prosecution of crime, the apprehension of offenders, the safe custody of prisoners and the maintenance of public order and of the safety of persons and property. A police officer, when in Israel, is for all purposes of the Ordinance considered to be always on duty, he may at any time be employed in any part of Israel and he may not engage in any employment or office whatsoever, other than his duties under the Ordinance, unless expressly permitted to do so in writing by the Inspector General of Police, who is charged with the superintendence, administration and disposition of the Force.

The Inspector General of Police may, as occasion arises, constitute Courts of Discipline for the trial of police officers who have committed one or more of the offences specified in the Police Ordinance. Such Courts will be constituted of three superior police officers appointed by the Inspector General of Police, and they may impose imprisonment for a term not exceeding two years or a fine not exceeding three months' pay, or both such penalties. Any sentence passed by a Court of Discipline will be subject to confirmation by the Inspector General of Police, who has power to confirm, reduce, or quash the sentence. If the sentence exceeds three months' imprisonment, it will be subject to confirmation by the Minister of Police, who has power to confirm, reduce, or quash it.

The Police Ordinance Amendment Law, 5723–1963, which came into force on the 20th June, 1963, repealed the provision of the Police Ordinance whereunder the procedure of Courts of Discipline for the trial of police officers had to be as nearly as might be, in accordance with the Rules of Procedure made under the British Army Act, and prescribes detailed provisions for such Courts of Discipline, contained in 117 sections, and, in addition, empowers the Inspector General of Police to appoint a police officer of the rank of inspector or above, who is an advocate, to act as legal adviser to the Court of Discipline, and such legal adviser may, whenever he thinks fit, during the course of proceedings before the Court of Discipline, express his opinion on questions of law, procedure and evidence.

Under the Police Ordinance, the Force included the prison service, but as from the beginning of 1946 the prison service was separated from the Police Force, and was re-established under the Prisons Ordinance, 1946. The Prison Service, headed by the Commissioner of Prisons, is employed for the administration of prisons and the safe custody of prisoners, and matters connected therewith.

The Minister of Police is charged with the implementation of the Police Ordinance and the Prisons Ordinance, 1946.

Nationality

The Nationality Law, 5712–1952, which was passed on the 1st April, 1952, and came into force on the 14th July, 1952, provides for the acquisition of Israel nationality in one of four ways—by virtue of return, residence in Israel, birth or naturalisation.

The law confers Israel nationality by virtue of return on every Jew who came to the country as an immigrant before the date upon which the Law of the Return, 5710-1950 (see pp. 39-40) came into force, every Jew born in the country, whether before or after that date, and every Jew settling in Israel after that date unless he ceased to be resident in Israel before the date of commencement of the law (14th July, 1952), or, being over 18 years of age, and a foreign national, he declared that he did not wish to be an Israel national, or, if he is under 18 years of age, he is included in such a declaration made by his parents.

Jews who immigrated before the date of the establishment of the State (15th May, 1948), or were born in the country before that date, acquire Israel nationality from that date. Jews immigrating to Israel after the date of the establishment of the State (15th May, 1948) acquire Israel nationality from the date upon which they immigrate, while Jews born in Israel after the 15th May, 1948, acquire Israel nationality from the date of their birth.

Special provisions are made for the automatic acquisition of Israel nationality by former Palestinian citizens who do not become Israel nationals by virtue of return. Such persons will become Israel nationals if they fulfil three conditions, namely, on the 1st March, 1952, they were registered as a resident under the Registration of the Inhabitants Ordinance, 5709–1949; they were resident in Israel on the date of the commencement of the Nationality Law, 5712–1952 (14th July, 1952); and, during the period from the 15th May, 1948, to the 14th July, 1952, they were resident in Israel or in territory which became Israel territory after the 15th May, 1948, or they legally entered Israel within that period. The law provides that all persons fulfilling those three conditions acquire Israel nationality as from the 15th May, 1948.

Persons born in Israel after the 15th May, 1948, and resident in Israel on the 14th July, 1952, one of whose parents was a former Palestinian citizen and acquired Israel nationality by fulfilling the conditions described above will become Israel nationals as from the date of their birth.

The third way in which Israel nationality may be acquired is by birth. If at the time a person is born his father or mother is an Israel national, such person acquires Israel nationality as from the date of his birth. If his father has died before he is born, he will be an Israel national as from the date of his birth if his father was an Israel national at the time of his death. Nothing is stated in the law as to the place of birth of a person acquiring Israel nationality by birth, nor is anything said about the manner of acquisition of Israel nationality by his father or mother, so that it would appear that a person born to a father or mother who is an Israel national, will be an Israel national from birth, wherever born and howsoever his father or mother acquired Israel nationality.

A person desiring to acquire Israel nationality by naturalisation must, in addition to being at least eighteen years of age, fulfil six conditions. He must be in Israel, and have been in Israel for three years out of the five preceding his application, and he must be entitled to reside permanently in Israel and have settled, or intend to settle, in Israel. In addition, he must have some knowledge of the Hebrew language and have renounced his former nationality or proved that he will cease to be a foreign national when he becomes an Israel national. After he has fulfilled all those conditions he must make a declaration that he will be a loyal national of the State of Israel, and his acquisition of Israel nationality will take effect as from the date of his declaration.

Some persons, however, may acquire Israel nationality by naturalisation without compliance with all those conditions. Thus persons who have served in the regular service of the Defence Army of Israel, or have served after the 29th November,

1947, in any other service proclaimed by the Minister of Defence in a proclamation published in *Reshumot* as a military service for the purposes of the Nationality Law, and have been duly released, as well as persons who have lost a son or daughter in such service, may become naturalised as Israel nationals on fulfilling only one of the six conditions, namely, that they have settled, or intend to settle, in Israel. A foreign national entitled to Israel nationality by virtue of return who has declared that he does not wish to become an Israel national, will, if he subsequently applies for Israel nationality by naturalisation, be exempt from complying with the condition of being in Israel for three years out of the five years preceding his application. A person who immediately prior to the establishment of the State was a Palestinian citizen may acquire Israel nationality by naturalisation without having any knowledge of the Hebrew language. Finally, the Minister of the Interior, who is charged with the implementation of the Nationality Law, may, if in his opinion there is a special reason justifying the exemption, exempt an applicant for naturalisation from all or any of the six conditions described above, other than the conditions that the applicant is entitled to reside permanently in Israel and has settled, or intends to settle, in Israel.

No provision is made in the law for the automatic acquisition of Israel nationality by a woman on marrying an Israel national, but it is provided that where a husband or wife is an Israel national, or has applied for naturalisation and fulfils the conditions for naturalisation or is exempt from them, his wife or her husband, as the case may be, may receive Israel nationality notwithstanding the fact that she or he is under eighteen years of age or does not comply with the conditions for naturalisation.

On the other hand, when a person becomes naturalised, his minor children become naturalised by virtue of his naturalisation. Furthermore, special provisions are made for the naturalisation of children under eighteen years of age whose parents are not in Israel, have died or are unknown. If such children are not Israel nationals and are resident in Israel, the Minister of the Interior may grant them a certificate of naturalisation on such conditions, and with effect from such date, as he may think fit.

Israel nationality may be lost in one of two ways, either by renunciation or by cancellation of naturalisation. No provision is made for depriving persons of their Israel nationality against their will if they acquired it otherwise than by naturalisation.

The only persons who may renounce Israel nationality are nationals over eighteen years of age who are not resident in Israel or, according to an amendment of the 13th March, 1958, intend to cease to be resident in Israel and the Minister of the Interior considers that there is a special reason justifying such renunciation, and then only in each case with the consent of the Minister of the Interior. An Israel national under eighteen years of age, under the said amendment, will lose his Israel nationality if his parents have renounced their Israel nationality, but if they renounced it, intending to cease to be resident in Israel, the Minister of the Interior may, if he considers that there is a special reason justifying his refusal, refuse to agree to the renunciation insofar as it relates to the cancellation of the minor's nationality. In no case will a minor lose his Israel nationality so long as one of his parents remains an Israel national.

There are three grounds upon which a naturalised Israel national may lose his nationality. The first ground is that he acquired his nationality on the basis of false particulars. The second ground is that he has been abroad for seven consecutive years and has no substantial connection with the country, and has not proved that such connection ceased against his will. The last ground is that he committed an act which constitutes a breach of loyalty to the State of Israel.

The cancellation of naturalisation will be effected by a District Court upon the application of the Minister of the Interior, and the Court may, upon such application, decide that the cancellation shall apply also to the children of the person whose naturalisation is being cancelled, if they acquired Israel nationality by naturalisation and are resident abroad.

Save in the case where a person acquires Israel nationality

by naturalisation and the Minister of the Interior has not waived the requirement of renunciation by the applicant of his foreign nationality, the acquisition of Israel nationality does not depend upon the renunciation of a former nationality. As a result, Israel nationals may have a double nationality by retaining their former nationality when acquiring Israel nationality, although as far as Israel law is concerned, they will be deemed to be Israel nationals.

Generally speaking, the effect of the Nationality Law has been that the vast majority of the persons resident in Israel, both Jews and Arabs, are Israel nationals, and only in exceptional cases will a resident of Israel lose his Israel nationality. There will, however, be many persons of double nationality in Israel unless, according to their foreign national law, they lose their foreign nationality on acquiring Israel nationality.

SOURCES OF THE LAW

THE LAW of Israel is by no means a homogeneous body of law. According to the Law and Administration Ordinance, 5708–1948, it consists of two distinct parts, namely, the law of Palestine obtaining on the 14th May, 1948, with modifications, and the legislation enacted by the Israel legislature.

The law of Palestine obtaining on the 14th May, 1948, was itself by no means a uniform body of law, being derived from three main sources: Ottoman law, English law and the law enacted by the Palestine legislature i.e. the High Commissioner for Palestine, who had full power and authority, subject to Royal Instructions, to promulgate such Ordinances as might be necessary for the peace, order and good government of Palestine, but did not restrict complete freedom of conscience and the free exercise of all forms of worship, save in so far as was required for the maintenance of public order and morals, or tend to discriminate in any way between the inhabitants of Palestine on the ground of race, religion or language, or were in any way repugnant to or inconsistent with the provisions of the Mandate.

Ottoman law, i.e. the law in force in Palestine on the 1st November, 1914, the date of the outbreak of hostilities between the Allied Powers and Turkey, of which Palestine at the time was a province, consisted of three large and entirely dissimilar elements: the Mohammedan law which had survived in the Ottoman Empire, French law adopted by the Ottomans and adapted to their own needs, and the personal law of the non-Moslem communities.

The Mohammedan law, based primarily on the Koran and custom, was, generally speaking, limited to the law covering civil transactions codified in the civil code known as the Mejelle, which, for the most part, is little more than a Turkish translation from the Arab authorities on Mohammedan law; the law relating to marriage, divorce, alimony, wills, and other matters of personal status of Moslems; and the land law adapted to suit the peculiar needs of the Ottoman Empire.

Apart from the Mohammedan element, French influence reigned supreme in the Ottoman Empire from the early part of the 19th century when the Turkish Sultans, who, in the absence of a parliament in Turkey, were the sole legislators, began to carry out the legal reforms insisted upon by the European Powers. In order to save time and trouble the Sultan borrowed almost en bloc the principal legal codes of France. such as the Commercial Code, the Maritime Code, the Civil Procedure Code, and the Criminal Code. This borrowing process continued almost without interruption down to 1914, when Turkey entered the First World War as a belligerent on the side of the Central Powers. This French influence was so strong that it is impossible fully to understand Ottoman legal principles without a study of French law, and Turkish lawyers and judges frequently adopted the practice of consulting French legal text books and decisions of the French Courts on difficult or disputed points of law. The Palestine Courts, too, when applying Ottoman law modelled on French law, based their decisions on the principles of French jurisprudence, and so do the Israel Courts.

The second main source of Palestine law is English law,

which consists of two elements: (1) Acts of the Imperial Parliament and Orders of His Majesty in Council applicable to Palestine; (2) English judge-made law, namely, the substance of the English Common Law, and the doctrines of equity in force in England.

That law, however, formed part of the law of Palestine only subject to the statute law, whether Ottoman, English or Palestinian, in force in Palestine, and so far as such law did not extend or apply, and as far only as the circumstances of Palestine and its inhabitants and the limits of His Majesty's jurisdiction permitted, and subject to such modifications as local circumstances rendered necessary (Article 46 of the Palestine Order in Council, 1922).

The third main source of Palestine law is the law enacted by the Palestine legislature. Generally speaking, that law is modelled upon English law and it cannot be fully understood without a thorough study of the principles of English law and the decisions of the English Courts on the English law upon which it is based. For the most part, by the time the Mandate was terminated, such legislation had replaced the Ottoman law which formed part of the law of Palestine on the 1st November, 1914, although some important parts of that Ottoman law, including part of the Civil Law (Mejelle) and the Land Law have not yet been replaced. Thus, for example, the commercial and criminal law and the law of civil and criminal procedure have been replaced by Palestine legislation modelled upon English law adapted to local circumstances. The process of replacing Ottoman law by Palestine legislation was begun right from the beginning of the Mandatory regime and continued with ever increasing speed throughout the period of that regime. On the other hand, in the early days of the Mandate the Palestine Courts were very reluctant to apply English judge-made law, although during the second half of the period of that regime, in view of certain decisions of His Britannic Majesty's Privy Council, which was an appellate Court from the Supreme Court of Palestine, they increasingly introduced English judge-made law into the law of Palestine, and re-

ferred more and more in their judgments to English legal text-
books and judicial decisions.

THE MEJELLE

THE MEJELLE, consisting of 1,851 articles, is an elaborate code
containing not only definite rules of law, many of which are
illustrated by examples, but also the maxims of Mohammedan
jurisprudence, set out in 99 articles. The substantive part of the
code consists of 1,751 articles arranged in 16 books, in which
the following subjects are dealt with: sale, hire, guarantee,
transfer of debt, pledges, trusts and trusteeship, gift, wrongful
appropriation and destruction, interdiction, constraint and pre-
emption, joint ownership, agency, settlement and release, ad-
missions, actions, evidence and administration of oath and
administration of justice by the court. In so far as they deal
with what are known in English law as 'torts' the provisions
of the Mejelle have been replaced by the provisions of the
Civil Wrongs Ordinance, 1944 (see pp. 96–8), which is a codifica-
tion of the English common law of torts as modified by the
Palestine legislature. Other provisions of the Mejelle were also
replaced by Palestine legislation. For example, the provisions
regarding partnership, by the Partnership Ordinance; certain
provisions regarding evidence, by the Evidence Ordinance
(see pp. 223–7); and the provisions regarding arbitration by the
Arbitration Ordinance. The Israel legislature, too, has replaced
provisions of the Mejelle. For example, certain provisions
regarding water have been replaced by the Water Law, 5719–
1959 (see pp. 141-3), certain provisions regarding limitation
of actions have been replaced by the Limitation Law, 5718–1958
(see pp. 212–3), and the provisions regarding agency, guarantee,
pledge and trusts and trusteeship have been replaced by the
Agency Law, 5725–1965 (see pp. 118–21), the Guarantee Law,
5727–1967 (see pp. 122–6), the Pledge Law, 5727–1967 (see pp.
126–31) and the Custodians Law, 5727–1967 (see pp. 132–5)
respectively.

CRIMINAL LAW

Criminal Code and Amendments Thereof

ON THE 1st of January, 1937, the Ottoman Criminal Code, together with twenty-four Ordinances and various sections of other Ordinances, was replaced by a comprehensive piece of legislation known as the Criminal Code Ordinance, 1936, based on the criminal law of England, with modifications and additions designed to render it suitable for application in Palestine. Comprising about 400 sections (including those added since the original enactment of the Ordinance), the Code is divided into forty-four chapters dealing with, *inter alia*, the general rules as to criminal responsibility, parties to offences, attempts, incitements, conspiracy and punishments, and defining offences against public order, offences against the administration of lawful authority, offences injurious to the public in general, offences against the person, offences relating to property, malicious injuries to property, forgery, coining, counterfeiting and similar offences, and miscellaneous minor offences. The Code, it is expressly provided, is to be interpreted in accordance with the principles of legal interpretation obtaining in England, and expressions used in it are to be presumed, so far as is consistent with their context and except as may be otherwise expressly provided, to have the meaning attaching to them in English law and are to be construed in accordance therewith.

The general rules as to criminal responsibility, set out in sections 8 to 21 of the Code, are as follows.

Ignorance of the law does not afford any excuse for any act or omission which would otherwise constitute an offence unless knowledge of the law by the offender is expressly declared to be an element of the offence (s. 8), but a person who does, or omits to do, an act under an honest and reasonable, but mistaken, belief in the existence of any state of things is not criminally responsible for the act or omission to any greater extent than if the real state of things had been such as he believed to exist, unless the express or implied provisions of the law relating to the subject excluded the operation of the latter rule (s. 12).

A person under the age of nine years is not criminally responsible for any act or omission, and a person under the age of twelve years is not criminally responsible for an act or omission, unless it is proved that at the time of doing the act or making the omission he had capacity to know that he ought not to do the act or make the omission (s. 9).

A person is not criminally responsible in respect of an offence relating to property, if the act done or omitted to be done by him with respect to the property was done in the exercise of an honest claim of right and without intention to defraud or injure (s. 10).

Subject to the express provisions of the Code relating to negligent acts and omissions, a person is not criminally responsible for an act or omission which occurs independently of the exercise of his will or for an event which occurs by accident. Unless the intention to cause a particular result is expressly declared to be an element of the offence constituted, in whole or in part, by an act or omission, the result intended to be caused by an act or omission is immaterial. Unless otherwise expressly declared, the motive by which a person is induced to do or omit to do an act, or to form an intention, is immaterial so far as regards criminal responsibility (s.11).

Every person is presumed to be of sound mind, and to have been of sound mind at any time which comes in question, until the contrary is proved (s. 13).

A person is not criminally responsible for an act or omission if at the time of doing the act or making the omission he is, through any disease affecting his mind, incapable of understanding what he is doing, or of knowing that he ought not to do the act or make the omission. But a person may be criminally responsible for an act or omission, although his mind is affected by disease, if such disease does not in fact produce upon his mind one of the effects above mentioned in reference to that act or omission (s. 14).

Intoxication, which is deemed to include a state produced by narcotics or drugs, will not constitute a defence to any criminal charge, unless by reason thereof the person charged did not know at the time of the act or omission complained of that such act or omission was wrong, or did not know what he was doing and   (a) the state of intoxication was caused without his consent by the malicious or negligent act of another person, or (b) the person charged was, by reason of intoxication, insane, temporarily or otherwise, at the time of such act or omission. Where such a defence is established, then in a case falling under paragraph (a) the accused must be discharged, and in a case falling under paragraph (b) the provisions of section 14 of the Code dealing with insanity must be applied (s. 15).

Except as expressly provided by the Code, a judicial officer is not criminally responsible for anything done or omitted to be done by him in the exercise of his judicial functions, although the act done is in excess of his judicial authority, or although he is bound to do the act omitted to be done (s. 16).

Except murder and offences against the State punishable with death, no act is an offence which is done by a person who is compelled to do it by threats which at the time of doing it reasonably cause the apprehension that instant death or grievous harm to that person will otherwise be the consequence, provided that the person doing the act did not, of his own accord, place himself in the situation by which he became subject to such constraint (s. 17).

An act or omission which would otherwise be an offence may be excused if the person charged can show that it was done or omitted to be done only in order to avoid consequences which could not otherwise be avoided, and which if they had followed would have inflicted grievous harm or injury to his person, or to his honour or his property, or to the person or honour of others whom he was bound to protect, or to property placed in his charge, provided that in so acting he did no more than was reasonably necessary for that purpose, and that the harm inflicted by the act or omission was not disproportionate to the harm avoided (s. 18).

A person is not criminally responsible for an act or omission if he does or omits to do the act in execution of the law or in obedience to the order of a competent authority which he is bound by law to obey, unless the order is manifestly unlawful. Whether an order is or is not manifestly unlawful is a question of law (s. 19).

A married woman is not free from criminal responsibility for doing or omitting to do an act merely because the act or omission takes place in the presence of her husband (s. 20).

Section 21 of the Code provided that a person cannot be twice criminally responsible, either under the provisions of the Code or under the provisions of any other law, for the same act or omission, except in the case where the act or omission is such that by means thereof he causes the death of another person, in which case he may be convicted of the offence of which he is guilty by reason of causing such death, notwithstanding that he has already been convicted of some other offence constituted by the act or omission. That section was repealed by s. 226 (14) of the Criminal Procedure Law, 5725–1965, but section 2 of that Law provides that a person may not be tried for any act (including an attempt or omission) if he was previously acquitted or convicted of an offence constituted thereby, but if the act (including an attempt or omission) caused the death of a person he may be tried therefor even if he was previously convicted of another offence constituted by such act (including an attempt or omission). For the purposes of section 2 of the Law conviction includes being placed on probation without conviction.

The Collective Punishments Ordinance and the Collective Fines Ordinance, 1936, were repealed by the Abolition of Collective Punishments Law, 5725–1964, which came into force on the 26th November 1964.

Punishment of Nazis and Their Collaborators
The Punishment of Nazis and their Collaborators Law, 5710–1950 renders liable to the death penalty any person who committed, in an enemy country, any of the following offences: (1) an act done during the period of the Nazi regime, that is,

the period beginning on the 30th January, 1933, and ending on the 14th August, 1945, which constitutes a crime against the Jewish people; (2) an act done during the period of the Nazi regime which constitutes a crime against humanity; (3) an act done during the period of the Second World War, that is, the period beginning on the 1st September, 1939, and ending on the 14th August, 1945, which constitutes a war crime.

'Enemy country' means (a) Germany during the period of the Nazi regime; (b) any other Axis state during the period of the war between it and the Allied Powers, that is, the states which signed the Declaration of the United Nations of the 1st January, 1942, or acceded to it during the period of the Second World War; (c) any territory which, during the whole or part of the period of the Nazi regime, was *de facto* under German rule, for the time during which it was *de facto* under German rule; (d) any territory which was *de facto* under the rule of any other Axis state during the whole or part of the period of the war between it and the Allied Powers, for the time during which that territory was *de facto* under the rule of that Axis state.

An 'Axis state', for the purposes of the Law, is defined as meaning a state which, during the whole or part of the period of the Second World War, was at war with the Allied Powers, and the period which began on the day of the beginning of the state of war between a particular Axis state and the first in time of the Allied Powers and ended on the day of the cessation of hostilities between that state and the last in time of the Allied Powers, is considered as the period of the war between that state and the Allied Powers.

A 'crime against the Jewish people' means any of the following acts, committed with intent to destroy the Jewish people, in whole or in part: (1) killing Jews; (2) causing serious bodily or mental harm to Jews; (3) placing Jews in living conditions calculated to bring about their physical destruction; (4) imposing measures intended to prevent births among Jews; (5) forcibly transferring Jewish children to another national or religious group; (6) destroying or desecrating Jewish religious or cultural assets or values; (7) inciting to hatred of Jews.

A 'crime against humanity' is defined as any of the following acts: murder, extermination, enslavement, starvation or deportation and other inhuman acts committed against any civilian population, and persecution on national, racial, religious, or political grounds.

A 'war crime' is defined as any of the following acts: murder, ill-treatment or deportation to forced labour or for any other purpose, of civilian population of, or in, occupied territory; murder or ill-treatment of prisoners of war or persons on the seas; killing of hostages; plunder of public or private property; wanton destruction of cities, town or villages; and devastation not justified by military necessity.

The Law also provides that if a person, during the period of the Nazi regime, committed in any enemy country an act which is such that, had he committed it in Israel territory, he would have been guilty of one of the thirteen specified offences against the person, or robbery, attempted robbery or demanding property with menaces with intent to steal, which are offences under the Criminal Code Ordinance, 1936, and he committed the act against a persecuted person, that is, a person belonging to a national, racial, religious or political group which was persecuted by an enemy administration, that is, the administration which existed in an enemy country, as a persecuted person, he will be guilty of an offence under the Law, and liable to the same punishment as that to which he would have been liable had he committed the act in Israel territory.

Any person who, during the period of the Nazi regime, in an enemy country, was a member of, or held any post or exercised any function in, an enemy organisation is liable to seven years' imprisonment. An 'enemy organisation' is one of two bodies of persons, namely, (1) a body of persons which, under Article 9 of the Charter of the International Military Tribunal, annexed to the Four-Power Agreement of the 8th August, 1945, on the trial of the major war criminals, has been declared by a judgment of that Tribunal to be a criminal organisation;

(2) any other body of persons, which existed in an enemy country and the object, or one of the objects, of which was to carry out, or assist in carrying out, actions of an enemy administration directed against persecuted persons.

The Law also provides for the punishment of persons guilty of certain offences committed in a 'place of confinement', that is, a place in an enemy country which, by order of an enemy administration, was assigned to persecuted persons, and includes any part of such a place. Any person who, during the period of the Nazi regime, in an enemy country, and while exercising some function in a place of confinement on behalf of an enemy administration, or of the person in charge of that place of confinement, committed in that place of confinement an act against a persecuted person which is such that, had he committed it in Israel territory, he would have been guilty of one of the seven specified less serious offences against the person, or theft, under the Criminal Code Ordinance, 1936, will be guilty of an offence under the Law and be liable to the same punishment as that to which he would have been liable had he committed the act in Israel territory.

Any person who, during the period of the Nazi regime, in an enemy country, was instrumental in delivering up a persecuted person to an enemy administration, will be liable to ten years' imprisonment, while any person who, during that period, in an enemy territory, received or demanded a benefit (a) from a persecuted person under threat of delivering up that person, or any other persecuted person, to an enemy administration, or (b) from a person who had given shelter to a persecuted person, under threat of delivering up that person or that persecuted person to an enemy administration, will be liable to seven years' imprisonment.

The provisions of sections 16, 17, 18 and 19 of the Criminal Code Ordinance, 1936, which provide defences to criminal charges for judicial officers, persons acting under constraint, or necessity, or with justification, in certain cases (see pp. 66–7), will not apply to offences under the Law. If, however, a persecuted person has done, or omitted to do, any act, and such act or omission constitutes an offence under the Law, the Court must release him from criminal responsibility if he did, or omitted to do, the act   (a) in order to save himself from the danger of immediate death threatening him, and the Court is satisfied that he did his best to avert the consequences of the act or omission, or   (b) with intent to avert consequences more serious than those which resulted from the act or omission, and actually averted them, save in the case of murder of a persecuted person or an offence punishable with death under the Law.

Furthermore, in determining the punishment of a person convicted of an offence under the Law, the Court may take into account as grounds for mitigating the punishment the following circumstances: (1) that the person committed the offence under conditions which, but for the non-applicability of sections 16, 17, 18 and 19 of the Criminal Code Ordinance, 1936, would have exempted him from criminal responsibility or constituted a reason for pardoning the offence, and that he did his best to reduce the gravity of the consequences of the offence;   (2) that the offence was committed with intent to avert, and was indeed calculated to avert, consequences more serious than those which resulted from the offence, but the Court may not, in the case of an offence punishable with death, impose a lighter punishment than ten years' imprisonment.

The Law expressly provides that a person who has committed an offence under the Law may be tried in Israel even if he has already been tried abroad, whether by an international tribunal or a tribunal of a foreign state, for the same offence, but if a person is convicted in Israel of an offence under the Law after being convicted of the same act abroad, the Israel Court must, in determining the punishment, take into consideration the sentence which he has served abroad.

The Law originally provided that there is no limit to the time for prosecuting a person for an offence punishable with death under the Law or murder of a persecuted person, and that no person may be prosecuted for any other offence under the Law if twenty years have elapsed since the time of the commission of the offence. Under the Abolition of Limitation of Offences against Humanity Law, 5726–1966, which came into force on the 23rd February, 1966, there is no limitation of offences under the Law.

All prosecutions for offences under the Law must be instituted by the Attorney General or his representative.

The Court in a trial for an offence under the Law may deviate from the rules of evidence if it is satisfied that by so doing it will promote the ascertainment of the truth and the just handling of the case. Whenever the Court decides to deviate from the rules of evidence it must place on record the reasons which prompted its decision.

Genocide

The Crime of Genocide (Prevention and Punishment) Law, 5710–1950, which is designed to give effect in Israel to the provisions of the Prevention and Punishment of the Crime of Genocide Convention adopted by the United Nations General Assembly on the 9th December, 1948, which was ratified by the State of Israel, came into force on the 7th April, 1950 and will remain in force whether or not that convention comes into force or remains in force.

The expression 'genocide' is defined, for the purposes of the Law, as any of the following acts committed with intent to destroy, in whole or in part, a national, ethnical, racial or religious group (referred to in the Law as a 'group') as such: (1) killing members of the group; (2) causing serious bodily or mental harm to members of the group; (3) inflicting on the group conditions of life calculated to bring about its physical destruction in whole or in part; (4) imposing measures intended to prevent births within the group; (5) forcibly transferring to another group persons of any group who are under eighteen years of age.

A person found guilty of genocide will be punishable with death, unless he committed the act constituting the offence in circumstances which, but for the provisions of section 6 of the Law, would exempt him from criminal responsibility or would be a reason for pardoning the offence, and he tried to the best of his ability to mitigate the consequences of the act, in which case he will be liable to imprisonment for not less than ten years. Section 6 of the Law provides that the provisions of sections 16, 17, 18 and 19 of the Criminal Code Ordinance, 1936 shall not apply to offences under the Law. Those sections provide defences to criminal charges for judicial officers, persons acting under constraint, or necessity, or with justification, in certain cases (see pp. 66–7).

A person guilty of conspiracy, incitement or attempt to commit genocide, or of complicity in genocide, will be treated like a person guilty of genocide, and a person guilty of an offence under the Law will be punishable whether he is a legally responsible ruler, a member of a legislative body, a public official or a private individual.

Any person who has committed outside Israel an act which is an offence under the Law may be prosecuted and punished in Israel as if he had committed the act in Israel, and, notwithstanding anything contained in any other law, in considering the extradition of a person charged with, or convicted of, genocide, or conspiracy, incitement, or attempt to commit genocide, or of complicity in genocide, the plea that the offence with which such person is charged, or of which he has been convicted, is an offence of a political character shall not be entertained.

Under the Abolition of Limitation of Offences against Humanity Law, 5726–1966, there is no limitation of offences under the Law.

Age of Marriage

The Age of Marriage Law, 5710–1950, of the 8th August, 1950, as amended on the 31st July, 1960, replaces the provisions of the Criminal Code Ordinance, 1936 as to marrying, or celebrating the marriage of, females under the age of fifteen and, in certain cases, eighteen years, and provides penalties for marrying or celebrating the marriage of females under the age of seventeen years completed. It provides, however, that the competent District Court may authorise the marriage of such a female to her husband on her or his application or on the application of one of her parents or guardians if she has given

birth to a child, or is pregnant, by her husband or if she is sixteen years of age and the District Court is of opinion that there
are special circumstances justifying the authorization of the
marriage; and if the marriage is so authorised no offence will
be committed by the husband or the person celebrating it.

Bigamy

The Criminal Law Amendment (Bigamy) Law, 5719–1959,
which came into force on the 30th July, 1959, replaces the
corresponding provisions of the Criminal Code Ordinance,
1936. That Law provides that a married man who marries
another woman and a married woman who marries another
man will be punishable with five years' imprisonment. A person
who was once married is deemed, for the purposes of that provision of the Law, to be married so long as he has not proved
that his previous marriage was dissolved or annulled, either by
the death of his spouse, or by virtue of a final judgment of a
competent Court, or by *Din Torah* (Jewish religious law) in
a manner approved by a competent Court, and he is not considered unmarried save at the time of the death or the giving
of the judgment or approval. For the purpose of those provisions, it is immaterial whether the validity of the previous marriage was according to the law of the state in which the marriage was celebrated or according to the religious law according
to which it was celebrated, or whether the new marriage is
valid or void, or the new marriage was celebrated outside of
Israel so long as at the time of the marriage the person marrying was a citizen or resident of Israel. In the event of the law
applicable to the new marriage being *Din Torah*, a person will
not be convicted of an offence under the Law if the new marriage is celebrated after a permit to marry has been given by
a final judgment of a Rabbinical Court which is confirmed by
the two Chief Rabbis of Israel, or, in the event of one of them
being unable to act, by the person appointed in that behalf by
the Council of the Chief Rabbinate of Israel. In the event of
the law applicable to the new marriage not being *Din Torah*,
a person will not be convicted of an offence under the Law if

the new marriage is celebrated after it has been permitted by a final judgment of a competent Court on the ground that the spouse of the previous marriage is incapable, by reason of mental illness, to agree to the dissolution of the marriage or its annulment, or to participate in any proceeding or act for its dissolution or annulment, or on the ground that the spouse of the previous marriage is absent in circumstances which arouse a reasonable suspicion that he is dead or there has been no trace of him for at least seven years.

The Law also provides that, if a man dissolves his marriage against the will of his wife without a judgment of a competent Court imposing the dissolution upon the wife, he will be punishable with five years' imprisonment, and that a person celebrating a marriage knowing that it is prohibited according to law or that one of the spouses is committing an offence, will be punishable with six months' imprisonment, and that a person arranging a divorce knowing that it is prohibited by law or that the person divorcing is committing an offence, will be punishable with six months' imprisonment. In addition, the Law provides that, notwithstanding anything contained in the Evidence Ordinance (see pp. 223–7), one spouse is competent to give evidence against the other spouse in a trial for an offence under the Law, but neither a spouse nor a person who has invalidly married the accused may be compelled to give evidence.

Other Amendments

The Criminal Code Ordinance, 1936, was further amended by Laws of the 6th March, 1952, and the 3rd April, 1952. The former amendment replaces the provisions of the Code with regard to bribery and kindred offences and makes it an offence not only for public employees to take bribes, but also for persons to give bribes to public employees. The punishment for the giver of the bribe will be one half of that for the public employee taking the bribe, while a conviction may be obtained on the evidence of an accomplice alone. The latter amendment replaces the provisions of the Code as regards assaults upon the police and interference with them in the execution of their duty, increasing the maximum penalties and providing for a minimum penalty of one month's imprisonment.

A more comprehensive amendment of the Criminal Code Ordinance, 1936 was effected by the Criminal Law Amendment (Modes of Punishment) Law, 5714–1954, which provides for many important changes in the law relating to punishment, and increases considerably the fines which can be imposed, a change long overdue owing to the decrease in the value of money. It also provides for the imposition of conditional sentences and for the production in Court of a pre-sentence report by a Probation Officer. In addition, it provides for the establishment of Release Boards composed of a District Court Judge (presiding), the Prisons Commissioner or his representative, and a medical practitioner or educator appointed by the Minister of Justice, and prescribes their powers and functions. It also repealed section 38 of the Criminal Code Ordinance, 1936, which provided that the punishment of death shall be inflicted by hanging the offender by the neck until he is dead, but that section was revived by the Courts (Offences Punishable with Death) Law, 5721–1961 (see p. 199).

The Criminal Law Amendment (Modes of Punishment) (Amendment No. 5) Law, 5723–1963, which came into force on the 13th June 1963, effected a number of amendments of the principal Law which had been found to be necessary by experience of the working of that law since it came into force.

The principal Law for the first time empowered the Courts to impose a conditional sentence, but it did not prescribe detailed provisions in that regard. The amending law prescribes much more detailed provisions and, in addition, for the first time, empowers a Court which imposes conditional imprisonment, also to make a probation order under the Probation of Offenders Ordinance, 1944, for the whole or any part of the period of the condition, that is to say, the period during which the convicted person must refrain from committing any offence specified by the Court imposing the conditional imprisonment in order to avoid having to serve the term of imprisonment imposed upon him. The Court is also granted a new power with regard to conditional imprisonment, namely, the power of extending the period of the condition instead of activating the sentence of imprisonment which was imposed conditionally, but that power may only be exercised if the Court does not impose a sentence of imprisonment after having convicted for an offence specified by the Court imposing the conditional imprisonment and, for reasons recorded by it, the Court is convinced that, in the circumstances of the case, it would not be just to activate the sentence of conditional imprisonment, and the convicted person is convicted for the first time of the additional offence. The period of the condition may not be extended for more than two years.

Among other amendments effected by the amending law are the increase, from six months to one year, of the period of imprisonment which may be imposed for non-payment of a fine imposed by the Court, the conferment upon the Court of a general power to extend the time fixed by the law or the Court for the carrying out of any sentence, the increase, from IL. 500 to IL. 1,500, of the amount of compensation which the Court may order a convicted person to pay to any person for any damage or suffering sustained as a result of the commission of the offence, and the maximum fine which may be imposed for a contravention was raised from IL. 5 to IL. 75 (see pp. 82–3).

An innovation introduced by the amending law is the provision whereunder, when a Court has sentenced a person to imprisonment unconditionally for a period of six months or more and it is satisfied, after hearing the opinion of a doctor for mental diseases, that the convicted person is suffering from an urge to take dangerous drugs and that there is ground to assume that he committed the offence of which he was convicted by reason of that urge and that that urge is liable to cause him to commit further offences, it is empowered, in its sentence, to order that the convicted person be detained in a closed institution in order that he may be cured of his urge. The Minister of Health, with the consent of the Minister of Police, may approve the Psychiatric Division of a prison as a suitable closed institution for that purpose. Such an order may not be made for a period exceeding three years or the period of imprisonment which the convicted person has to serve, whichever is the longer. The period of detention of the convicted person in such a closed institution will be deducted from the period of imprisonment which the convicted person has to serve, unless the Court orders that the period of such detention, either in whole or in part, shall not be so deducted. The Minister of Police is empowered to appoint a committee of three persons, one of whom, who is to serve as chairman of the committee, must be a District Court Judge, and at least one of whom must be a doctor of mental diseases. If the committee is satisfied that the person who has been ordered to be detained in a closed institution is no longer in need of treatment in a closed institution or that he cannot be cured, it may order his release from the closed institution at any time before the termination of the period of the order for his detention, and it may also, for any reason it sees fit from the point of view of his cure or rehabilitation, order his release for such period and upon such conditions as it deems fit. The Attorney General or his representative is required once every six months to bring the matter of the patient before the Court which made the detention order, and the Court may cancel the order if it is satisfied that there is no justification for continuing the detention of the patient in the closed institution. In whichever way the patient is released from detention in the closed institution his release will not release him from the sentence of imprisonment which he has to serve. A patient who leaves a closed institution without lawful permission, and any person who assists him to do so, will be liable to one year's imprisonment.

The Minister of Health is empowered, in consultation with the Minister of Police, to make regulations with regard to the conditions of detention of persons in respect of whom a detention order is made and the methods of treating them, and two months after such regulations come into force the above provisions regarding detention in closed institutions will come into force.

The Criminal Law Amendment (Prohibited Games, Lotteries and Betting) Law, 5724–1964, which came into force on the 29th January, 1964, replaced the provisions of the Criminal

Code Ordinance, 1936 with regard to gaming houses and lotteries.

For the purposes of the Law a 'prohibited game' is defined as a 'game in which a person is likely to win money, money's worth or some benefit according to the results of the game, and the results depend upon chance more than understanding or skill', a 'place of prohibited games' is defined as 'premises in which prohibited games are usually conducted, whether the premises are open to the public or open only to particular persons, and it is immaterial whether they are occupied also for some other purpose', a 'lottery' is defined as 'any arrangement by which it is possible, either by drawing lots or any other means, to win money, money's worth or some benefit, and the winning depends upon chance more than understanding or skill', and 'betting' is defined as 'any arrangement by which it is possible to win money, money's worth or some benefit, and the winning depends upon guessing something.'

Any person who organises or arranges a prohibited game, lottery or betting is liable to one year's imprisonment or a fine of IL 5,000, and any person who plays a prohibited game is liable to three months' imprisonment or a fine of IL 1,000. Any person who offers, sells or distributes tickets or anything else which is evidence of a right to participate in a lottery or in a bet, and any person who prints or publishes any notice regarding a lottery or a bet is liable to a fine of IL 2,000. Any person who occupies or manages any place of prohibited games or a place for the conducting of lotteries or betting is liable to one year's imprisonment or a fine of IL 5,000, while any person who leases or permits the use of such place knowing that it will serve as a place of prohibited games or for the conducting of lotteries or betting is liable to six months' imprisonment or a fine of IL 2,000.

The foregoing provisions will not apply to any game, lottery or betting in respect of which the three following conditions are fulfilled: (1) they are intended for a group of specified persons; (2) they do not exceed the bounds of entertainment or amusement; (3) they are not held in a place of prohibited games or in a place for holding lotteries or betting.

The Law will not apply to those classes of lottery or betting or to any particular lottery or bet in respect of which a permit has been given in advance by the Minister of Finance or a person authorised by him in that behalf. Notice of the grant of such a permit must be published in *Reshumot*.

Furthermore, the Law did not apply until the 1st January, 1965, to such lotteries and betting as had been lawfully begun before the Law came into force.

In a case brought for an offence regarding a prohibited game under the Law, the Court may convict the accused on the basis of evidence of an accomplice even if there is no corroboration, and where a person is convicted of an offence under the Law the Court may order that the devices, articles or other things which served for the conducting of the lottery or betting shall be forfeited to the State Treasury, and it is immaterial whether the accused is the owner thereof or not.

For the purposes of the Law, and without detracting from any other mode of proof—(1) where a person is found in a place of prohibited games and a police officer has reason to assume that at that time prohibited games are being played there, that person is deemed to be playing there a prohibited game so long as he has not proved that he was there for another purpose only; (2) a game with cards, dice or a machine is deemed to be a game in which a person is likely to win money, money's worth or a benefit, so long as the contrary is not proved;   (3) premises are deemed to be a place in which prohibited games are usually conducted if a prohibited game is conducted there at least twice within the six months preceding the commission of the offence by the accused, so long as the contrary is not proved, and it is immaterial, as regards the person accused of occupying them, whether he occupied them during all that period or only part of it, or if the premises served as a club for card games and a prohibited game is conducted there at least once within the six months preceding the commission of the offence by the accused.

Within the last few years there has been a considerable increase in cases of 'joy-riding' in motor vehicles but no adequate action could be taken against the offenders as the only offence with which they could normally be charged was stealing the petrol consumed while driving the vehicle.

A new offence was therefore created by the Criminal Law Amendment (Use of Vehicle without Permission) Law, 5724–1964, which came into force on the 2nd April 1964. Under that Law a person who uses a vehicle for a journey without obtaining permission from the owner of the vehicle or the person in lawful possession of the vehicle will be liable to three years' imprisonment. For the purposes of the Law, a 'vehicle' is defined as a motor vehicle within the meaning of the Road Transport Ordinance, including a boat or ship propelled by mechanical power and a cart hitched to an animal.

The Criminal Law Amendment (Offences of Fraud, Extortion and Exploitation) Law, 5723–1963, which came into force on the 15th August, 1963, replaced the provisions of the Criminal Code Ordinance, 1936 with regard to extortion, false pretences, frauds by trustees and persons in a position of trust, false accounting, and forgery, other than forgery of bank notes, and imposes less severe penalties for such offences. In addition, it created new offences regarding cheques. A person who draws a cheque knowing that on the date fixed therein as the date on which it was drawn the banker upon whom the cheque was drawn is not under an obligation to pay it, will be liable to one year's imprisonment, and for that purpose there is a presumption that the drawer knows that on the date fixed in the cheque as the date on which it was drawn the banker is not under an obligation to pay it if (1) at that time the drawer does not have an account with the banker (2) the cheque is presented within sixty days of the date fixed therein as the date on which it was drawn and the banker does not pay it, either because there was no cover for the cheque or for any other reason, and the drawer does not pay the cheque within ten days of the day upon which he was required to do so by the holder of the cheque, or (3) after the cheque was drawn the drawer unlawfully does any act with intent to prevent payment of the cheque, but such presumption does not preclude proof in any other way that the drawer knew at the date fixed in the cheque as the date upon which it was drawn that the banker was not under an obligation to pay it. It will be a good defence for a person charged with such an offence to prove that on the date fixed in the cheque as the date upon which it was drawn, there were, in the circumstances of the case, reasonable grounds for assuming that the banker was under an obligation towards the drawer to pay the cheque. Criminal liability under the above provisions is expressly stated not to derogate from criminal liability under any other enactment.

Another new offence created by this law is the offence of exploitation, which consists of exploiting by any person of the straits, bodily or mental weakness, lack of experience or light-mindedness of another person in order to demand or receive something to which he is not lawfully entitled, or to demand or receive for a commodity or service a consideration which exceeds to an unreasonable degree the usual consideration, or to give for a commodity or service a consideration which is to an unreasonable degree less than the usual consideration. The penalty for such an offence is one year's imprisonment.

The Law also provides that, for the purposes of the Law, a person who orders commodities or services in a restaurant, hotel or similar place, is deemed to represent that he has money to pay the price of the commodities or the services, and a person who pays by cheque is deemed to represent that as from the date fixed in the cheque until a reasonable date for presentation of the cheque for payment, there is with the banker upon whom the cheque is drawn sufficient money to the order of the person delivering the cheque to meet it.

The Criminal Code Ordinance Amendment (No. 28) Law, 5726–1966, which came into force on the 28th July, 1966, amends the definition of 'contravention' appearing in the Ordinance and also in the Interpretation Ordinance, and makes comprehensive changes in the penalties prescribed for offences under the Ordinance, in some cases increasing them, while in other cases decreasing them. The former definition of a 'contravention' was 'any offence punishable with imprisonment for not more than a week or, if with fine only, with a fine not exceeding seventy five Pounds', while the new definition is 'any offence punishable with imprisonment for not more than a month, and if it is punishable with a fine only—a fine not exceeding two hundred Pounds'. The amending law also provides that, wherever the penalty prescribed by the Criminal Code Ordinance, 1936 is a fine or imprisonment, the Court may impose a fine of the amount prescribed by the Criminal Law Amendment (Modes of Punishment) Law, 5714–1954, whatever be the amount of the fine prescribed by the Criminal Code Ordinance, 1936.

In addition to amending the penalties prescribed by the Criminal Code Ordinance, 1936, the amending law abolishes several offences prescribed by that Ordinance, including challenging another to fight a duel, attempting to provoke another to fight a duel, attempting to provoke any person to challenge another to fight a duel, unlawful administration by a woman to herself of any poison or other noxious thing, or using any force of any kind, or any other means whatever, or permitting any such thing or means to be administered or used to her, with intent to procure her own miscarriage, whether she is or is not with child, and attempting to kill oneself.

The Prevention of Infiltration (Offences and Jurisdiction) Law, 5714–1954, which came into force on the 26th August, 1954, prescribes heavy penalties for infiltrators and persons harbouring them or trading with them, and provides for the establishment of special tribunals composed of officers of the Defence Army of Israel to try offenders. That Law also provides that any person who, knowingly and unlawfully, departs from Israel for Lebanon, Syria, Egypt, Trans-Jordan, Saudi Arabia, Iraq, Yemen or any part of Palestine outside Israel, is liable to four years' imprisonment or a fine of five thousand Pounds.

Concealment of Offences

The Criminal Law Amendment (Concealment of Offences) Law, 5719–1959, which came into force on the 14th August, 1959, provides that no person shall take part in any 'trial proceeding' as from the time when, during the course of the proceeding, it is apprehended that one of the offences set out in the Schedule to the Law has been committed, unless notice has been given to the Attorney General to the Government or his representative. For the purposes of the Law, 'trial proceeding' is defined as a proceeding designed to bring about the expulsion of a person from a body of which he is a member, or his being deprived of any of his rights in that body, or the publication of the disgrace of a person for his acts, or the imposition of any other sanction which constitutes a denunciation, not being merely of religious significance. The offences set out in the schedule to the Law are offences against the Criminal Law Amendment (Security of the State) Law, 5717–1957, offences against the Criminal Law Amendment (Bribery Offences) Law, 5712–1952, offences against life or the person or morality punishable with imprisonment for three years or more, and offences under Chapter XII of the Criminal Code Ordinance, 1936 (Corruption and Abuse of Office), Chapter XV of that Ordinance (Miscellaneous Offences against Public Authority), and a number of other sections of that Code, which affect property or rights of the State or of an inspected body within the meaning of the State Comptroller Law, 5718–1958 (Consolidated Version). When a notice has been delivered to the Attorney General or his representative as required by the Law, or a person has been charged with an offence under the Law, and the Attorney General or his representative has decided to institute proceedings in a Court, the Attorney General or his representative may order that the trial in question be stayed until the conclusion of the proceedings in Court. It will be a good defence for a person charged with an offence under the Law to prove either that a notice regarding the act in question had already been delivered to the Attorney General or his representative or to the Police, or that in respect of that act there had already been a police inquiry or that some person had been charged. A person convicted of an offence under the Law will be liable to imprisonment for one year.

Protection of Holy Places

On the 27th June, 1967, the Knesset passed the Protection of Holy Places Law, 5627–1967, which came into force immediately. The Law provides that the holy places shall be protected against desecration and any other injury and against anything likely to affect the freedom of access of members of those faiths for whom those places are sacred or their feelings towards those places, and it prescribes a maximum penalty of seven years imprisonment for a person desecrating or otherwise howsoever injuring a holy place, and a maximum penalty of ten years imprisonment for a person doing anything likely to affect the freedom of access of members of those faiths for whom those places are sacred or their feelings towards those places.

The Law is in addition to, and does not derogate from, any other law.

The Minister for Religious Affairs is charged with the implementation of the Law and he may, after consultation with representatives of members of those faiths concerned, or upon their proposal, and with the consent of the Minister of Justice, make regulations for its implementation.

Pardon

On the 10th February, 1949, the Provisional Council of State, immediately prior to its dissolution passed the Amnesty Ordinance, 5709–1949, which came into force on that day.

The Ordinance provided that any person who on the 10th February, 1949 was under arrest or detention should be released unless he was under arrest or detention by reason of his having been sentenced for, or charged with, murder or any other offence for which the maximum penalty prescribed by law was death or imprisonment for life, or he was a prisoner of war in a prisoner of war camp or an insane person in a place of detention.

It also provided that where a person before the 10th February, 1949, had committed an offence other than murder or an offence for which the maximum penalty prescribed by law was death or imprisonment for life he should not be arrested, detained or prosecuted for it or, if he was already being prosecuted, the proceedings should be discontinued and he should not be punished.

On the 12th July, 1967, following upon the cease fire in the Six Day War (5th–10th June, 1967) between Israel and neighbouring Arab States, the Pardon Law, 5727–1967, was passed by the Knesset and came into force upon its publication in *Reshumot* on the 14th July, 1967.

The Law provides that a person who, before the 5th June, 1967, committed a criminal offence and on the date of commencement of the Law was serving the sentence of imprisonment imposed upon him for that offence should be released from prison, and that if a sentence of imprisonment as aforesaid was imposed upon him and on the date of the commencement of the Law he had not yet begun to serve his sentence he should be released, but the Law contains a long list of offences to the imprisonment for which the Law shall not apply. Among those offences are those for which the penalty is imprisonment for life or for ten years or more, and various offences against the security of the State and offences against the Genocide Law, 5710–1950 or the Punishment of Nazis and their Collaborators Law, 5710–1950.

The Law contains special provisions as regards income tax offences, and provisions as regards exemption from the payment of certain fines of an amount less than IL. 10,000.

It is also provided by the Law that no proceedings shall be taken in any Court for an offence committed before the 5th June, 1967, unless the offence is one of those to the imprisonment for which the Law does not apply, and if proceedings have been commenced they must be stayed, and that a person against whom, on the date of the commencement of the Law (14th July, 1967), there was a charge pending in any Court for any of the said offences, or who had been convicted for such an offence and on the date of the commencment of the Law was entitled to appeal or to file an application for leave to appeal against the judgment, or there was an appeal or such an application pending on that date, is entitled to waive the pardon under the Law by giving a written notice to the Court within thirty days from the date of commencement of the Law.

The Law will not derogate from any result of any offence, conviction or sentence, unless it is expressly provided otherwise in the Law, and it will not derogate from any disciplinary or civil liability, but a disqualification for holding or obtaining a driving licence resulting from a conviction under section 4(2) of the Motor Vehicles Insurance (Third Party Risks) Ordinance, 1947 (under which it is an offence to use a motor vehicle on a public road unless there is in force in relation to the use of the motor vehicle a policy of insurance as required by the Ordinance) and which is in force immediately prior to the date of the commencement of the Law will cease as from that date.

DEFAMATION

THE DEFAMATION LAW, 5725–1965, which came into force upon its publication in *Reshumot* on the 30th July, 1965, was subjected to a considerable amount of criticism, expecially from the journalists, who alleged that it seriously restricted the freedom of the Press. A three man committee presided over by a Supreme Court Justice was appointed by the Prime Minister to hear the objections to it and propose amendments to it for consideration by the Sixth Knesset. Its proposals were brought before the Sixth Knesset which, after considering them, passed the Defamation Amendment Law, 5727–1967, which came into force on the 14th August, 1967. That law amended the Defamation Law, 5725–1965, as hereinafter explained and changed its title to the Prohibition of Defamation Law, 5725–1965.

The Law defines defamation as 'anything the publication of which is likely (1) to degrade a person in the eyes of human beings or to make him the object of hatred, contempt or ridicule on their part; (2) to cause a person to be regarded with contempt for acts, conduct or characteristics imputed to him; (3) to injure a person in his office, whether a public office or any other office, or in his business, occupation or profession; (4) to cause a person to be regarded with contempt because of his origin or religion. For the purpose of this definition a 'person' means an individual or a corporation.

For the purpose of defamation, publication may be by spoken word, or in writing or print, including painting, effigy, gesture, sound or any other means, and, without excluding any other methods of publication, there is deemed to have been a publication of a defamation if it was (1) intended for a person other than the injured person and reached that person or any person other than the injured person; (2) in writing and the writing was likely, in the circumstances, to reach a person other than the injured person.

It is immaterial whether the defamation was expressed directly and completely, or whether it and its being imputed to the person who claims that he was injured by it can be understood from the publication or external circumstances, or partly from one and partly from the other.

Under Section 4 of the Law defamation of a body of persons or any group which is not a corporation, is to be treated as is defamation of a corporation, save that it does not constitute a ground for a civil action or a complaint.

The amending law adds that no information may be filed for an offence under that section save by the Attorney General or with his consent.

Under Section 5 of the Law defamation of a person published after his death is to be treated as is a defamation of a living person, and the spouse of the deceased person, his child, parent, brother and sister are deemed to be the injured persons.

The amending law replaces the words after the words 'living' person by the following : "but it shall not be a ground for a civil action or a complaint and no information may be filed for an offence under the section save upon the request of the spouse of the deceased or one of his children, grand-children, parents, brothers or sisters.

Where the person who is injured by a defamation dies within six months after its publication without having filed an action or a complaint therefor, his spouse, child or parent, or if he left no spouse, children or parent, his brother or sister, may file an action or complaint therefor within six months after his death, while if the injured person himself has filed an action or complaint for the defamation and dies before its termination, his spouse, child or parent, or if he left no spouse, children or parent, his brother or sister may notify the Court, within six months after his death, of their desire to continue the action or complaint, and if they do so they will replace him as plaintiff or complainant.

Any person who, with intent to injure, publishes a defamation to two or more persons other than the injured person, will be liable to one year's imprisonment, while publication of a defamation to one or more persons other than the injured person, constitutes a civil wrong.

The offence of defamation is added by the Law to the list of offences in respect of which the injured person may file a complaint in Court.

The Law empowers the Court, in addition to imposing any penalty or granting any relief, in a civil or criminal case for defamation, to order (1) the prohibition of the distribution of copies of the publication which contains the defamation or its confiscation; if it orders confiscation the order will apply to any person in whose possession there are copies of the publication for sale, distribution or storage, even if that person was not a party in the case; (2) the publication of a correction or denial of the thing constituting the defamation or the publication of the judgment, in whole or in part, and the publication must be made at the expense of the accused or the defendant, in such place, to such extent, and in such manner, as the Court may direct.

Public libraries, archives and the like may, however, be in possession of a copy of the publication unless the Court otherwise orders in the confiscation order. An individual, too, may be in possession of a copy.

Where the accused or the defendant admits that some of the things published are defamatory or untrue, the Court may, at any stage of the proceedings before judgment, order the publication of a correction or denial in respect thereof. .

Under Section 11 of the Law, where a defamation has been published in a newspaper within the meaning of the Press Ordinance the following persons will be liable criminally and civilly for the defamation: the person who brought the defamatory matter to the newspaper and thus caused its publication, the editor of the newspaper and the person responsible for the publication of the defamation in the newspaper. In addition, the publisher of the newspaper will be civilly liable.

The amending law substituted 'the person who actually decided on the publication' for 'the person responsible for the publication'.

A newspaper within the meaning of the Press Ordinance means any publication containing news, intelligence, reports of occurrences, or any remarks, observations or comments, in relation to such news, intelligence or occurrences, or to any other matter of public interest, printed in any language and published in Israel for sale or free distribution at regular or irregular intervals, but does not include any publication published by, or for, the Government of Israel.

In a criminal charge against an editor of a newspaper for the publication of a defamation in the newspaper it will be a good defence for him that he took reasonable steps to prevent the publication of the defamation and that he did not know of its publication.

For the purposes of the Law an editor of a newspaper includes an acting editor and any person who heads the editorial board of the newspaper.

Under Section 12 of the Law, where a defamation is published in print, except in a daily newspaper published under a valid permit, the following persons will also be criminally and civilly liable for the defamation: the person in possession of the printing press in which the publication was printed, and the person who sells or otherwise distributes the publication, save that such seller or distributor will not be liable unless he knew, or ought to have known, that the publication contains a defamation.

The amending law replaces 'a daily newspaper' by 'a newspaper appearing every forty days or less' and the words after the word 'save' by 'that they shall not be responsible unless they knew or ought to have known'.

There are eleven classes of publication enumerated in section

13 of the Law, which will not be a ground for any criminal or civil case. They are: (1) publication of proceedings at an open meeting of the Knesset, or publication of proceedings at a closed meeting of the Knesset permitted by the Standing Rules of the Knesset, under the Basic Law: The Knesset, and publications by a member of the Knesset in respect of which he has immunity under section 1 of the Immunity, Rights and Duties of Knesset Members Law, 5711–1951 (see p. 35); (2) publication at a meeting of the Government; (3) publication by the Government, or a member of the Government, by virtue of his office, or a publication upon the instruction of the Government, or of a member of the Government, by virtue of his office; (4) publication by, or on behalf of, the State Comptroller by virtue of his office; (5) publication by a Judge, Judge of a Religious Court, arbitrator, or any other person with judicial or quasi-judicial powers according to law, made in the course of the proceedings before him and for the purposes of, and in connection with, such proceedings, or in his decision, or a publication by a party, his attorney or witness, in the course of such proceedings and for the purposes of, and in connection with, such proceedings; (6) publication by a member of a commission of enquiry within the meaning of section 22 of the Basic Law: The Knesset or the Commissions of Enquiry Ordinance, made in the course of the proceedings before the commission and for the purposes of, and in connection with, such proceedings, or in its report, or a publication by any person whose matter serves as the subject-matter of the inquiry of the commission, his attorney or a witness, made in the course of such proceedings and for the purposes of, and in connection with, such proceedings; (7) a correct and fair report of what was said, or what occurred, as stated in the foregoing paragraphs (5) and (6) at a public hearing save where the publication is prohibited under section 21 of the Law: (8) a correct and fair report of what was said, or occurred, at a public meeting of an international organisation of which the State of Israel is a member, or of an international conference to which the State of Israel sent a representative, or of an international court, or of any of the elected institutions of the World

Zionist Organisation—Jewish Agency for Palestine; (9) publication which the person publishing it is obliged to make according to law, or according to a direction from an authority authorised by law in that behalf, or which he is authorised to make by a permit from such authority; (10) a copy or correct and fair summary of a register kept in accordance with any enactment or other document open to inspection by any person asking to inspect it according to any enactment; (11) a correct and fair publication, whether in full, or partial, or a summary of what was previously published in the circumstances described in the foregoing paragraphs (1), (3), (4), (7), (8), (9) or (10), and a repetition of what was published at a meeting of the Government if the Government permitted its publication.

The amending law deleted the words 'and for the purposes of and in connection with such proceedings' appearing in paragraphs (5) and (6).

Under Section 14 of the Law, in a criminal or civil case for defamation it will be a good defence that the thing that was published was true and it was in the public interest to publish it, provided that the publication did not go beyond what was necessary in the public interest. Such a defence will not be denied by reason only of the fact that the truth of an incidental particular which does not cause a substantial injury is not proved to be true.

The amending law deleted the words: 'it was in the public interest to publish it, provided that the publication did not go beyond what was necessary in the public interest' and replaced them by the words: 'there was a public interest in the publication'.

In a criminal or civil case for defamation it will be a good defence if the accused or defendant made the publication in good faith in one of the following circumstances, enumerated in Section 15 of the Law: (1) he did not know, and was not obliged to know, of the existence of the injured person; (2) the relations between him and the person at whom the publication was directed imposed upon him a legal, moral or social obligation to make the publication; (3) the publication was made for the protection of a legitimate personal interest of the accused or defendant, of the person at whom the publication was directed or of someone in whom that person had a legitimate personal interest;   (4) the publication was an expression of opinion on the conduct of the injured person in a judicial, official or public office, in a public service or in connection with a public matter, or on the character, past, acts or opinions of the injured person in so far as they were revealed in such conduct;   (5) the publication was an expression of opinion on the conduct of the injured person   (a) as a party, attorney of a party or witness at a public hearing of proceedings referred to in Section 13(5) of the Law, provided that the publication was not prohibited under Section 21 of the Law, or   (b) as a person whose matter constitutes the subject-matter of an enquiry, or his attorney or as a witness at a public hearing of a commission of enquiry referred to in Section 13(6), or on the character, past, acts or opinions of the person injured in so far as they are revealed in such conduct; (6) the publication was a criticism of a literary, scientific, artistic or other work which the injured person exhibited publicly, or of any act which he did publicly, and in so far as the matter is bound up with such a criticism, or expression of opinion on the character, past, acts or opinions of the injured person in so far as they are revealed in such work or act;   (7) the publication was an expression of opinion on the conduct or character of the injured person in a matter in which the accused or defendant was in charge of the injured person, by virtue of any law or contract, and the publication was justified by reason of his being so in charge of him;   (8) the publication was a complaint against the injured person, by virtue of any law or contract, or a complaint made to an authority competent to receive complaints against the injured person or to investigate the matter forming the subject-matter of the complaint;   (9) the publication was a correct and fair report of a public meeting or of a meeting of a corporation to which the public had access, and the publication was in the public interest;   (10) the publication was made only in order to condemn or deny a defamation previously published; (11) the publication was only the delivery of information to an editor of a newspaper for him to examine the question of its publication in the newspaper.

The amending law added at the end of paragraph (1): 'or of the circumstances in which the defamation is understood or its connection with the injured person as stated in Section 3' and after the words 'to an editor of a newspaper' in paragraph (11), the words 'or to his representative'.

Where the accused or defendant who made the publication in one of the circumstances specified in Section 15 of the Law and the publication did not go beyond reasonable bounds in such circumstances, it is presumed that he made the publication in good faith. On the other hand, it is presumed that the accused or defendant who made the publication did not do so in good faith if (1) the thing that was published was not true and he did not believe it to be true; or (2) the thing that was published was not true and before the publication he did not take reasonable steps to ascertain whether it was true or not; (3) he intended by means of the publication to injure to a greater extent than was reasonable for the protection of the matters protected by Section 15 of the Law.

Where a defamation has been published in a newspaper the defence of good faith will not be available to the editor, the person responsible for the publication of the defamation in the newspaper or to the publisher of the newspaper, if he has been requested by the injured person, or one of the injured persons, to publish a correction or denial by the injured person, and he has not published the correction or denial in a manner as similar as possible to that of the publication of the defamation and within a reasonable time after the receipt of the request, provided that the request was signed by the injured person, that the correction or denial did not contain any defamation or other unlawful content, and its length was not unreasonable in the circumstances.

The amending law replaced the words 'the person responsible for the publication' by the words 'the person who actually decided upon the publication' and added the following paragraph: 'Where the newspaper appeared less than once a week the correction or the denial shall be published upon the demand of the person injured also in a daily newspaper.'

Where the accused or defendant adduces any evidence, or himself gives evidence, in order to establish one of the defences specified in the Law the prosecutor or plaintiff may bring rebutting evidence.

In imposing sentence, or awarding damages, the Court may also take into consideration for the benefit of the accused or defendant the following: (1) the defamation was but a repetition of what had already been said, and he specified the source upon which he relied; (2) he was convinced of the truth of the defamation; (3) he did not refer to the injured person; (4) he apologised for the publication, corrected or denied the thing constituting the defamation or took steps to stop the sale or distribution of a copy of the publication which contains the defamation, provided that the apology, correction or denial was published in the place, to the extent and in the manner in, or to, which the defamation was published and contained no reservation.

The Law empowers the Court in a criminal or civil case for defamation to prohibit the publication of the Court proceedings, including the information and the pleadings but excluding the judgment, to such extent as it considers necessary for the protection of the name of the person affected by the case, and any person who contravenes the prohibition will be liable to six months' imprisonment or a fine of IL. 5,000.

The amending law replaces the words 'to prohibit the publication of the Court proceedings including the information and the pleadings but excluding the judgment' by the words 'on its own motion or upon the application of a party to prohibit or postpone temporarily, for reasons to be recorded, the publication of the Court proceedings, including the pleadings but excluding an information and a judgment.'

In a criminal or civil case for defamation no evidence may be adduced, and no witness may be examined, with regard to the bad reputation of the person injured or with regard to his defective character, past, acts or opinions, save to the extent to which those particulars directly concern the defamation constituting the subject-matter of the case, or to which the Court permits the adduction of that evidence or the examination of that witness (1) in a criminal case after the conviction of the accused—for the mitigation of his sentence; (2) in a civil case, after the decision that the defendant has to pay damages—for the mitigation of damages; (3) to the extent that the injured person on his part has given evidence, or has adduced evidence, or examined a witness, with regard to his good character, past, acts or opinions; (4) if the Court is satisfied that the thing is necessary for discovering the truth and doing justice in the case.

The amending law replaces paragraph (4) by the following: '(4) if the Court is satisfied that it is necessary for doing justice and the discovery of the truth, either by ascertaining the reliability of the evidence of the person injured or otherwise'.

In a civil case for defamation which is tried after the termination of a criminal case against the same person for the same defamation the Court is empowered by the Law to rely upon the findings of fact, in whole or in part, made in the criminal case in accordance with the evidence taken therein, without having to retake that evidence.

The Law repeals sections 201–3, and 205–9, of the Criminal Code Ordinance, 1936 and sections 16–22 of the Civil Wrongs Ordinance, 1944.

CIVIL WRONGS

THE QUESTION whether the English law of torts was applicable in Palestine was argued in the Palestine Supreme Court for the first time in 1940 and it was decided by a majority that it was not applicable and that if it was desired to introduce a law of torts in this country then it should be done by Ordinance. As a result the Civil Wrongs Ordinance, 1944, was enacted, but it was not put into force until the 15th July, 1947, as it was considered necessary to ensure first that suitable insurance facilities were available to enable effect to be given to the Motor Vehicles Insurance (Third Party Risks) Ordinance, 1947. Before it was put into force it was amended in 1947 in order to bring its provisions

regarding contributory negligence into line with the then
recent English Law Reform (Contributory Negligence) Act,
1945.

The Civil Wrongs Ordinance, 1944, codifies the English law
of torts with certain modifications. Section 3 thereof provides
that matters enumerated therein shall be civil wrongs and, subject to the provisions of the Ordinance, any person who suffers
any injury or damage by reason of any civil wrong committed
in this country will be entitled as against the person committing
or liable for such civil wrong to the remedies specified in the Ordinance, namely, compensation and injunction. The Israel Courts
have interpreted that section as restricting the matters which
constitute civil wrongs to those enumerated in the Ordinance,
and in consequence have refused to apply the English law of
torts in respect of any matter not so enumerated. Section 60 of
the Ordinance provides that where the plaintiff has suffered
damage, which is defined as meaning 'loss of life, or loss of, or
detriment to, any property, comfort, bodily welfare, reputation or other similar loss or detriment', compensation shall
only be awarded in respect of such damage as would naturally
arise in the usual course of things, and which directly arose from
the defendant's civil wrong.

Section 2(1) of the Ordinance provides that the local Interpretation Ordinance shall apply to it, and subject thereto, expressions used in it shall be presumed, so far as is consistent with
their context, and, except as may be otherwise expressly provided, to be used with the meaning attaching to them in English
law, and shall be construed in accordance therewith. As a result
the Israel Courts are required to refer to English decisions in
order to construe expressions used in the Ordinance if they are
not defined by local legislation.

Apart from defamation, the provisions of the Ordinance in
respect whereof were repealed by the Defamation Law, 5725–
1965 (see pp. 87–96), the Ordinance contains provisions regarding the following civil wrongs: injurious falsehood, as-
sault, false imprisonment, malicious prosecution, unlawfully
causing breach of contract, passing off, fraud, unlawful detention

of property, conversion, trespass to immovable property, trespass to movable property, public nuisance, private nuisance, interference with daylight, negligence and breach of statutory duty.

Under section 67 of the Ordinance it will be no bar to any action in respect of a civil wrong that the facts upon which such action is based constitute a criminal offence; but when, at any stage of any action in respect of a civil wrong, it appears to the Court before which the action is pending that the facts upon which the action is based constitute, or may constitute, a felony, the Court must stay further proceedings in the action until it is satisfied that either those facts have been reported to a police officer or a police officer is aware of those facts.

Section 4(1) of the Ordinance provided that, save where otherwise expressly provided, no action in respect of any civil wrong shall be brought against His Majesty or the Government of Palestine. That section was repealed by the Civil Wrongs (State Liability) Law, 5712–1952, which came into force on the 31st August, 1952. Under that Law, for the purposes of civil liability, the State is, with certain exceptions specified in the Law, regarded as a corporate body. The Law provides that the State is not civilly liable for an act done within the scope of lawful authority, or bona fide in the purported exercise of lawful authority, although it is liable for negligence in connection with such an act. Nor is it liable for defamation, an act done in the course of a war operation of the Defence Army of Israel, an injury sustained by a person during and in consequence of his military service within the meaning of the Invalids (Pensions and Rehabilitation) Law, 5709–1949, the death of a person resulting from injury sustained by him during and in consequence of his military service within the meaning of the Fallen Soldiers' Families (Pensions and Rehabilitation) Law, 5719–1949, or as owner of property vested in it solely by operation of law, so long as it has not taken possession thereof. For the above purposes act includes omission.

Reparation for Bodily Injury

For the purposes of the Civil Wrongs Law Amendment (Reparation for Bodily Injury) Law, 5724–1964, which came into force on the 2nd April, 1964, 'reparation for injury' is defined as 'expenses incurred, or service given, in order to make good bodily injury, to save the person injured from a worsening of the injury or additional injury or to relieve his suffering, including assistance given to the injured person for his subsistence or that of his family required as a result of the injury, and also, if the injured person has died, such assistance given to a person entitled to compensation by reason of his death from the person who caused the injury' and 'bodily injury' is defined as including 'illness, physical or mental defect, and death'.

Where a person causes bodily injury to another person, the Law entitles the person who has made good the injury to recover the reparation for the injury from the person who caused the injury up to the amount which the person who caused the injury would have had to pay to the beneficiary under any law for the causing of the bodily injury if the injury had not been made good by the person who made it good.

Where the bodily injury is caused also by the contributory negligence of the person injured or is caused entirely by the negligence of the person injured the person making good the injury may recover from the beneficiary the reparation for the injury, wholly or partially, in accordance with the degree of negligence of the person injured.

For the purposes of the Law it is immaterial whether the person making good the injury acted in accordance with a duty imposed upon him by law or by contract or whether he acted voluntarily. It is also immaterial that the person making good the injury is a cooperative society of which the beneficiary is a member, but if the person making good the injury is a corporation carrying on insurance business, other than a corporation which insures only its own members, and acted under an insurance contract with the person injured or the beneficiary, the person making good the injury will not be able to recover under the Law, but without prejudice to any right he may have under any other law.

All that may be recovered under the Law is a reasonable amount for expenses, fee for service and assistance. Any salary or wage which an employer continues to pay to his employee during the period when the employee is incapable of working by reason of his bodily injury, is deemed for this purpose to be a reasonable expense but there cannot be recovered more than the salary or wage which the employee would have received if he were able to work. The food supplied and the pay given by the State to a soldier while he is unfit for service are also deemed to be a reasonable expense.

Where the person causing the injury is insured against his liability to the beneficiary, the person making good the injury may recover under the Law from the insurer to the extent to which the insurer is liable to the person causing the injury.

The person making good the injury will not be entitled to claim from the person causing the injury under the Law any sum of the reparation for the injury paid to him by the beneficiary, but the beneficiary may recover that sum from the person causing the injury.

The Law does not affect the right of the person making good the injury from claiming the reparation for the injury on any other ground, but he may not collect in all his claims more than the amount of the reparation for the injury.

A Court dealing with a claim under the Law may, at the request of the person making good the injury, receive as evidence of the liability for injury and contributory negligence any finding in the matter in any unappealable judgment given in an action for compensation by reason of the injury.

It is expressly provided that the Law shall apply also to the State.

Under the Reward for Soldier Injured in Saving the Life of Another Person Law, 5725–1965, which came into force on the 1st August, 1965, where a soldier has become disabled or has sacrificed his life as a result of saving another person from the danger of losing his life, he is to be treated for all purposes as if he were a disabled person of the Defence Army of Israel or a soldier killed in battle, as the case may be.

Under the Rewards for Persons Injured in Saving Life Law, 5725–1965, which came into force on the 1st January, 1965, where a person becomes disabled, or loses his life in the course of an act of rescue, that is, an act done for saving the life of another person of the classes which the Minister of Labour, with the approval of the Labour Affairs Committee of the Knesset, has declared to be an act of rescue for the purpose of the Law, the provisions of the Third Chapter of the Second Part of the National Insurance Law, 5714–1953 will apply to such person or his dependants, as if he were an insured person who suffered an employment injury within the meaning of section 13 of the National Insurance Law and as if the State were his employer, even if he was not entitled to any benefits under the said Chapter but for the Law.

The benefits under the Law will be paid through the National Insurance Institute, and the State Treasury must reimburse the Institute upon its demand for any expenditure incurred by it for the granting of the benefit.

The Minister of Labour is charged with the implementation of the Law, and is empowered to make regulations as respects any matter touching its implementation. He may also appoint, by notice in *Reshumot*, Certifying Commissioners who are empowered to certify that an act is an act of rescue. The certification by a Certifying Commissioner that an injury has been caused as the result of an act of rescue is a condition precedent to any claim under the Law. The National Insurance Tribunal has exclusive jurisdiction to deal with, and adjudicate upon, any claim for a benefit under the Law.

CONTRACTS

MOHAMMEDAN law, and consequently the Mejelle, does not deal specifically with contract as a branch of law. There is only one formal definition of a contract in the Mejelle, namely, that contained in Article 103, in which contract is defined as being 'What the parties bind themselves and undertake to do with reference to a particular matter. It is composed of the combination of offer and acceptance'.

The different rules govening the subject are scattered throughout the various books of the Mejelle, and many are to be found in the Book dealing with Sale which apply to every class of contract. Such rules have been considerably affected and amplified by Articles 64, 80 -82 and 106 -112 of the Ottoman Code of Civil Procedure, the provisions whereof are hereinafter set out.

Freedom of contract is considerably limited by the terms of Mohammedan law as reproduced in the Mejelle. In order to remedy that defect, and, it appears, in order to avoid the reproach of seeking to change the terms of the Mejelle, the origin whereof is claimed by Moslems to be divine as it is based on Mohammedan law, the Ottoman legislative authorities introduced modifications to Article 64 of the Ottoman Code of Civil Procedure, dated the 10th May, 1914, which, in effect, have had the desired result.

The following are the terms of Article 64:

'(1) The terms of all contracts and agreements which are not forbidden by special laws and regulations and which are not contrary to morality and which do not disturb public order nor conflict with matters of personal status, such as the capacity of the contracting parties, and the rules of law relating to inheritance and succession, and to any disposition of money or real property dedicated to pious purposes and immovable property, are valid as regards the contracting parties. Provided, however, that if the subject matter of the contract cannot be produced, such contract may be declared null and void.

(2) Any matter which possesses some specific value may be the subject of contract. Any determinate object, interest, or right which is generally recognised as being capable of transmission is regarded as possessing some specific value. Agreements relating to things to be produced in the future are also void.

(3) Should the parties have agreed as to the fundamental points of a contract, such contract shall be regarded as being completely concluded, even though subsidiary matters may have been passed over in silence. In cases where the parties have not been able to arrive at an agreement concerning subsidiary matters, the Court shall give a decision thereon, bearing in mind the nature of the business.'

The Mejelle does not insist upon any contract being reduced to writing, but Article 80 of the Ottoman Code of Civil Procedure provides:

'Claims relating to undertakings and contracts of any nature whatsoever, which it is customary to reduce to writing, and claims relating to partnerships, farming out and loans, which exceed one thousand piastres (Ten Israel Pounds), must be proved by a document. Any action brought in respect of a document relating to the matters mentioned above must be proved by a document or by the admission of the defendant or by an entry in a register, even though it does not exceed one thousand piastres (Ten Israel Pounds).

Article 81 of the said Code provides that the procedure set forth in Article 80 shall be in force and apply in cases where interest added to the principal sum, or where the amount obtained by adding a number of items together which are actually claimed, exceeds one thousand piastres.

Article 82 of the said Code provides that the subject matter of the claim may be proved by the evidence of witnesses and the procedure set forth in Article 80 shall not apply in the following circumstances:

(1) Transactions between husband and wife, ascendants and descendants, brother and sister or their children, or father and mother and her sister, and father-in-law and mother-in-law;

(2) Claims which could not be reduced to writing on account of *force majeure* or for any reason which is legally acceptable;

(3) Where the document in the possession of the creditor has been lost accidentally;

(4) Where the parties are in a village and there is no person in that village able to write out a document.

Articles 106–111 of the Ottoman Code of Civil Procedure, the provisions whereof are hereinafter set out, deal with the circumstances under which damages for breach of contract may be awarded.

Article 106 provides that damages claimed on account of non-performance or delay in the performance of the terms of any special contract drawn up with a view to the doing of any particular thing or the delivery of any specific quantity of things at any fixed place by one party to the contract from the party upon whom the obligation falls shall not be awarded unless the party making the claim has officially served upon the other party, in accordance with the usual procedure, a protest, i.e. a warning, served through the official channel, calling upon such other party to carry out the obligation which he has undertaken to perform. Such a warning is known as a 'notarial notice' and is sent by a Notary Public (see pp. 244–5).

If a stipulation be inserted in the contract itself to the effect that if, at the expiration of the period of the contract, the person upon whom an obligation falls fails to carry out the same, notice shall be dispensed with, and the expiration of the prescribed period shall be considered to take the place of a notice, such stipulation shall take the place of a protest, i.e. warning, at the expiration of the period, (Article 107).

Judgment may be given that a contracting party who has failed to carry out, or has delayed in carrying out, what he has undertaken to do, is to make good the loss sustained by the payment of damages, although he may not in any way have acted in bad faith. If his failure to carry out, or his delay in carrying out, his undertaking arose out of *force majeure* i.e. from some cause which cannot be attributed to him or which is not within his control, judgment may not be given against him. (Article 108).

If the failure to carry out an undertaking is not due to bad faith on the part of the person who has undertaken to perform it, the loss to be made good by him shall consist of the ascertained amount of injury suffered by the other party owing to such failure. (Article 109).

If the failure to carry out the contract is due to bad faith on the part of the person upon whom the obligation falls, the loss to be made good by such person on account of failure to carry out his obligation shall consist of the direct injury sustained by the other party and the profit of which he has been deprived. (Article 110).

If the contract contains a clause to the effect that whoever of the two parties fails to carry out his undertaking shall pay to the other party a definite fixed sum by way of indemnity, that sum and no more and no less is payable. (Article 111).

The Privy Council, in appeals from judgments of the Supreme Court of Palestine, held that, in view of the provisions of Article 46 of the Palestine Order-in-Council, 1922 (see p. 62), regard must be had to the English law applicable in the case of concurrent obligations so that in an action to recover damages for breach of contract the plaintiff is bound to establish his readiness and willingness to perform his part, and that the said Article 111 will only apply to an agreement which represents 'a genuine pre-estimate of damages' and if the Court applying the well-known rules of English law has to conclude that the sum agreed was a penalty, whatever it may be called in the agreement, then the penal stipulation will not be enforced. Another doctrine of English law, the doctrine of specific performance, was also applied by the Palestine Courts.

Article 112 of the said Code, which contained provisions with regard to the payment of interest in the case of delay in the payment of money contracted to be paid, was repealed by section 13 of the Adjudication of Interest Law, 5721–1961 (see pp. 111–2), which also provided that the provisions of the said Article 106 shall not apply to the adjudication of interest under the said Law.

Generally speaking, in matters connected with contracts,

including the rules for the interpretation thereof, the Palestine Courts, in view of the provisions of the said Article 46, applied the rules of English law, both common law and equity, in the absence of relevant legislation and the Israel Courts do the same.

Standard Contracts

The Standard Contracts Law, 5724–1964, was passed by the Knesset on the 12th February, 1964, and came into force three months later.

For the purposes of the Law, a 'standard contract' is defined as 'a contract for the supply of a commodity or the giving of a service all or any of the conditions whereof have been fixed in advance by the supplier of the commodity or the giver of the service (the supplier), or on his behalf, in order that they should serve as the conditions of many contracts between him and persons unspecified in number or identity (the customers)'. Commodity is defined as including land and rights in land, rights of letting and leasing, and a condition of the contract is defined as including a condition specified in the contract and every condition, waiver or other matter which is part of the engagement although not specified in the contract itself, other than a condition upon which the supplier and the customer have agreed especially for the purposes of a specific contract.

The Law contains a list of what are known for the purposes of the Law as 'restrictive conditions'. According to that list a 'restrictive condition' is one which (1) rejects or restricts the responsibility of the supplier towards the customer, either under a contractual obligation or by law as it would have existed but for the condition; (2) confers upon the supplier a right to cancel the contract or to vary its conditions or suspend its execution, solely of his own accord, or otherwise brings about the rescission of the contract or the cancellation or restriction of any right of the customer arising out of the contract, unless the above were made conditional upon a breach of the contract by the customer or other causes independent of the supplier; (3) makes the exercise by the customer of any of his rights arising out of the contract conditional upon the consent of the supplier or any other person on his behalf; (4) requires the customer to be dependent upon the supplier or any other person in a matter which is not directly connected with the subject-matter of the contract or makes it a condition of any right of the customer arising out of the contract that he should be so dependent, or restricts the freedom of the customer to enter into any agreement in such matter with a third party; (5) constitutes a waiver in advance on the part of the customer of any of his rights which would have arisen out of the contract but for the condition; (6) authorises the supplier or any other person on his behalf to act in the name of the customer or in his stead in order to exercise a right given to the supplier as against the customer; (7) makes the books of account or other documents drawn up by the supplier, or on his behalf, binding upon the customer, or otherwise places upon the customer a burden of proof which would not be placed upon him but for the condition; (8) makes as a condition of the right of the customer to any lawful relief the fulfilment of a condition or acting within a specified time, or restricts the customer in his pleas or the legal proceedings at his disposal, other than a condition of arbitration; (9) submits a dispute between the parties to arbitration when the supplier has greater influence than the customer upon the fixing of the arbitrator or arbitrators or the place of the arbitration, or which confers upon the supplier a right to select, solely of his own accord, the Court in which the dispute will be adjudicated.

Where a supplier enters into, or is about to enter into, a standard contract with customers, he may apply to the Board appointed for the purposes of the Restrictive Trade Practices Law, 5719–1959, (see p. 114) and ask it to approve the restrictive conditions in the contract, and when such an application is made to it the Board may, after hearing the applicant and the Attorney General or his representative, and after having given to every person specified in regulations made by the Minister of Justice as a respondent to such an application an opportunity of stating his arguments, approve a restrictive condition in the contract or refuse to approve it. In order to decide upon the validity of a restrictive condition the Board must consider whether, having regard to all the conditions of the contract and all the other circumstances, the condition prejudices the customers or confers an unfair advantage upon the supplier which is calculated to prejudice the customers. The applicant, the Attorney General and any respondent to the application may appeal to the Supreme Court against the decision of the Board within 60 days.

The approval of the Board will remain in force for a period of five years from the date when it is given or for such shorter period as the Board may fix in its decision, and a restrictive condition in a standard contract which the Board has approved will be valid in any contract made in accordance with the standard contract before the giving of the approval or within the period during which the approval is in force.

A restrictive condition in a standard contract which the Board has refused to approve is void, but if before the refusal the standard contract was approved by the Board, the refusal will not affect a contract made in accordance with the standard contract before the approval or within the period during which the approval is in force.

The Board is required to keep a register of its decisions which will be open to inspection by any person, and the Board may publish its decisions in such form as appears to it to be suitable for the benefit of the public.

If the Board approves the conditions of a standard contract, the supplier must indicate the fact of the approval on the face of every contract which he makes with a customer after the grant of the approval and within the period during which the approval is in force, and if there is no such indication on the face of any particular contract the Court may, despite the approval of the Board, exercise its powers with regard to such contract.

The Law provides that a Court, when it finds during the course of a legal proceeding between a supplier and a customer that a condition in a standard contract, having regard to all the conditions of the contract and all the other circumstances, prejudices the customers or confers an unfair advantage upon the supplier which is calculated to prejudice the customers, may regard the condition, wholly or partially, as a void condition, and order the return to the customer of what he gave under that condition.

The Board may not entertain any application for approval which has been submitted after an argument against a restrictive condition has been put forward in a case between the supplier and one of its customers, nor may it entertain any application for approval of a condition which a Court, in the exercise of its powers under the Law, has decided to regard as a void condition.

The invalidation of a condition in a contract by the Board or by a Court will not of itself affect the remaining conditions of the contract.

It is expressly provided in the Law that for the purposes of the Law, when the State is a supplier it is to be treated as is any other supplier.

The provisions of the Law will not apply to any condition which is consonant with the conditions fixed or approved by any enactment in force immediately prior to the coming into force of the Law or under any such enactment, or which are fixed by an international agreement to which Israel is a party or in an agreement between an Israel corporation which has been approved for the purpose by the Government and a foreign supplier, nor will they apply to any condition more favourable to the customer than those conditions.

COMMERCIAL LAW

IN THE field of commercial law the Ottoman law was almost completely replaced by Palestine legislation based upon the corresponding English law. Of the Ottoman Commercial Code only a few articles—those dealing with traders' accounts and common carriers—still remain in force. The provisions relating to bankruptcy were replaced by the Bankruptcy Ordinance, 1936, those relating to bills of exchange by the Bills of Exchange Ordinance, to which the Bills of Exchange Ordinance Amendment (No. 2) Law, 5724–1953, which came into force on the 1st June, 1964, added a new provision whereunder a cheque which is issued before the date stated in it as the date of the cheque, or is issued without a date, will be payable upon issue, and for all intents and purposes, the date of the day of issue will be declared to be the date of the cheque, and those relating to companies, by the Companies Ordinance, to which the Companies Ordinance Amendment Law, 5710–1950, of the 18th August, 1950, has added a new Section (s. 119A) relating to the transfer of an undertaking of a foreign company to an Israel company, first used for the transfer of the undertaking of the Anglo-Palestine Bank Ltd., an English company, to the Bank Leumi le-Israel B.M., an Israel company. Each of the said Ordinances contains an express provision that it is to be interpreted by reference to the law of England relating to the subject matter of the Ordinance. In addition, the Palestine legislature enacted a comprehensive Cooperative Societies Ordinance, which regulates societies having as their objects the promotion of thrift, self-help and mutual aid among persons with common economic needs so as to bring about better living, better business and better methods of production, and societies established for the purpose of facilitating the operations of such societies.

Interest

The Ottoman law relating to interest remained in force until replaced by the Interest Law, 5717–1957 as from the 1st March, 1957. Under the Ottoman law the maximum rate of interest which could be charged was 9% per annum, compound interest could not be charged except in certain specified cases, and the amount of interest chargeable could not exceed the principal sum upon which it was chargeable. Palestine legislation, however, provided for the grant of exemptions in certain cases from compliance with the provisions of the Ottoman law. The Interest Law, 5717–1957 authorises the Minister of Finance, after consultation with the Governor of the Bank of Israel, and with the approval of the Finance Committee of the Knesset, to fix, by order, either generally or in relation to any particular class of credit transactions, the maximum rate of interest which the lender is entitled to receive from the borrower, as well as the conditions and periods for accumulation of interest, and no person may demand any interest the rate of which exceeds the maximum so fixed, and no person may demand or receive compound interest save to the extent permitted by an order of the Minister of Finance. The new law, for the first time, imposes a penalty—a fine of IL. 10,000 or five times the excessive interest —for giving a loan at excessive interest or receiving excessive interest. The penalty will not, however, be imposable in respect of deposits with a banking institution.

Furthermore, under section 56 of the Bank of Israel Law, 5714–1954, the Governor of the Bank of Israel may, after consultation with the Advisory Committee appointed by the Government under the Law and with the approval of the Government, and the Finance Committee of the Knesset, by order, fix either generally or for any particular class of deposits or credit transactions, the maximum rate of interest which a banking institution may pay upon deposits as well as the maximum rate of interest which a banking institution may receive for discounting bills and upon loans and other credit transactions.

The Minister of Finance may not make an order in respect of any class of credit transaction in respect of which the Governor of the Bank of Israel has made an order, and vice versa.

The Adjudication of Interest Law, 5721–1961, which came into force on the 23rd June, 1961, provides for the awarding of interest by a judicial authority, which is defined for the purposes of the Law as meaning 'any Court, tribunal or other authority competent by law to award a payment to a party or to fix a sum payable to a party, and includes an arbitrator'.

Under that law, a judicial authority which awards a sum of money to a party, or which orders the enforcement of such an award, or which fixes a sum of money due under any enactment, may, at its discretion, award interest on the whole or a part of the sum, and it may also award interest on costs and advocate's fees awarded by it to a party. The rate of interest will be eleven per cent per annum unless the judicial authority fixes a lower rate. If the judicial authority does not fix a shorter period, the period of interest in the case of an award of costs will be from the day on which the costs were incurred to the day of payment, in the case of an award of advocate's fees it will be from the date of the award to the day of payment, and in all other cases it will be from the date of the submission of the claim to the day of payment.

Interest under the Law may not be awarded where an agreement as to the payment of interest or other compensation for delay in payment exists between the parties, or where an enactment provides for the payment of interest or other relief as compensation for delay in payment and so long as the relief can be granted.

Interest awarded under the Law will not bear interest.

Where a party has paid to his opponent, subject to the decision of the judicial authority, the whole or part of the sum which he may become liable to pay, or where a party has offered so to pay and the opponent has rejected the offer, interest on the sum paid or offered as aforesaid may not be imposed under the Law in respect of the period subsequent to the payment or offer.

The Law is expressly made applicable to the State.

Restrictive Trade Practices

The Restrictive Trade Practices Law, 5719–1959, which came into force on the 28th January, 1960, and was amended on the 25th February, 1961 and the 6th October, 1963, contains provisions relating to two classes of restrictive trade practices, namely, cartels and monopolies. For the purposes of the Law, a 'cartel' is defined as an arrangement, other than one of the arrangements specified in the Law, between persons carrying on business, which is expressly or impliedly designed to impose on any of the parties to it, in respect of any commodity or service, any preventive or restrictive provisions, referred to in the Law as 'restraints', as to any of the following matters: (1) the consideration or any other recompense (referred to in the Law as 'price') to be demanded, accepted, offered, or given, whether it be a fixed price, or a minimum or maximum price; (2) the profit to be derived; (3) the conditions, methods, volume, qualitative standard, or nature of, the business to be carried on; (4) the persons or class of persons with, or for whom, business is to be carried on; (5) the place where business is to be carried on; (6) the amount, quality, conditions, and methods of investments to be made for the purposes of the business.

An arrangement will be regarded as a cartel under the Law where, in pursuance thereof, a person obtains a benefit if he observes, or incurs a liability if he does not observe, any restraint within the meaning of the Law, and a determination by a body of persons, whether incorporated or unincorporated, of a policy for its members or for a particular class of its members, as to any of the matters specified in the definition of a cartel, whether or not the determination is binding on them, will also be regarded as a cartel, and every member of that body will be regarded as a party to the cartel. On the other hand, the following arrangements will not be regarded as cartels: (1) an arrangement imposing restraints all of which are prescribed by law (2) an arrangement imposing restraints relating to the right to use any patent, design, trade mark, or copyright (3) an arrangement to which an organisation of employees or employers is a party and which imposes restraints all of which relate to the employment and conditions of employment of employees (4) an arrangement imposing restraints all of which relate to certain specified locally produced agricultural commodities and all the parties to which are producers or wholesale distributors of the commodity to which the arrangement applies (5) an arrangement the parties to which are a parent company and not more than one subsidiary for the whole or any particular part of the territory of the State. For this purpose a company which holds in another company fully paid-up shares, including stock, the nominal value of which exceeds one half of the registered capital of the other company, is a parent company, and the other company is a subsidiary (6) an arrangement the parties to which are only two persons, one of whom supplies a particular commodity or service and the other acquires it for the purposes of supply, and who are not a 'commercial combination', that is to say, a combination of the owners of two or more businesses for the purpose of furthering their business interests, and under the arrangement the supplier undertakes to supply the commodity or service to that acquirer only and the acquirer undertakes to acquire that or any similar commodity or service from that supplier only (7) an arrangement imposing restraints all of which relate to international carriage by sea or by air and notified to the Minister of Transport on a form prescribed by him by regulations.

The Law provides for the appointment by the Government of a Board and a Controller of Restrictive Trade Practices. The Board will consist of a least five members. The chairman will be a District Court Judge and at least half of its members, excluding the chairman, must be persons other than State employees, of whom at least one must be a person who, in the opinion of the Government, is a representative of the consumers. The Controller will have the status of a State employee.

Every cartel must be registered in the Register kept by the Controller. Registered cartels are to be open to inspection by the public, but the Board is empowered to direct that any particular cartel, or part of it, shall not be open to inspection if the Board is of opinion that it should so direct, having regard to the security or interests of the State or the interests of any person in a commercial or industrial secret. Notice of every registered cartel and of every direction issued by the Board in respect of it must be published by the Controller in *Reshumot* and in two daily newspapers.

Every person who considers himself aggrieved by a cartel may lodge with the Board an opposition to the cartel. The Board may not approve a cartel unless it is of the opinion that the cartel is in the public interest. In deciding whether a cartel is in the public interest the Board must consider every point which in its opinion is of importance and especially whether there is a reasonable need for the cartel in order to do certain things specified in the Law. Every decision of the Board or of the Supreme Court in respect of a cartel must be entered in the Register by the Controller, and notice of the decision must be published in *Reshumot*.

The Law also contains provisions for the control of monopolies. A monopoly is defined, for the purposes of the Law, as the supply or acquisition of a commodity or service by one person to an extent exceeding the extent designated by the Minister of Commerce and Industry, by order, as monopolistic with regard to the supply of that commodity or service, either generally or in respect of a particular area, and for that purpose the following are regarded as one person (1) a company and its subsidiaries; (2) the subsidiaries of one company; (3) companies most of the directors of which are the same persons; (4) a company and the persons controlling it; (5) companies controlled by one person, and the term 'company' includes a cooperative society.

If it appears to the Controller that a monopoly exists in respect of the supply of a particular commodity or service, and that, but for the monopoly, the price level of that commodity or service would be lower, or that the quality or the methods of production or marketing of that commodity or service supplied would be more satisfactory, or that the quantity of that commodity or service supplied would be greater, he may, with the approval of the Board, propose to the Minister of Commerce and Industry that he make provisions, by order, as to the maximum prices, or the quality or the methods of production or supply, of that commodity or service, and the Minister may so order.

Decisions and orders of the Board under the Law will be appealable on a point of law to the Supreme Court sitting as a High Court of Justice.

In addition to imposing penalties for offences under the Law, the Law provides that any damage caused to a person by a contravention of any of its provisions, or of any direction or order issued or made under the Law, shall be regarded as damage for which compensation may be claimed under the Civil Wrongs Ordinance, 1944, and for that purpose it will be immaterial whether the damage was caused directly or indirectly, or whether it consisted of actual loss or loss of profits, or whether or not the offender has been criminally prosecuted, and whether or not the offender intended to cause the damage or could have foreseen it.

Banking

The transaction of banking business is regulated by the Banking Ordinance, 1941, under which only registered companies may transact such business. The incorporation of a company which has as its object, or one of its objects, the carrying on of banking business may not be authorised unless its authorised capital is not less than fifty thousand pounds. No foreign company which has as its object, or one of its objects, the carrying on of banking business may be registered unless it is proved to the satisfaction of the Governor of the Bank of Israel that it has a paid-up capital of a sum which in his opinion is equivalent to an amount of not less than one hundred thousand pounds. The Governor of the Bank of Israel may, however, vary those requirements in respect of any company when he considers it to be in the interest of the public so to do. General supervision and control over the carrying on of banking business is exercised by an Examiner of Banks appointed by the Governor of the Bank of Israel, and provison is made for an Advisory Committee to be appointed by the Governor of the Bank of Israel to advise him on matters relating to banking business.

The Bank of Israel Law, 5714–1954, of the 3rd September, 1954, provides for the establishment of a Bank of Israel, prescribing its powers and functions. The bank is the sole banker and fiscal agent of the Government of Israel, and represents Israel in every matter connected with its membership in the International Monetary Fund and in the International Bank of Reconstruction and Development.

Insurance

Insurance is regulated by the Ottoman Law of Insurance, 1905, which deals with insurance of property (but not life or personal accident insurance), Articles 175 to 240 inclusive of the Ottoman Maritime Code, which are based on the relevant articles of the French Commercial Code with certain modifications and additions taken mainly from the Dutch and Portuguese Commercial Codes, and the Motor Vehicles Insurance

(Third Party Risks) Ordinance, 1947, based on the corresponding English law. In addition, the Control of Insurance Business Law, 5711–1951, provides for the licensing and control of insurance businesses. The control is exercised by a Superintendent of Insurance appointed by the Minister of Finance, and provision is made for an Insurance Committee to advise the Minister of Finance on insurance matters.

The National Insurance Law, 5714–1953, which came into force on the 1st April, 1954, provides for old-age insurance, survivors' insurance, industrial injuries insurance, maternity insurance and insurance of families with many children, and for the setting up of the necessary organisations and tribunals for its implementation. The provisions with regard to industrial injuries insurance replace those of the Workmen's Compensation Ordinance, 1947, which has accordingly been repealed. As from the 1st July, 1957, self-employed persons are covered by the Law upon certain conditions in respect of accidents while engaged in their occupation.

Miscellaneous

Other Ordinances dealing with commercial law include the Copyright Ordinance, the Trade Marks Ordinance, 1938, the Merchandise Marks Ordinance and the Registration of Business Names Ordinance, 1935, all modelled on the corresponding English law.

The Control of Commodities and Services Law, 5718–1957, which came into force on the 31st December, 1957, replaced the control legislation regarding food, essential commodities, and services and anti-profiteering legislation enacted by the Mandatory authorities in Palestine during the Second World War. It will only be in force so long as a proclaimed state of emergency exists, and no Minister may exercise his powers thereunder unless he has a reasonable ground for assuming that it is necessary for him to do so for the maintenance of an essential operation or the prevention of profiteering and speculation.

AGENCY

THE AGENCY LAW, 5725–1965, is one of a series of laws prepared in the Ministry of Justice with the assistance of prominent Israel jurists which are designed to constitute an original Israel Code which is to replace the Mejelle, the Ottoman Civil Code. It came into force three months after its publication in *Reshumot* on the 23rd July, 1965, but relations between a principal and his agent created before the date of the commencement of the Law will continue to be governed by the provisions of the law previously in force.

Agency is defined by the Law as being the empowering of an agent to do in the name of, or in place of, a principal any legal act vis-a-vis a third person, and any legal act may be the subject of agency unless by its nature or according to law it has to be done personally.

A person's agent is like the person himself and any act of the agent, including his knowledge and intention, creates an obligation, or a right, of the principal, as the case may be.

Agency is created by a written or verbal authorisation of the agent by the principal, or by notice thereof from the principal to the third party, or by conduct of the principal vis-a-vis one of them.

When any person is required to be dependent upon the act of an agent, he may refuse to recognise the agency so long as a written authorisation has not been produced to him and a copy thereof delivered to him.

Every person is legally competent to be an agent to do any act which he himself has the intelligence to do, save that as regards his rights and obligations the general law regarding legal competence will apply.

Subject to any restriction in the authorisation, agency extends to any act reasonably necessary for the proper performance of the subject of the agency, but, in the absence of a specific authorisation in that behalf, it does not extend to any proceedings before any Court, tribunal or arbitrator, or to any compromise or waiver or act without consideration. An agent, however, may do any urgent and unforeseen act reasonably necessary for the protection of the interests of the principal in connection with the subject of the agency, even if the act exceeds the limits of his authorisation.

Where a person has acted as an agent of another person without authorisation, or in excess of the authorisation of that person, that other person may ratify the act retroactively, and such a ratification is equivalent to prior authorisation, save that it may not affect any right which any other person may have acquired in good faith and for consideration prior to the ratification. If, however, the third party did not know at the time the act was done that the agent was acting without authorisation, or in excess of his authorisation, he has an option, so long as he does not know of the ratification of the act, either to treat the agent as the principal or to cancel the act and claim damages from the agent.

The Law expressly empowers a corporation to ratify an act done on its behalf before it was formed and the foregoing provisions as to ratification will apply.

If the third party did not know at the time of the act of the existence of the agency, or did not know the identity of the principal, the act of the agent will bind the principal and the agent jointly and severally and will confer rights only on the agent, but the principal may arrogate to himself the rights of the agent vis-a-vis the third party, unless that would be repugnant to the right by reason of its nature, conditions, or the circumstances of the case.

Where a person has taken upon himself to be an agent he must act towards his principal faithfully and according to his instructions, and, save where a contrary intention appears from the nature of the agency, or the conditions thereof, it will be the duty of the agent: (1) to disclose to his principal all information, and deliver to him every document, concerning the subject of the agency and to give him a report on his activities;   (2) not to be the agent of different principals for one subject of agency without the authority of his principal;   (3) not to do any act of agency with himself;   (4) not to receive from any person any benefit or promise of any benefit in connection with the subject of the agency without the consent of his principal; (5) not to use to the detriment of his principal any information or documents which he has received by reason of the agency, and generally to refrain from doing anything in which there is a conflict between the interests of his principal and his own interests or those of any other person.

If the agent commits a breach of any of his duties towards his principal the latter will be entitled to the remedies available for a breach of contract, and if the agent does any act vis-a-vis a third party by reason of his breach of duty to his principal upon the authority of the third party, then the principal will be entitled, in addition to the remedies for a breach of contract, to cancel the act and claim from the third party the damages due to him from his agent.

Any property which the agent receives by reason of his agency must be held by him as a trustee for his principal, and that will be so even if the agent has not disclosed to the third party the existence of the agency or the identity of his principal.

The principal will be entitled to any profit or benefit received by the agent in connection with the subject of the agency.

The principal must indemnify his agent for any reasonable expenses he has incurred and for any obligations he has reasonably undertaken by reason of the agency.

The agent will have a right of lien on property of his principal which he has received by reason of the agency, including property held by him as a trustee for his principal, for the amount of his remuneration and the other sums due to him from his principal by reason of the agency.

The debts which the principal and the agent owe to each other by reason of the agency may be set off.

An agency is terminated when it is cancelled by either the principal or the agent, and also by the death of either of them, or by a diminution of his legal competence or by his bankruptcy in the case of an individual or its being wound up in the case of a corporation, save where the authority has been given to secure the right of some other person or of the agent himself and that right depends upon the performance of the subject of the agency.

So long as the agent does not know of the termination of the agency he is entitled vis-a-vis his principal to regard it as continuing. If the third party does not know of the termination of the agency he is entitled to regard it as continuing, and if the agent knows of its termination, the third party is also entitled, so long as he does not know of the termination of the agency, to regard the agent as the principal or to cancel the act and claim damages from the agent.

An agent may not appoint an agent for the subject of the agency unless he is authorised to do so either expressly or by implication, or he does so in order to do an urgent and unforeseen act reasonably necessary for the protection of the interests of his principal in connection with the subject of the agency.

Where an authorisation is given to several agents there is a presumption that they must act together, and where an authorisation is given by several principals there is a presumption that the agent has to act upon the authority of all of them together.

For the purposes of the Law, a person is deemed to know something if as a reasonable man he ought to have known it, or if he was notified of it in the ordinary way.

Finally, it is provided that the Law will not derogate from the provisions of any law which regulates a special class of agency.

Protection of Entrusted Property

The Protection of Entrusted Property Law, 5725–1964, which was passed by the Knesset on the 30th December, 1964, and came into force on the 8th January, 1965, provides that where property has been delivered to the administration or control of any person for the benefit of any other person by any authorisation, or appointment, or as a trustee, the first mentioned person must give notice in writing to the Administrator General of particulars of the property and of the latter mentioned person, if ten years have elapsed since the authorisation, appointment, or commencement of the trusteeship, or from the day upon which the latter mentioned person gave instructions regarding the property or agreed in writing that the said notice should not be given, whichever is the latest date.

The penalty for not giving the required notice within six months of the expiration of the ten year period is a fine of IL. 2,000 and an additional IL. 500 for each month during which the default continues.

In addition to the penalty for default the Law provides that no transaction the validity of which depends on registration may be registered in any land register or other register kept pursuant to any enactment if a party to the transaction is represented by any person appointed or authorised by any revocable appointment or authorisation and ten years have elapsed since the appointment or authorisation, unless there has been submitted the written consent to the transaction of the appointor or person giving the authorisation and one year has not elapsed since the giving of the consent or unless a Court has permitted the registration.

The provisions of the Law will not apply to any person authorised or appointed to administer any property or exercise control over it, or to do any transaction in relation to it, or who is a trustee of the property, by virtue of any law or regulation having legislative effect, or by any Court.

GUARANTEE

THE GUARANTEE LAW, 5727–1967 replaces all the provisions of the third Book of the Mejelle dealing with guarantee, with the exception of Articles 656 and 658. Article 656 provides that if a person who has contracted debts repayable at some future definite date wishes to leave for some other country before such debts fall due for payment, such person must find a guarantor upon the creditor applying to the Court to that effect, and Article 658 provides that if any party to a contract based upon consideration deceives another party thereto, such party must make good any loss caused to the other.

The Law defines guarantee as 'the undertaking of a person to perform the obligation of another person towards a third person', and it provides that a guarantee may be for the whole, or part, of an obligation, for an existing or future obligation, a recurrent or conditional obligation, or a definite or indefinite obligation, and it can only be for a valid obligation.

A guarantee is created by an agreement between the guarantor and the creditor, or by the undertaking of the guarantor notice whereof is given to the creditor, and, if the guarantee is pursuant to an order of an authority, when the document of guarantee is delivered to the authority (Section 3).

The guarantor is not under any obligation greater or more onerous than that of the debtor. He is obliged to pay also interest, expenses and damages which the debtor was obliged to pay in respect of the guaranteed obligation, and such interest, expenses and damages will be treated as is the guaranteed obligation, unless some other intention appears from the guarantee. Should the scope of the guarantee be limited the guarantor is liable only within the limits of his guarantee.

The Law also provides for changes in the guaranteed obligation. Should the guaranteed obligation be reduced, by agreement between the debtor and the creditor, or by waiver of the creditor, then the guarantor will be discharged to the extent to which the debtor is discharged. Should the guaranteed obligation be increased by agreement between the debtor and the creditor, the obligation of the guarantor will not be altered thereby. Should there be any other alteration in the guaranteed obligation, by agreement between the debtor and the creditor, the obligation of the guarantor will be altered by the alteration, but the guarantor will have the choice of performing the obligation without alteration, if that is possible, or cancelling his guarantee if the alteration is a fundamental alteration which affects the rights of the guarantor.

If the creditor causes the non-performance of the guaranteed obligation the guarantor will be discharged, while if the creditor causes the extinction of a security given for the securing of the guaranteed obligation and damage is thereby caused to the guarantor, the guarantor is discharged to the extent of the amount of the damage.

Every claim which the debtor has against the creditor in connection with his obligation will also be available for the

guarantor, and if the claim against the debtor has become prescribed, the claim against the guarantor will also be prescribed,
if it has not become prescribed previously.

The Law goes on to provide that the guarantor and the debtor
are jointly and severally liable to the creditor, but that the creditor
may not demand from the guarantor the performance of his
guarantee without previously having demanded from the debtor
the performance of his obligation save in one of the following
circumstances: (1) the guarantor waived the demand from the
debtor;   (2) a receiving order or a winding up order was given
against the debtor;   (3) the debtor has died, or is out of Israel,
or the making of the demand involves special difficulties.

As regards the guarantor's right of recourse against the debtor,
Section 9 of the Law provides that, unless the guarantee was
given without the consent of the debtor, the guarantor has a
right of recourse against the debtor and to recover from him
what he has given in performance of his guarantee, together with
reasonable expenses which he has expended by reason of the
guarantee and interest at the full rate under the Adjudication of
Interest Law, 5721–1961 (see pp. 111–2), from the date of the
performance of the guarantee or from the date of the expenses.
The guarantor will not have a right of recourse against the debtor
to the extent to which he could have been discharged by a claim
which was available to the debtor against the creditor in connection with the obligation and the claim was known to the guarantor and he did not plead it in his defence, but the guarantor's right
of recourse against the debtor will not be affected if, in the exercise
of his choice in the case of an alteration in the guaranteed obligation, he performed his guarantee without alteration as explained
above, or if he performed his obligation after sending to the
debtor a notice of his intention of doing so and gave the debtor a
reasonable time for applying to the Court.

The guarantor, before he has performed his guarantee, will
have the same remedies for securing his right of recourse against
the debtor as are given to a creditor for securing a debt which
has not yet become due (Section 11).

If the guaranteed obligation was also secured by a charge on the

property of the debtor, under Section 12 of the Law the charge
will pass to the guarantor after he has performed his obligation,
for securing his right of recourse against the debtor, and the
person giving the charge and the creditor must do, upon demand
by the guarantor, all the acts necessary in order that the transfer
may be valid for all purposes, in so far as the rights of the creditor
are not affected.

Where two or more persons have guaranteed one obligation,
either together or separately, they will be jointly and severally
liable, and if the scope of the guarantees is different, they will be
liable as aforesaid within the limits of the joint guarantee, unless
some other intention appears from the guarantees.

Where a person has given to a creditor an undertaking to
perform the guarantee of a guarantor, the guarantee of the
guarantor towards the creditor will be treated as a guaranteed
obligation both as regards the relations between that person
and the creditor and the relations between him and the guarantor.

Where a guarantee has been given for a future obligation the
guarantor may, so long as the guaranteed obligation has not been
created, cancel the guarantee by giving notice in writing to the
creditor, but he must compensate the creditor for any damage
caused to him by the cancellation. If the guarantee was given as
aforesaid with the consent of the debtor and the guarantor cancels
his guarantee without giving the debtor notice thereof a reasonable time in advance, the guarantor must compensate the debtor
for the damage caused to him by failure to give the notice.

The provisions of sections 3, 9, 11 and 12 of the Law will apply,
mutatis mutandis, to the obligation of a person to indemnify a
creditor for non-fulfilment of the obligation of a debtor towards
a creditor, where the obligation is not a guarantee.

A guarantee of an obligation the validity whereof is defective
only as regards the capacity or representation of the debtor will
be deemed to be an obligation to indemnify, and the provisions
of sections 9, 11 and 12 of the Law will not apply to an obligation
to indemnify for non-fulfilment of such an obligation.

The provisions of the Law will apply where there are no special
provisions in any other law as regards the matter in question,

and where no other intention appears from the agreement between the parties.

As regards guarantees and indemnities given before the commencement of the Law (1st October, 1967), the previous law will continue to apply.

PLEDGE

THE PLEDGE LAW, 5727–1967 replaces all the provisions of the fifth Book of the Mejelle dealing with pledge and also Articles 118–9 and 396–403 of the first Book of the Mejelle dealing with Sale which deal with sale subject to a right of redemption.

The provisions of the Law will apply where there are no special provisions for the matter in question in any other law and also to every transaction the intention whereof is a charge on property as a security for an obligation by whatever name the transaction be called, but they will not derogate from the provisions of any law relating to a floating charge on property of a corporation.

As regards pledges created before the commencement of the Law the previous law will continue to apply.

A pledge is defined as a charge on property as a security for an obligation, and the Law provides that it entitles the creditor to recover from the pledge if the obligation is not discharged. The security may be for the whole, or part, of an obligation, for an existing or future obligation, a recurrent or conditional obligation, or a definite or indefinite obligation.

A pledge is created by an agreement between the debtor and the creditor, and any restriction or condition applicable, according to any law or agreement, upon the transfer of the ownership of any property will also apply to a pledge thereof.

The effect of the pledge vis-a-vis other creditors of the debtor depends on the property pledged. If the property is property in respect whereof there are special provisions in some other law for the matter in question, the effect will be in accordance with those provisions. If the property is movable property or securities in respect whereof there are special provisions in some other law for the matter in question and it has been deposited with the creditor, or with a custodian on behalf of the creditor other than the debtor, the effect will be upon the deposit thereof as aforesaid and so long as it is deposited. If the property is movable property or securities which have not been deposited as aforesaid, and in every other case, the effect will be upon the registration of the pledge in accordance with regulations made by the Minister of Justice under the Law, but as regards a creditor who knew, or ought to have known, of the pledge, the pledge will have effect even without registration.

Section 5 of the Law provides that where movable property is pledged while in the possession of the pledgor and deposited or registered as aforesaid, the pledge will have effect for all purposes even if the pledgor was not the owner of the property pledged, or was not entitled to pledge it, provided that the creditor acted in good faith and the property came into the hands of the pledgor with the knowledge of the owner thereof, or with the knowledge of the person entitled to possession thereof.

The Law permits the debtor to pledge the pledged property by an additional pledge without obtaining permission from the creditor, but an additional creditor may recover from the pledge only after the discharge of the obligation which was secured by the prior pledge, in the absence of some other provision in the prior agreement of pledge. It also permits the debtor, with the consent of the creditor, to pledge the property pledged by an additional pledge ranking equally with the pledge of that creditor or having priority over it.

The pledge serves as security also for interest, expenses and damages which the debtor is obliged to pay in respect of the obligation and the expenses of the preservation of the pledge and its realisation, and such interest, expenses and damages will be treated as is the obligation, if there is no other provision in the agreement of pledge. If the scope of the obligation is increased in accordance with an agreement between the debtor and the creditor, the pledge will not serve as security for the addition, unless an additional pledge has been created as security for the addition.

Where the pledge has been deposited with the creditor, or

with a custodian on behalf of the creditor, the pledge will also apply to the fruits of the pledge, if there is no other provision in the agreement of pledge.

If the pledge is lost, damaged or expropriated and as a result thereof the debtor has a right to compensation or an indemnity from a third party, the pledge will apply to the said right. When a pledged right, including such a right to compensation or an indemnity, is realised, the pledge will apply to what is obtained from the realisation of the right, but the sum which the creditor received from the realisation of the right will be treated as on account of the obligation if there is no other agreement between the parties in the matter. If the pledge is exchanged in accordance with the above provisions the debtor must, upon demand of the creditor, do all the acts necessary in order that the pledge may have effect vis-a-vis other creditors of the debtor.

Where the pledge has been deposited with the creditor, or with a custodian on behalf of the creditor other than the debtor (each of whom is referred to as "the possessor"), the possessor may not use the pledge and will have no right to its fruits, unless the debtor has so permitted in the agreement of pledge or there-after, and if the debtor has so permitted the possessor must pay him an appropriate consideration therefor in the absence of any other agreement. If the pledge bears fruits which by their nature cannot be preserved, the debtor is presumed to have permitted the possessor to have a right to them.

Where an undefined part of property is pledged the joint owners may not divide the property without the consent of the creditor or the permission of the Court, and the right of the debtor to claim the division of the property will also be vested in the creditor from the time the debtor may claim the realisation of the pledge. Where the property has been divided in accordance with those provisions the pledge will apply to what fell to the debtor.

Where property of one person has been pledged as security for the obligation of another person, the owner of the property will be treated as a person who guaranteed the obligation, but there may be recovered from the owner of the property only the realisation of the pledge as provided in the Law.

As regards the redemption of a pledge, the Law provides that the debtor and every person whose right is likely to be affected by the giving of the pledge or its realisation, may redeem the pledge by performing the obligation after the time for its performance, unless there is some other provision in the agreement of pledge. Every such person may also redeem the pledge by performing the obligation before the time for its performance, provided that if the obligation is to pay a sum of money bearing interest he pays to the creditor also the interest due to him up to the time for the performance of the obligation or for six months after the payment, whichever is the shorter period, unless there is some other provision in the agreement of pledge or the pledge is given for securing a series of debentures.

Where property is pledged in the circumstances described in section 5 of the Law, the owner of the property, or the person who was entitled to possession thereof, may redeem the pledge before the time for performance of the obligation even if there is some other provision in the agreement of pledge.

The above provisions will not confer any right to redeem part of a pledge by performance of part of the obligation unless it has been so agreed in the agreement of pledge.

Where a person who redeems a pledge is not the debtor, such person will have a right of recourse against the debtor and may recover from the debtor as if he were a guarantor who performed his guarantee, and if such person was not the owner of the property the pledge will be a security for his said right.

Upon the cessation of the obligation the pledge will be extinguished, and when the pledge is extinguished the debtor may demand the return of the pledge if it was deposited with the creditor, or a custodian on behalf of the creditor, and if the pledge was registered the debtor may demand the cancellation of the registration, but such provisions will not affect a pledge which serves as security for a recurrent obligation.

Where the obligation is not performed in due time the creditor may realise the pledge, but the parties may not stipulate for resort to methods of realisation other than those under the Law so long as the date for performance of the obligation has not arrived.

The Law lays down a general rule that the realisation of a pledge must be in accordance with a Court order, but it provides for the following four exceptions to the rule: (1) where the pledge is one to which special provisions of another law apply in the matter then the realisation must be in accordance with those provisions;   (2) where the pledge is of movables or securities and has been deposited with the creditor, or a custodian on his behalf, or has been registered, as provided in section 4 of the Law as described above, the realisation may be in accordance with an order of the Chief Execution Officer;   (3) where the pledge is of movables or securities and has been deposited with the creditor, or a custodian on his behalf, as provided in section 4 of the Law as described above, and it serves as security for an obligation due to a banking institution within the meaning of the Bank of Israel Law, 5714–1954, the realisation may be effected by the institution itself without an order as aforesaid;   (4) where the pledge is a right the realisation may be effected as provided in section 20 of the Law, whereunder, where a right which the debtor has as against another person is pledged, the creditor may realise it just as the debtor may realise it, and he may do so even if the date for the exercise of the right falls before the date for performance of the obligation secured, unless there is some other provision in the agreement of pledge.

The realisation of a pledge in accordance with a Court order or an order of a Chief Execution Officer will be by way of realisation of property upon which an attachment has been placed in execution of a judgment, unless the Chief Execution Officer directs that it shall be in some other way which appears to him to be more effective and just in the circumstances of the case.

The realisation of a pledge by a banking institution will be by sale in the manner usual in the market in which property of the same kind is sold, and, in the absence of such a market, in a reasonable commercial manner. The banking institution may only commence the realisation of the pledge after it has given the debtor and every person whose right is likely to be affected by the realisation, and he and his address are known to the institution, a notice a reasonable time in advance of the steps which it is about to take for the realisation of the pledge.

The banking institution will be liable towards the debtor, and every person whose right is likely to be affected by the realisation of the pledge, for any damage caused to him by realisation of the pledge otherwise than in accordance with the provisions of the Law.

The Court may, under section 21 of the Law, upon the application of the debtor, the creditor or the possessor of the pledge, order the realisation of the pledge before the date for the performance of the obligation, or give such other directions as it may deem fit, if it is satisfied that the property pledged is likely to become spoiled, or lose a considerable part of its value, or that the rights of the parties are likely to be affected for any other reason. In any such case the realisation will be in such manner as the Court may direct.

The amount which the creditor receives before the date of performance of the obligation as a result of realisation under section 20 or 21 of the Law will be credited to the account of the obligation if there is no other agreement between the parties in the matter.

Finally, the Law provides that the giving of a pledge will not derogate from the right of the creditor to collect the obligation otherwise than by its realisation, and the realisation of the pledge will not derogate from his right to collect the balance of the obligation which was not discharged by the realisation.

For the purposes of the Law, "other creditors of the debtor" include the trustee in bankruptcy of the debtor, and, if the debtor is a corporation in liquidation, the liquidator, and "securities" are defined as "a certificate, bill or other document issued according to law or custom, to order or bearer, conferring on the holder the right specified therein," and "debtor" is defined as including the owner of property pledged as security for the obligation of another person.

CUSTODIANS

THE CUSTODIANS LAW, 5727–1967 replaces all the provisions of the sixth Book of the Mejelle dealing with trusts and trusteeship, with the exception of Article 770, which provides that the finder of lost property must make known the fact that he has found such property, and must keep it in his possession on trust until such time as the owner appears, and that if any person appears and proves that such property is his, the property in question must be handed over to him.

The provisions of the Law will apply to the custody of property where there are no special provisions for the matter in question in any other law and if no other intention appears from the agreement between the parties.

As regards custody of property which existed before the commencement of the Law (1st October, 1967) the previous law will continue to apply.

Custody of property is defined as the lawful possession thereof otherwise than by virtue of ownership. A custodian of property who has no benefit for himself from the custody is known as an 'unpaid custodian', a custodian of property who receives consideration for his custody, or has some other benefit for himself, and is not a borrower, is known as a 'paid custodian', while a custodian of property in order to use it or enjoy it without giving consideration therefor is known as a 'borrower'.

The Law prescribes the liability of each class of custodian as follows.

An unpaid custodian is liable for the loss of the property or any damage to it, if the loss or damage was caused by his negligence.

A paid custodian is liable for the loss of the property or any damage to it, unless this was caused by circumstances which he was not obliged to foresee and the results whereof he could not prevent, but where the purpose of the custody of the property was subsidiary to the main purpose of its possession, the custodian is exempt if the loss or damage was not caused by his negligence.

A borrower is liable for the loss of the property, or damage thereto, whatever may be the causes thereof, provided that the liability shall not be greater than that of a person who possesses property unlawfully.

Where a custodian learns that damage to property for which he is not liable, either as a paid custodian or a borrower, is likely to be caused to the property, and he does not give notice thereof to the owner of the property within a reasonable time or does not take reasonable steps to notify him, he will be liable for such damage to the extent to which the notice would have enabled the owner of the property to prevent the damage.

Section 3 of the Law provides that, where an unpaid custodian, or a paid custodian, has received property in order to keep it in his personal custody, and he delivers it to another person without having been expressly, or impliedly, authorised in that behalf, his liability for the loss of the property, or damage thereto, will be that of a borrower.

A custodian is not liable for the loss of property, or damage thereto, which is caused as a result of ordinary use of the property in accordance with the conditions of the custody, or as a result of natural wear and tear or a defect which was in it at the beginning of the custody, but such provisions will not lessen his liability for negligence.

Where a custodian is liable for the loss of the property, or damage thereto, the owner of the property is entitled to such damages as are given for a breach of contract, while if the custodian is not liable for the loss of the property, or damage thereto, but he has for the loss or damage a right to compensation or indemnity from a third party, the owner of the property may claim his damage from the custodian out of the compensation or indemnity due to the custodian.

Where a custodian has delivered the property to a sub-custodian, the acts and omissions of the sub-custodian are deemed to be the acts and omissions of the custodian, and the sub-custodian is liable also towards the owner of the property to the same extent as he is liable to the custodian. Such provisions will apply whether the delivery of the property was with the permission of the owner or without his permission, provided that nothing shall derogate from the liability of a custodian under section 3 of the Law or any other law.

The owner of the property must indemnify an unpaid custodian, and also the holder of a pledge or other security, for the reasonable expenses which they have expended and for the liabilities which they have reasonably undertaken as a result of the custody, and every custodian is entitled to an indemnity as aforesaid as a result of an act which he has done under section 6 of the Law, which provides that a custodian may do any urgent and unforeseen act which is reasonably necessary for preventing damage which is likely to be caused to the property as if the owner had given him an authorisation to do so.

The Law confers upon the custodian a right of lien on the property for the amount due to him from the owner of the property as a result of the custody, and provides that the debts which the owner of the property and the custodian owe to each other as a result of the custody be set off one against the other.

Where a custodian is entitled to return the property to its owner and he has done what it is incumbent upon him to do in order to return it but the owner has not received it, he may ask the Court for directions what shall be done with the property and he will be exempt from all liability if he acted in good faith in accordance with the directions of the Court, but if he is a paid custodian, or a borrower, his liability for the loss of the property, or damage thereto, and his right to indemnity, will be the same as those of an unpaid custodian without his having asked the Court for directions.

Finally, the Law contains special provisions with regard to hotels, which are defined as including pensions and other guest houses. As regards property in a hotel of a guest, who is defined as a person who is given a place to sleep in a hotel, the owner of the hotel, who is defined as including the person who is in charge of the management of the hotel, will be treated as a paid custodian, save as regards money, securities and other valuables, unless the guest has notified the owner of the hotel thereof and he has, upon the demand of the owner of the hotel, delivered them into his custody.

The owner of a hotel is exempt from liability under the above provisions if he has not been given notice of the loss of the property or damage thereto, within a reasonable time after the guest has learned thereof, or ought to have known thereof.

The owner of a hotel will have a right of lien on the property of the guest which is in the hotel, or which was delivered into his custody as aforesaid, for the amount due to him, either as a result of the custody or as a result of the lodging.

For the purposes of the Law, "owner of the property" vis-a-vis a custodian is defined as every person for whom the custodian holds the property.

LAND LAW

Ottoman Law

THE SUBSTANTIVE Land Law which was in force in Palestine on the 1st November, 1914, was not, on the whole, greatly modified by the Palestine Legislature, and it has not been greatly modified by the Israel legislature, although a comprehensive draft Israel Land Code has been prepared by the Ministry of Justice.

In addition to the Ottoman Land Code, the following are the most important Ottoman Land Laws which are still in force:

(1) The law concerning the rights of certain corporate bodies to own immovable property (1913).

(2) The law concerning the mortgaging of immovable property (1913).

(3) The law regulating the right to dispose of immovable property (1913).

(4) The law of partition of jointly owned immovable property (1914).

(5) The law of leasing of immovable property (1914).

Land Settlement

The Palestine legislature, however, introduced an important innovation in the land law, namely, settlement of title to land, and the subsequent registration of title thereon, by the Land (Settlement of Title) Ordinance, in accordance with a system based on the Torrens system in use in Australia and other parts of the British Commonwealth. Under that Ordinance, which was enacted in 1928, the High Commissioner (whose powers are now vested in the Minister of Justice) from time to time declared certain areas, known as 'settlement areas', to be areas within which the settlement of rights to land and registration thereof were to be effected, and settlement officers were appointed to carry out the settlement of land in those areas with power to hear and decide any dispute with regard to the ownership or possession of land in the settlement area. In accordance with the provisions of the Ordinance, a new register of title to land is opened for each village under settlement. On the completion of the prescribed settlement procedure by the settlement officer, all settled land is registered in this register in accordance with the decisions of the settlement officer and the plan transmitted by him. By an amendment of the Ordinance which came into force on the 28th April, 1960, the judicial powers of land settlement officers were vested in the District Courts. Except as provided in the Ordinance, the registration of land in the new register invalidates any right conflicting with such registration, and no disposition of land registered in the new register, other than a lease for a period of not more than three years, and no transmission of land on death, is valid until it has been recorded in the register.

Land Transfer

In September, 1920, an Ordinance, entitled the Land Transfer Ordinance, was enacted and is still in force. Under that Ordinance, no disposition of immovable property is valid until the consent of the Director of Land Registration to the disposition has been obtained and the other provisions of the Ordinance have been complied with. No guarantee of title or of the transaction is implied by such consent and the registration of the appropriate deed in the land registry, but every disposition to which the consent has not been obtained is null and void and any person who is a party to such disposition and either enters into possession, or permits the other party to enter into possession, of the immovable property is guilty of an offence and is liable to a fine of one fourth of the immovable property, although any person who has paid money in respect of a disposition which is null and void may recover such money by action in the courts.

'Disposition' is defined for the purposes of the Ordinance as meaning 'a sale, mortgage, gift, dedication of *wakf* of every description, and any other disposition of immovable property, except a devise by will or a lease for a term not exceeding three years, and includes a transfer of mortgage and a lease containing an option by virtue of which the term may exceed three years', and 'land' is defined as including 'houses, buildings and things permanently fixed in the land.'

Acquisition for Public Purposes

Acquisition of land for public purposes is effected under the Land (Acquisition for Public Purposes) Ordinance, 1943, whereunder the Minister of Finance, in whom the Government has vested the powers vested by the Ordinance in the High Commissioner, if he is satisfied that it is necessary or expedient for any public purpose so to do, may (a) acquire the ownership of any land, (b) acquire the possession or use of any land for a definite period, (c) acquire any easement on any land or any other right thereon or thereover, (d) impose any easement on any land or any other restraint on the exercise of any right incidental to ownership thereof, paying such compensation or consideration as may be agreed upon or determined under the provisions of the Ordinance.

If any person (including any local authority) applies to the Minister to acquire any land on his behalf and for his use, the Minister may proceed to acquire it under the provisions of the Ordinance as if it were land to be acquired for a public purpose, if in the opinion of the Minister the acquisition of the land on behalf and for the use of such person is likely to prove useful to the public. If the applicant is a local authority, the Minister may authorise the applicant itself to take the necessary steps for the acquisition of the land.

Tenant Protection

Restrictions on eviction and the raising of rents were imposed by the Rent Restrictions (Dwelling Houses) Ordinance, 1940, and the Rent Restrictions (Business Premises) Ordinance, 1941. The former Ordinance applied the restrictions throughout the country with respect to houses, or parts of houses, let as a separate dwelling and also prohibited the requirement of payment of any fine, premium, or other like sum in addition to the rent, in consideration of the grant, renewal, or continuance, of a tenancy of any dwelling house to which the Ordinance applied. The latter Ordinance applied the restrictions to premises other than dwelling houses to which the former Ordinance applied, although only in those areas to which it had been applied by an order made under the Ordinance.

The Key Money Law, 5718–1958, which came into force on the 14th August, 1958, repealed the provision of the Rent Restrictions (Dwelling Houses) Ordinance, 1940, whereunder a person was forbidden in consideration of the grant, renewal, or continuance, of a tenancy of any dwelling house to which the Ordinance applied to require the payment of any fine, premium, or other like sum in addition to the rent, as that prohibition had for many years been ignored or evaded, while there was no corresponding prohibition as regards business premises, and a public committee set up to consider whether it was desirable to legalise and regulate the payment of key money reported that it was desirable to do so and made detailed proposals to that end. The Law gives effect to those proposals, and provides, among other things, that an outgoing tenant of any premises is entitled to a share in the key money paid by a proposed tenant, the amount of his share being fixed by the Law according to the time during which the outgoing tenant was in occupation, and that the share of the landlord is the balance remaining after payment of the share of the outgoing tenant. Special provisions are made for the division of the key money where there is a payment for goodwill of a business, or where the outgoing tenant or a previous tenant has invested money in fundamental structural alterations or improvements.

The provisions of the Law may be waived by agreement with regard to key money for business premises, but not dwelling houses.

The Tenant Protection (New Buildings) Law, 5713–1953, exempts, for five years from the date the first leasing commences, from the Rent Restrictions Ordinances dwelling houses and premises in buildings or additions to buildings completed after the 1st January, 1953, and factories and workshops erected by approved undertakings within the meaning of the Encouragement of the Capital Investments Law, 5710–1950, while the Tenant Protection (New Buildings) Law, 5715–1955 provides a similar exemption for ten years in respect of buildings completed after the 1st April, 1954. The Tenant Protection Law, 5714–1954, of the 16th April, 1954, provides for increases in rents for both dwelling houses and business premises, and prescribes a set of rules with regard to the obligations of landlords and tenants in connection with services and repairs.

The Tenant Protection Law, 5715–1955, of the 8th July, 1955, repealed the Rent Restrictions (Business Premises) Ordinance, 1941, and much of the Rent Restrictions (Dwelling Houses) Ordinance, 1940, and replaced their provisions by more comprehensive provisions, and also empowered the Courts to refuse to order eviction even if a ground for eviction is proved, if they are satisfied that it would not be just to order eviction.

The Cooperative Houses Law, 5713–1952, which came into force on the 19th March, 1953, contains detailed provisions for separate registration in the Land Registry of flats in cooperative houses, the settlement of rates and taxes on each flat separately, and rules for the management of such houses.

Town Planning

Legislation concerning town planning was enacted during the first year of the British civil administration. It was replaced by the Town Planning Ordinance, 1936, whereunder every plot of land in this country is subject to town planning control, and no building may be erected, or road constructed, without a permit from the competent town planning authority.

The Planning and Building Law, 5725–1965, which came into force six months after its publication in *Reshumot* on the 12th August, 1965, replaced the Town Planning Ordinance, 1936.

At the end of 1947 a comprehensive Planning and Building Ordinance was published in draft form, but it was not enacted before the termination of the Mandate. As a result of the discussions and developments which took place since then many changes were made in that draft until the text finally enacted by the Knesset was evolved, although to a great extent the new law is based on the same principles as those of the former law, save that under the new law provisions are made for the establishment of a National Council, as well as District and Local Commissions, and for a national outline scheme in addition to district and local outline schemes.

The function of the National Council is to advise the Government on everything concerning the general policy for the implementation of the Law, including matters of legislation, and to perform the duties imposed upon it by the Law or any other law. The chairman of the National Council will be the Minister of the Interior, or his representative.

The provisions of the Law other than those relating to offences and penalties will also be binding on the State, but the State will be exempt from fees for building for public purposes.

Among the innovations introduced by the Law are the prohibition of the use of agricultural land save in accordance with with the provisions of the First Schedule to the Law, and the prohibition of the doing of any act in territorial waters for which a permit is required save in accordance with the provisions of the Second Schedule to the Law. There are also entirely new provisions with regard to security installations and aviation obstacles, while the provisions for the enforcement of the Law have been tightened up.

Oil

The Oil Law, 5712–1952, of the 31st August, 1952, which replaces the Oil Mining Ordinance, 1938, contains comprehensive provisions regarding oil prospecting and mining.

Water

The waters of all rivers, streams and springs and of all lakes and other natural collections of still water in Israel have been vested in the Government in trust for the State since the 19th April, 1950, under Article 16E of the Palestine Orders in Council, 1922–1947, and a Proclamation of the Government of the 12th April, 1950.

The Drainage and Defence against Floods Law, 5718–1957 provides for the declaration of drainage areas, the establishment of drainage authorities and the making and carrying out of drainage schemes. The Minister of Agriculture is charged with the implementation of the Law and he will be advised by a National Drainage Council established by the Law.

The Water Law, 5719–1959, which came into force on the 13th August, 1959, is a comprehensive law with 159 sections. It provides that the water resources in the State are public property subject to the control of the State and destined for the requirements of its inhabitants and for the development of the country, and defines such resources, for the purposes of the Law, as meaning springs, streams, rivers, lakes and other currents and accumulations of water, whether above ground or underground, whether natural, regulated or made, and whether water rises, flows or stands therein at all times or intermittently, and includes drainage water and sewage water. Every person, the Law declares, is entitled to receive and use water subject to the provisions of the Law. On the other hand, the right of a person in any land does not confer upon him a right in a water resource situated therein or crossing it or abutting thereon, and the right of a person to receive water from a water resource is valid so long as the receipt of water from that water resource does not lead to the salination or depletion thereof. Every right to water, the Law provides, is linked to one of the following water purposes, namely, domestic purposes, agriculture, industry, handicraft, commerce and services, and public services. For the purposes of the Law, it is immaterial whether a right to water was created by law, including the

Law itself, or by agreement or custom, or in any other manner, or whether it was created before or after the coming into force of the Law.

The Minister of Agriculture is charged with the implementation of the Law, and he will be the chairman of the Water Board appointed by the Government under the Law to advise him on questions of water policy and to carry out the functions assigned to it by the Law. The vice-chairman of the Board will be the Water Commissioner appointed by the Government under the Law to manage water affairs in the State. The Water Board will consist of not less than 27, and not more than 55, members, including the chairman and vice-chairman, representatives of the World Zionist Organisation and its institutions.

The Law contains detailed provisions as to the regulation of the use of water, including preservation of water norms and rules for the use of water, control of production and supply of water, and rationing areas, provisions as to water supply systems, including supply systems and authorities, planning of water supply systems, establishment of water supply systems, compensation, supply of water by a water authority, and transfer of water supply systems, provisions as to water charges, including control of water charges and the establishment of the Adjustment Fund, a corporation managed by the Water Commissioner, the purpose of which is to reduce the differences between water charges in different parts of the country and which may not be used for any other purpose, and also provisions as to organisation, including provisions as to the Water Board and other bodies, the Water Commissioner, tribunals for water affairs, the Water Register to be kept by the Water Commissioner in which are to be entered determinations and apportionments made, and rights of use of water recognised, under the Law.

The provisions of the Law will not affect any existing custom of occasionally taking water, in a vessel for drinking, for the watering of animals or for the operation of vehicles, so long as private property is not trespassed upon.

Among the powers conferred upon the Minister of Agriculture by the Law are the power to prescribe, after consultation with the Water Board, norms for the quantity, quality, price, conditions of supply and use, of water within the scope of the purpose thereof, and rules for the efficient and economic utilisation of water, and, upon his so doing, no person may supply or use water otherwise than in accordance with such norms and rules. Where the Minister of Agriculture is satisfied that the water resources in a particular area are not sufficient for the maintenance of the existing consumption of water, he may, after consultation with the Water Board and the supply committees, declare, in *Reshumot*, such area to be a 'rationing area', that is, an area in which the consumption of water shall be rationed. The Minister of Agriculture may also, with the approval of the Government and the Knesset, empower a corporation to be the National Water Authority, provided that a majority of the controlling shares of such corporation are held by the State and by the World Zionist Organisation or its institutions. The functions of the National Water Authority will be to establish and manage the national water system, to supply water therefrom, to maintain it in proper condition, to improve and enlarge it and to do any other act necessary for the supply of water therefrom. The Minister of Agriculture is obliged to submit to the Knesset once a year a report on the activities of the water authorities.

Israel Lands

The Basic Law: Israel Lands, which came into force on the 29th July, 1960, provides that the ownership of Israel Lands, namely, the lands in Israel of the State, of the Development Authority and of the Keren Kayemeth LeIsrael (Jewish National Fund) shall not be transferred, by sale or otherwise, and defines 'land' for the purposes of the Law, as land, houses, buildings and everything permanently attached to land.

It is expressly provided in the Law, however, that the Law shall not apply to such categories of land and such categories of transactions as may be prescribed in that behalf by any law.

Two other laws came into force simultaneously with the

coming into force of that Basic Law. The first, the Israel Lands Law, 5720–1960, prescribes certain categories of transactions to which that Basic Law will not apply, while the second, the Israel Lands Administration Law, 5720–1960, provides that the Government shall establish an Israel Lands Administration for the administration of lands as defined in that Basic Law. The Government is also required to appoint a director of the Israel Lands Administration, who will be directly subordinate to the Minister of Agriculture, and also an Israel Lands Council, which is to fix the land policy according to which the Israel Lands Administration is to act, and is to supervise the activities of that Administration and approve the draft of the budget which is to be fixed by law. The Director is required to submit to the Council at least once every year a report on the activities of the Administration, and the Government is required to submit to the Knesset at least once every year a report on those activities.

TAXATION
Palestine Taxes

ON THE eve of the establishment of the State five kinds of taxes were payable in this country. They were urban property tax (under the Urban Property Tax Ordinance, 1940), rural property tax (under the Rural Property Tax Ordinance, 1942), animal tax (under the Animal Tax Ordinance, 1944), income tax (under the Income Tax Ordinance, 1947) and company profits tax (under the Company Profits Tax Ordinance, 1947).

Urban property tax was payable by owners of house property and land in areas declared to be 'urban areas' at a rate not exceeding fifteen per cent of its net annual value, as prescribed annually, although provisions were made for exemptions and remissions in certain cases.

Rural property tax was payable by owners of rural lands. It was a tax per dunum at varying rates on categories of land arranged according to the estimated productivity of the soil, and in some relation to the net annual yield.

Animal tax was payable on buffaloes, camels, cattle, goats, sheep and swine by their owners.

Income tax was first introduced into Palestine by the Income Tax Ordinance, 1941, which came into force on the 1st September, 1941, and which, with the amendments made to it during the period 1941–47, was replaced by the Income Tax Ordinance, 1947. The original system was adopted in part from that operated in India and in part from that operated in the United Kingdom and the British Colonial Empire, with such modifications as were found desirable for its application in Palestine. The tax is levied on income accruing in, derived from, or received in, this country. Individuals are charged at rates varying with the amount of their chargeable income.

Company profits tax was payable by companies and co-operative societies on their profits which, during any chargeable accounting period, accrued in, or were derived from, or were received in, this country of an amount equal to ten per centum of such profits.

Encouragement of Capital Investments

The Encouragement of Capital Investments Law, 5710–1950, which came into force on the 6th April, 1950, provided for certain reliefs and exemptions from such taxes for 'approved undertakings' within the meaning of the Law, with a view to encouraging economic initiative and capital investment in this country. That Law was amended in 1955, and replaced by the Encouragement of Capital Investments Law, 5719–1959, which came into force on the 16th August, 1959, and took into account the experience gained in the working of the first mentioned Law. The object of the new law, as stated therein, is to attract capital to Israel and to encourage economic initiative and investments of foreign and local capital with a view to (1) the development of the productive capacity of the national economy, the efficient utilisation of its resources and economic potential and full utilisation of the productive capacity of existing enterprises; (2) the improvement of the balance of payments of the State, the reduction of imports and the increase of exports; (3) the absorption of immigration, the planned distribution of the population over the area of the

State and the creation of new sources of employment. The new Law provides for considerably greater benefits to investors than the previous Law, especially in regard to tax exemptions and currency exchange regulations.

Further benefits for approved undertakings, including State grants, are provided for by an amending law published in *Reshumot* on the 21st April, 1967.

New Taxes

Nine new kinds of taxes, some temporary, have been introduced by the Israel legislature. They are the luxuries tax (under the Luxuries Tax Ordinance, 5709–1949), replaced, since the 1st September, 1952, by a purchase tax (under the Purchase Tax Law, 5712–1952); estate tax (under the Estate Tax Law, 5709–1949); absorption tax (under the Absorption Tax Law, 5709–1949); land betterment tax (under the Land Betterment Tax Law, 5709–1949 and the Land Betterment Tax Law, 5723–1963; the foreign travel tax (under the Foreign Travel Tax Law, 5711–1950); defence levy (under the Defence Levy Law, 5716–1956, the Defence Levy (Amendment and Extension of Period of Charge) Law, 5717–1957, and the Defence Levy Law 5717–1957), and the defence stamp (under the Defence Stamp Law, 5716–1956, and the Defence Stamp (Amendment and Extension of Period of Charge) Law, 5718–1958); property tax (under the Property Tax and Compensation Fund Law, 5721–1961 (which repealed the Urban Property Tax Ordinance, 1940, the Rural Property Tax Ordinance, 1942, and the War Damage Compensation Levy Law 5711–1951, whereunder the war damage compensation levy was payable)), and the building levy (under the Levy on Large Apartments Law, 5724–1964).

Purchase tax is payable upon the importation and sale of such goods, other than certain specified goods, and at such rates, as the Minister of Finance may, by order, determine. The Minister of Finance may also, by order, determine which goods are luxuries. The tax is a percentage of the wholesale price of the goods, and if the goods are not luxuries, the tax may not exceed

$7^1/_2$ per cent of the wholesale price or 5 per cent of the retail price. The tax is payable, in the case of imported goods, by the importer, and, in the case of sale, by the vendor.

Estate tax is payable in respect of the whole of a deceased person's estate wherever situated, if at the date of his death he was a resident of Israel, and in respect of that part of his estate which is situated in Israel, if at the date of his death the deceased was not a resident of Israel. The amount depends on the value of the estate and on who are the heirs of the deceased, such heirs, for the purposes of the Law, being divided into three classes: (1) spouse, children, and descendants of children, of the deceased; (2) parents of the deceased and their descendants; (3) heirs not included in either of the first two classes.

Absorption tax was chargeable and collectable in accordance with the rules relating to the imposition and collection of income tax, but was not chargeable upon companies. The rate of the tax was 30 prutot on each of the first IL. 300 of the chargeable income, 40 prutot on each of the second IL. 300, and 50 prutot on each pound thereafter. It was chargeable in the years of assessment 1949/50, 1950/51, and 1951/52.

Land betterment tax is payable under the Land Betterment Tax Law, 5723–1963, which came into force on the 26th August, 1963, on the betterment on the sale of a right in immovable property in Israel, which is defined as ownership, or a lease, or sub-lease, for a period exceeding ten years, and betterment is defined as the amount by which the value of the sale exceeds the value of the acquisition after the addition of the additions thereto and the deduction of the permitted deductions therefrom as specified in the Law. The tax is also payable in certain specified circumstances on a 'transaction in an immovable property association'. A 'transaction in an association' is defined as a conferment of a right in an association, the assignment or transfer of such a right, or the waiver thereof, or an alteration in the rights flowing from a right in an association, with or without consideration, an 'association' is defined as a company or foreign company within the meaning of the Companies Ordinance, a society registered under the Cooperative Societies Ordinance, a partnership registered under the Partnership Ordinance, and an association to which the Ottoman Law of Associations, 1909 applies, and an 'immovable property association' is defined as an association the major part of the assets whereof consists of rights in immovable property.

The rates of the tax are as follows: (1) on that part of the betterment which does not exceed 200% of the value of the acquisition—20% of that part of the betterment (2) on that part of the betterment which exceeds 200% but does not exceed 400% of the value of the acquisition—30% of that part of the betterment (3) on that part of the betterment which exceeds 400% of the value of the acquisition—40% of that part of the betterment. Where the period which has elapsed between the date of acquisition and the date of sale exceeds two years, there will be deducted from the amount of the tax calculated as above $\frac{1}{2}$% for every additional month during the thirteen years following those two years, and thereafter 1% for each additional year, and there are special deductions in a case in which the owner of immovable property has built upon it.

In the case of the sale by an individual of all the rights in immovable property which he has in his dwelling, and in the case of expropriation, the vendor will be entitled to deduct from the tax payable the following amounts: (1) 100% of the first IL. 1,000 of the tax, 75% of the next IL. 1,000 of the tax, $66\frac{2}{3}$% of the next IL. 1,000, and 50% of every additional amount of the tax, while in certain cases no tax is payable upon the sale of a dwelling which is owned or leased by an individual and in which he or his relative lives for the greater part of the year.

The Law contains detailed provisions in respect of exemptions from payment of the tax, including cases of sale of a right in immovable property the profit from which is assessable to income tax, and the sale of a right in immovable property without consideration to public institutions, and in certain cases the sale of a right in immovable property by a public institution. A waiver of a right without consideration is also exempt from the tax. A sale of a right in immovable property by a local authority, the Development Authority, the Jewish National Fund or Hemnutah

Ltd., so long as it is controlled by the Jewish National Fund, is also exempt from the tax.

The Law also contains detailed provisions regarding the assessment of the tax, objections to assessments and appeals, payment and collection of the tax, the powers of the Director of Land Betterment Tax appointed by the Minister of Finance, offences and penalties, and miscellaneous provisions, including a provision whereunder estate tax payable on an estate in which there is included a right in immovable property or a right in an association in respect of the sale whereof, or a transaction therein, land betterment tax is payable, will be credited with the amount paid for land betterment tax in respect of such sale or transaction.

Every person who holds in his own name for any other person a right in immovable property or a right in an immovable property association, is required to notify the Director of Land Betterment Tax within three months of the commencement of the Law, of every right which he so holds and the name of the person for whom he holds it and also the time when he acquired the right for the beneficiary.

The foreign travel tax is payable on the price of the ticket obtained in Israel for a journey to Israel from abroad, or from Israel to a place abroad, or from one place abroad to another place abroad. The rate, which may not exceed 100 per cent of the price of the ticket, is fixed by the Minister of Finance, with the approval of the Finance Committee of the Knesset, while the Minister of Finance may grant either total or partial exemptions from the tax to certain classes of persons.

The defence levy, payable upon income in the years 1956/57, 1957/58, was a progressive levy depending upon the amount of the income of the taxpayer, varying from 3.8% upon the lowest income to 11.4% upon the highest income. Incomes of childless persons not exceeding IL. 1,200 a year were exempt from the levy. In addition, there was an indirect tax upon tickets for entertainments, possession of wireless sets, possession of a telephone and its use, beer, wines, soft drinks, methylated spirits, cigarettes, cigars and tobacco, gas and crude oil, consumption of electricity, imported electrical appliances and possession of private cars. The object of the levy was to finance the acquisition of arms and equipment, the building of fortifications and shelters and security requirements. The defence stamp was originally payable during the period 30th November, 1956—31st March, 1958, on telephone accounts, bus journeys, railway journeys, documents, private car licences and taxi journeys, and will be payable for an additional period until the 31st March, 1970, upon those items and certain other items.

Property tax is payable by the owners of property, in respect of any tax year, on the property which they have in that year. Property is defined as meaning 'immovable property, stock-in-trade, and equipment, situated in the area of the State and vessels and aircraft, registered in Israel, even if not situated therein.' The tax is a percentage of the value of the property as specified in the Property Tax and Compensation Fund Law, 5721–1961.

Forty per cent, or such higher percentage as the Minister of Finance with the approval of the Finance Committee of the Knesset may prescribe, of the property tax collected in any year will be a special fund for the payment of compensation for damage, which is defined as meaning 'war damage, indirect damage and drought damage.' War damage means 'physical damage caused to property by war operations of the regular armies of the enemy or by other hostile acts or by war operations of the Defence Army of Israel, and indirect damage is defined as meaning 'loss, or loss of profits resulting from war damage in the area of a border settlement or from inability to utilise property' owing to such operations or acts.

The Minister of Finance determines by regulations, with the approval of the Finance Committee of the Knesset, who is entitled to compensation and the rates of compensation for every class of property, class of persons affected and class of damage.

The building levy is payable under the Levy on Large Apartments Law, 5724—1964, which came into force on the 7th August, 1964, where a person has been granted a building permit to build an apartment, or an addition to an apartment, or to combine existing apartments, and the area of the floors as fixed for the purposes of the building permit for the apartment or of the apartment together with the addition, or of the combined apartment, exceeds 125 square metres. The amount of the levy is IL. 100 for each of the first 125 square metres of the excess over 125 square metres, IL. 150 for each of the succeeding 50 square metres and IL. 200 for each additional square metre. The moneys of the levy will be transferred to the treasury of the local authority having jurisdiction in the area in which the apartment is situated and they will serve as a special fund for the abolition of dangerous buildings and slums, to be expended by the local authority for that purpose and for the rehabilitation of the tenants of the dangerous buildings and slums within the area of jurisdiction of the local authority in accordance with regulations made by the Minister of the Interior.

An 'apartment' is defined for the purposes of the Law as a 'set of rooms intended, in accordance with a town planning scheme or the building permit, for the dwelling of a family, together with its service rooms, corridors and balconies', and it is immaterial whether the building permit has been given especially for the apartment in question or for a building of which the apartment in question is intended to form part.

If the building permit has been cancelled and the apartment is not erected the building levy will be returned.

The United Nations Organisation and foreign states are exempt from payment of the levy, and the Minister of the Interior is empowered, with the approval of the Finance Committee of the Knesset, to prescribe by notice in *Reshumot* that the Law shall not apply to an area the boundaries whereof are set out in the notice. Under an amendment which came into force on the 16th August, 1967, immigrants are granted exemption in certain cases.

The Company Profits Tax Ordinance, 1947 was repealed by the Income Tax Ordinance Amendment Law, 5713–1953, and its provisions, with amendments, were incorporated in the Income Tax Ordinance, 1947.

The Income Tax Ordinance, 1947, has been amended by the Israel legislature nearly every year and sometimes more than once in certain years. A new Hebrew version of the Ordinance was published on the 25th April, 1961.

Under the Tax Laws Amendment (Exchange of Information between Tax Authorities) Law, 5727–1967, which came into force on the 16th August, 1967, the Income Tax Commissioner, the Director of Customs and Excise, the Director of Land Betterment Tax and the Director of Estate Tax, and State employees subordinate to them are authorised to supply to each other any information which they are empowered by any law to demand or receive from any other source notwithstanding the provisions of the tax laws as to the duty imposed upon them to treat such information as secret.

Import and Excise Duties

Import duty is levied and collected in respect of each of about 800 different classes of articles, and at the rates, specified in the Schedule to the Customs Tariff and Exemption Ordinance, 1937, in which the generally accepted tariff nomenclature and system of classification of imports have been adopted. Exemption from import duties in certain cases is provided for in the Schedule, while the Minister of Finance may, subject to Knesset control, vary such duties or grant exemptions.

Excise duty is levied on local products under the Tobacco Ordinance, the Intoxicating Liquors (Manufacture and Sale) Ordinance, the Matches Excise Ordinance, the Salt Ordinance, the Playing Cards Excise Ordinance, 1944, the Methylated Spirits Ordinance, the Tyres Excise Law, 5713–1953, the Sugar Excise Law, 5717–1957, and the Fuel Excise Law, 5718–1958.

Under the Customs, Excise and Purchase Tax (Cancellation of Special Exemption) Law, 5717–1957, as from the 1st October, 1957, no provision of the law regarding the grant of exemption from, or reduction of, customs duty, excise duty or purchase tax, to any particular person or class of persons may be acted upon, and no regulations may be made granting such exemption or reduction, unless the person concerned is one of those specified in the Law, including the President of the State, foreign diplomatic and consular representatives, certain international organisations, and Israel residents returning from abroad. In addition, the law provides that the State will be liable to pay customs duty, excise duty and purchase tax.

LOCAL GOVERNMENT

Classes of Local Authorities

THE MUNICIPAL CORPORATIONS Ordinance, 1934, the Local Councils Ordinance, 1941, and the Village Administration Ordinance, 1944, provide for three different categories of local authorities, namely, municipal councils, local councils and village councils. Municipal corporations are of two kinds, namely, those established by the Municipal Corporations Ordinance, 1934, in replacement of the municipalities and townships constituted under the Ottoman Law, and municipal corporations established by proclamation of the High Commissioner for Palestine, or the Minister of the Interior, as the case may be.

Local Councils and Village Councils were established by order of the High Commissioner for Palestine, and are established by order of the Minister of the Interior in Israel. No Village Councils have so far been established by the Minister of the Interior.

Considerable changes in the Municipal Corporations Ordinance, 1934, and the Local Councils Ordinance, 1941, have been made by the Israel legislature with a view to making local authorities much more democratic than they were under the Mandatory regime and a new Hebrew version of those Ordinances as amended has been published. Elections to municpal and local councils are general, direct, equal, secret and proportional. The persons eligible for inclusion in the register of voters for elections to municipal councils are persons permanently resident on the appointed day for six months in the area of the local authority and eighteen years of age on the 31st December immediately preceding the appointed day. Those eligible for election as councillors are persons registered in the register of voters and 20 years of age on the 31st December immediately preceding the appointed day, unless they ceased to be permanently resident in the municipal area before the date fixed for the sub-mission of lists of candidates or before the date of the elections.

Village councils consist of the mukhtar (headman) or mukhtars of the village *ex officio* and a prescribed number of persons chosen in the approved manner, by approved categories of persons ordinarily resident in the village area provided that they are Israel citizens of not less than 21 years of age, ordinarily resident in the village area, and their appointment has been approved as provided in the Ordinance.

The Mayors and Deputy Mayors of municipal corporations are elected by the municipal councils from among their mem-bers, while the Presidents and Vice-Presidents of local councils are appointed or elected as provided in the order constituting the local council. The Chairman and Deputy Chairmen of village councils are appointed, as provided in the Ordinance, from among the members of the village council.

The Local Authorities (Benefits for Head of Authority and his Deputies) Law, 5719–1959, passed by the Knesset on the 6th August, 1959, but having effect as from the 1st April, 1958, provides for pensions and gratuities for Mayors of Municipal Corporations and Presidents of Local Councils, and their De-puties, and their survivors.

By-Laws

All three classes of local authorities exercise their authority in the main by means of by-laws approved by the Minister of the Interior or his representative, under which they provide for such matters as water and conservancy, regulate markets and the slaughter of animals, maintain roads and parks, provide scavenging services, and generally undertake the normal duties of a local authority. If any such by-laws are repugnant to any law, or are unreasonable, the Courts will declare them to be invalid.

Under Section 77 of the Road Transport Ordinance a local authority may, with the consent of the Minister of the Interior and the Minister of Transport, make by laws as regards fares for journeys in public vehicles within their area, the regulation of

stationary vehicles within their area, animal-drawn vehicles and
the licensing of bicycles and tricycles other than motorbicycles
and motor-tricycles, and fees payable therefor.

The Local Authorities (Special Authorisation) Law, 5717—
1956 empowers local authorities to make by-laws which restrict,
or prohibit, the breeding of pigs and the possession and sale
of pig flesh and its products which are destined for food, notwithstanding anything contained in any other law. Such restriction
or prohibition may be imposed throughout the area of jurisdiction of the local authority, or any particular part of that
area, but the restriction or prohibition must be applied to all
the inhabitants of the area, or that particular part. The Law
validates any by-law made by a local authority and published
in *Reshumot* before the commencement of the Law (16th
December, 1956), which would have been valid had the Law been
in force at the time, but no person may be prosecuted for any
offence against the by-law committed before the commencement
of the Law.

The Prohibition of Pig Breeding Law, 5722–1962, which
came into force one year after its being passed by the Knesset
on the 23rd July, 1962, prohibits the breeding, keeping, and
killing for food, of pigs in any part of Israel save those areas
specified in the Law, unless the breeding, keeping or killing is in
institutes for science, research and public zoological gardens.
Any person contravening the prohibition will be liable to a fine
of IL. 10,000, while the owner of any structure or other place
who lets it, or renews the lease of it, or permits the use of it,
or renews permission to use it, knowing that the structure or
place is used, or will be used, for the breeding, keeping, or killing
for food, of pigs will be liable to a fine of IL. 5,000.

The Law also contains provisions regarding the seizure, forfeiture and destruction of pigs in respect of which a policeman,
or person authorized by the Minister of Police, has reasonable
ground for believing to be bred, kept, or killed, contrary to
the provisions of the Law, or in respect of which a person has
been convicted of an offence under the Law, but the owners
and keepers of pigs seized under the Law may apply to a com-

petent Magistrates' Court, and if it is not proved that there was a reasonable ground for seizing the pigs, or that an offence was committed in respect thereof under the Law, then the Magistrates' Court may order payment of their value to the applicant or to any other person entitled thereto, or, should they have not yet been destroyed, their restoration to the applicant or other person entitled thereto, as the Court deems fit, and an appeal will lie from that order as if were a judgment of a Magistrates' Court in a criminal case.

The Minister of the Interior is charged with the implementation of the Law.

Social Welfare Service

The Social Welfare Services Law, 5718–1958, which came into force on the 28th March, 1958, imposes a duty upon every local authority to maintain a Social Welfare Office for the social treatment of the needy and for providing them with aid. Such offices are to be organised in accordance with regulations made by the Minister for Social Welfare in consultation with the Minister of the Interior. Under an amendment of the Law which came into force on the 1st August, 1965, provision was made for the establishment of Objections Committees to which any person who considers himself affected by the lack of an answer from a Social Welfare Office within a reasonable time or any decision of such an office, may lodge an objection, and the powers of such committees are prescribed.

Where a social welfare officer is satisfied that a person is a needy person, he may interrogate the person who is liable, or likely to be liable, to pay maintenance for such needy person, as to his capacity to provide such maintenance, and in so far as such needy person has not claimed maintenance from such person, or has not collected it from him, the Minister for Social Welfare, or the local authority, may claim and collect it from him in the name of the needy person with his authority, and even without such authority in the case of a minor or insane person, or if he is receiving social treatment from the social welfare officer. When the Minister for Social Welfare, or local authority, has collected maintenance, he or it must hand it over to the needy person or use it in accordance with the directions of the Court which ordered payment of maintenance for the needs of the needy person. Should there be no need for, or possibility of, so using the maintenance, it must be returned to the person who paid it.

If the Minister for Social Welfare, or a local authority, has given aid to a person and subsequently discovers that at the time the aid was given the income of such person was sufficient for the needs for which the aid was given, such person must return the aid given to him, and, for that purpose, aid given to a child of any person up to sixteen years of age is deemed aid given to that person himself. Provision is also made for the repayment to the Minister for Social Welfare, or a local authority, of aid given by them to a person whose income has subsequently sufficiently increased, but no person may be required to repay aid given to him while he was under sixteen years of age. All claims for repayment must be made within six years of the giving of the aid.

Local Revenue

Generally speaking, the revenue of the local authorities is derived from rates imposed with the approval of the Minister of the Interior, or his representative. The municipal councils may impose (a) a property rate assessed on the rateable value of buildings, occupied and unoccupied land, levied on the owners; (b) a general rate assessed on the rateable value of buildings, agricultural land, and occupied land and levied on the occupier.

The majority of local councils impose general rates and property rates or rates on houses and/or land of varying percentages. A number impose, in addition, rates for specific services, e.g. education, watch and ward and scavenging.

Both the Municipal Corporations Ordinance and the Local Councils Ordinance provide that no disposition of any property within the area of jurisdiction of a local authority may be registered in any land register until there has been produced to the Land

Registrar a certificate, signed by the Head of the local authority, to the effect that all the debts owing to the local authority in respect of such property have been paid in full, or that there are no such debts.

Under the Local Authorities (Additional Income Tax) Law, 5712–1952, of the 3rd September, 1952, a local authority was empowered to impose upon local residents and companies, in the assessment year 1952/53 and in each subsequent assessment year up to 1957, a payment of $7\frac{1}{2}\%$ of the income tax or company profits tax, as the case may be, payable to the local authority and for its use.

The Local Authorities (Social Welfare and Recreation Charge) Law, 5719–1959, which came into force on the 16th August, 1959, empowers local authorities, by by-law, to impose a charge in respect of certain specified services provided in certain specified classes of establishments, such as hotels and restaurants. It kept in force for one year by-laws made prior to its commencement and in force at that date under the previous law, as doubts had arisen as to their validity. The Minister of the Interior may grant certain exemptions from the payment of the charge, and has exempted tourists as respects lodging and food in hotels.

The Law requires the local authority to devote the charge to purposes of social welfare in its area, but, under an amendment which came into force on the 8th January, 1965, where the Minister of the Interior has, by order, declared that the area of a particular local authority is resorted to in certain seasons for the purposes of recreation or recuperation, such local authority may devote the charge, or part thereof, also for the development and upkeep of enterprises for recreation and vacation in its area.

The Local Authorities (Land Transfer Fee) Law, 5719–1959, which came into force at the expiration of thirty days from the day on which it was passed by the Knesset (the 1st April, 1959) requires a person liable to pay a land transfer fee to pay, together with that fee, an additional fee to go to the local authority in the area in which the land in respect whereof the transfer fee is payable is situated at the rate of half of the amount of the land transfer fee paid by him as aforesaid.

The Local Authorities (Business Tax) Ordinance, 1945, as amended by the Local Authorities (Business Tax) Ordinance Amendment (No. 5) Law, 5727–1966, which came into force on the 1st November, 1966, provides that a local authority may, by by-law, impose upon any person engaged within its area of jurisdiction, in any of the trades or businesses specified in the by-law at a rate fixed by the by-law, not exceeding five thousand Pounds a year for each place in which that person is engaged in the said trade or business, but such business tax may not be imposed in respect of any trade or business which does not have within the area of jurisdiction of the local authority a place such as a workshop, factory, office, shop, store, installation, stop for picking up passengers, or a like place, but such provision will not preclude the imposition of business tax in respect of contracting works.

The building levy payable under the Levy on Large Apartments Law, 5724–1964, is transferred to the local authority having jurisdiction in the area in which the apartment is situated (see pp. 150–1).

PERSONAL STATUS

Matters of Personal Status

MATTERS OF PERSONAL status are defined, for the purposes of the Palestine Orders-in-Council, 1922–1947, by Article 51 thereof, as meaning 'suits regarding marriage or divorce, alimony, maintenance, guardianship, legitimation and adoption of minors, inhibition from dealing with property of persons who are legally incompetent, successions, wills, and legacies, and the administration of the property of absent persons'. Upon the coming into force of the Adoption of Children Law, 5720–1960 (see pp. 161–4) adoption of minors was excluded, and upon the coming into force of the Inheritance Law, 5725–1965, (see pp. 167–75), successions, wills and legacies were excluded.

The law applicable in matters of personal status depends upon whether or not the persons concerned are Jews, Moslems or members of one of the recognised religious communities, and whether or not they are foreigners, which include stateless persons, as 'foreigner' is defined as any person who is not an Israel citizen.

The nine recognised Christian religious communities are: the Eastern (Orthodox), Latin (Catholic), Gregorian Armenian, Armenian (Catholic), Syrian (Catholic), Chaldean (Uniate), Greek Catholic Melkite, Maronite, and Syrian Orthodox. In addition, since the 21st April, 1957, the Druze community has been recognised as a religious community.

Generally speaking, the law applied in matters of personal status by the Religious Courts is the religious law, and the law applied in such matters by the Civil Courts is the personal law of the parties concerned, which, in the case of an Israel citizen is the religious law, and in the case of a foreigner, is expressly declared to be the law of his nationality, unless that law imports the law of his domicile, in which case the law of his domicile is applied.

No provision is made for civil marriage or civil divorce in Israel, although foreigners may be married by their consuls in Israel if their national law permits of such a marriage. It is doubtful, however, whether foreigners who are Jews may be so married in view of the provisions of section 2 of the Rabbinical Courts' Jurisdiction (Marriage and Divorce) Law, 5713–1953, (see pp. 207–8), under which marriages of Jews must be celebrated in Israel in accordance with *Din Torah* (Jewish religious law).

Most of the other powers which foreign consuls had had under the Personal Status (Consular Powers) Regulations since the 1st December, 1922, were taken away from them by the Personal Status (Consular Powers) Regulations Amendment Law, 5717–1956, of the 13th December, 1956.

Equality of Women's Rights

Under the Equality of Women's Rights Law, 5711–1951, of the 26th July, 1951, the law shall apply equally to men and women in respect of every legal transaction, and no provision of law which discriminates against a woman, by reason of her being a woman, as regards any legal transaction may be applied.

A married woman shall be as fully competent to acquire, or dispose of, property as is an unmarried woman, and her property acquired before marriage will not be affected by her marriage.

Both the father and mother are declared to be the natural guardians of their children, and in the event of the decease of either parent the surviving parent is declared to be the natural guardian. A competent court or tribunal may, however, when dealing with matters of guardianship of children, whether over their person or property, have regard solely to the good of the children.

All courts and also all tribunals are to act in accordance with the provisions of the Equality of Women's Rights Law, 5711–1951. If, however, all the parties are eighteen years of age or more, and agree before a tribunal competent to try matters of personal status that the tribunal should apply the law of the community, that law is to be applied.

Adoption of Children

Until the Adoption of Children Law, 5720–1960 came into force on the 19th August, 1960, there was no general legal basis for adoption in this country. The Civil Courts in Israel, owing to the urgent need for making adoption orders in many cases, made such orders in anticipation of the passing of appropriate legislation which would, *inter alia*, validate those orders. The Adoption of Children Law, 5720–1960 expressly validates such orders by providing that, if a person has been adopted in accordance with such an order, he will be deemed to have been adopted in accordance with that Law.

The Law empowers a District Court to make an adoption order upon the application of an adopter who is a resident of Israel, if it is satisfied that the adoption will be for the good of the adoptee. An adoptee must be under 18 years of age and of the same religion as that of the adopter, and the adopter must be at least 18 years older than the adoptee, but, if the spouse of the adopter is the parent of the adoptee, or previously adopted the adoptee, the Court may make an adoption order in the absence of such difference between the age of the adopter and the adoptee.

There may be no adoption save by a husband and wife together, but the Court may make an order for adoption by one adopter alone if the spouse of the adopter is the parent of the adoptee or previously adopted the adoptee, or if the adopter is an unmarried relative of the adoptee and is at least 35 years old.

The Court may not make an adoption order unless the adoptee was supported by the adopter for at least six months prior to the making of the order, which period is to be counted from the day upon which notice was given to a social welfare officer within the meaning of the Social Welfare Services Law, 5718–1958 (see pp. 156–7), that the adopter has taken the adoptee into his home with a view to adopting him. If the adoptee is capable of understanding the matter, the Court may not make an adoption order unless it is satisfied that the adoptee wishes to be adopted by the adopter, nor may the Court make an adoption order unless it is satisfied that the parents of the adoptee agree to the adoption, although it is not necessary that they should know who the adopter is. The Court is empowered to cancel the consent of a parent given before the birth of the adoptee, or if it was obtained by improper means, and it may permit a parent to retract his consent so long as the adoption order has not been made. On the other hand, the Court is empowered to make an adoption order despite the absence of the consent of a parent if it is satisfied that the parent has abandoned the adoptee, or has permanently failed to carry out his obligations towards him, or is unable to express his opinion, or if there is no reasonable possibility of ascertaining his opinion, or if his refusal to agree to the adoption is due to immoral causes, or for an unlawful purpose.

Adoption will create, as between the adopter and the adoptee, the same duties and rights as exist between parents and their children, and confers upon the adopter as respects the adoptee the same powers as are given to parents as respects their children, and it terminates the duties and obligations as between the adoptee and his parents and other relatives and the powers given to them as respects the adoptee, but the Court may, in its order, restrict those consequences and the adoption will not affect the laws regarding prohibition and permission in matters of marriage and divorce. The consequences of adoption will have effect as from the date of the adoption order, unless the Court determines, in the order, that those consequences, or any of them, shall have effect from some other date.

The Court may cancel an adoption order by reason of circumstances which were not known, or did not exist, at the time of the making of the order, if it is satisfied that it is proper so to do and that the good of the adoptee so requires. The cancellation of an adoption order brings to an end the duties and rights as between the adopter and the adoptee and the powers of the adopter as respects the adoptee, and restores the duties and rights as between the adoptee and his parents and other relatives and their powers as respects the adoptee, as from the date fixed therefor in the order cancelling the adoption order, but the Court may, in the former order, direct otherwise, either generally or as respects any particular right, duty or power, and order what shall be done to the adoptee after the cancellation of the adoption.

Proceedings under the Law are to be held in camera unless the Court decides that they shall be conducted in open Court, although the Court may permit a person, or class of persons, to be present during the whole, or any part, of the proceedings.

The Court may not make an adoption order save after having received a written report from a social welfare officer, and it is empowered to vary certain specified provisions of the Law if in special circumstances it is satisfied that it is for the good of the adoptee so to do.

In addition to the District Court, Religious Courts are given jurisdiction in matters of adoption under the Law if the parents, the adopters and the adoptee have consented in writing to their jurisdiction. Should the adoptee not be capable of understanding the matter, or be under the age of 13 years, the consent of a social welfare officer and of the Attorney General to the Government is required.

Every adoption order, and every order cancelling an adoption order, must be entered in a register to be kept by a registrar appointed in that behalf by the Minister of Justice. The register will be open to inspection only by the Attorney General to the Government or his representative, a marriage registrar or other person authorised in that behalf, when the inspection is necessary for the performance of his official duty, and an adoptee after he has reached the age of 18 years.

Any person who offers, or gives, and any person who asks for, or receives, any money or money's worth for an adoption, or for mediation for adoption, without permission of the Court will be liable to three years' imprisonment, while any person who publishes, without permission of the Court, the name of any adopter or adoptee or an adoptee's parent, including the names of those persons in respect of whom any application has been made to the Court under the Law, or who publishes anything else which is likely to lead to their identification, will be liable to imprisonment for three months.

Where in any enactment or document made after the coming into force of the Law, mention is made of the child of any person, an adopted child of that person will be included, and if mention is made of the parent of any child, an adopter of that child will be included, unless there is an express or implied intention to the contrary. In addition, for the purpose of certain specified enactments in force before the coming into force of the Law, it is provided in the Law that a child shall include an adopted child.

Maintenance

The Family Law Amendment (Maintenance) Law, 5719–1959, which came into force on the 12th March, 1959, deals with maintenance payable to spouses, minor children and other relatives. It does not apply to maintenance payable by any person to his or her spouse which is regulated by the personal law applicable to such person, but it imposes an obligation to pay maintenance to his or her spouse, upon a person who is not a Jew, Moslem or Druze, or a member of one of the nine recognised Christian religious communities (see p. 160), or to whom there is no personal law applicable. Nor does it apply to maintenance payable by a person to his or her minor children, that is, children under eighteen years of age, and the minor children of his or her spouse, which is regulated by the personal law applicable to such person, but if a person is not obliged by the personal law applicable to him or her to pay maintenance to his or her spouse, or if he or she has no personal law applicable to him or her, then such person must pay maintenance for such children in accordance with the provisions of the Law.

The Law imposes an obligation upon a person to pay maintenance for the following relatives, namely, parents-in-law, adult children (eighteen years of age and upwards) and their spouses, grandchildren, grandparents and grandparents-in-law, brothers and brothers-in-law, sisters and sisters-in-law, if the following conditions are fulfilled: (a) such person is able to pay maintenance after satisfying his or her own needs and those of his or her spouse and the minor children of his or her spouse; (b) such relative, despite his or her efforts, cannot supply his or her needs from work, property or any other source; (c) such relative cannot receive maintenance from a relative preceding him in the above list.

The scope and amount of the maintenance and the manner of providing it will be determined, in default of agreement between the parties, by a District Court having regard to the circumstances and, save in the case of maintenance for minor children, in accordance with the needs of the person liable to pay it. Should there be two or more persons liable to pay maintenance to any person, the Court may fix the extent of liability of each of them. The Court may also exempt, in whole or in part, any person from liability to pay maintenance by reason of disgraceful conduct towards such person by the person entitled, if it considers it just and equitable to do so.

The Court may dismiss a claim for maintenance made more than one year after the period in respect of which it is claimed if it finds no reasonable ground for the delay, while if judgment is given for the payment of maintenance and no steps are taken to collect the maintenance within two years of the period for which it was awarded, it may not be collected without leave of the Court.

No agreement regarding maintenance for a minor child or waiver of such maintenance will bind the minor child so long as it has not been confirmed by the Court, while an agreement regarding maintenance for an adult and waiver of such maintenance must be in writing and may be confirmed by the Court. Furthermore, the Court is empowered to vary the terms of any agreement, waiver or judgment as regards maintenance, if it deems fit to do so because of circumstances which have become known to the applicant for variation, or have changed since the agreement, waiver or judgment.

The Law also provides that maintenance may not be transferred, charged, set-off, or attached, save in favour of the person who supplied the person entitled thereto with the means of livelihood in the form of services or commodities, and that the right to maintenance ceases with the death of the person entitled thereto or the person liable to pay it.

The liability of a spouse to pay maintenance will be determined by the law of the place of his or her residence, while the liability of a person to pay maintenance for a minor child will be determined by the law of the place of residence of the person liable to pay. For the purposes of the Law, a child means a child born in or out of wedlock, and includes an adopted child.

The jurisdiction of the Religious Courts is not affected by the Law, and in those cases in which the Religious Courts have jurisdiction, they may exercise the powers conferred by the Law upon District Courts. Furthermore, the Law supplements the rights to maintenance conferred by religious law applied by Religious Courts, or by the personal law applicable to the parties, and does not derogate from any right to maintenance conferred by any agreement in excess of the amount or scope under the Law.

For the purposes of computing the chargeable income of a person who pays maintenance in accordance with a judgment or agreement confirmed by the Court, a deduction not exceeding the rate fixed by the Income Tax Ordinance, will be allowed in respect of the class of relative to whom maintenance is paid, but without any restriction upon the number of such relatives in respect of whom a deduction may be claimed under that Ordinance.

Inheritance

The original draft of the Inheritance Law, 5725–1965, which came into force nine months after its publication in *Reshumot* on the 10th February, 1965, was published in *Reshumot* in 1958. It met with considerable opposition from the religious parties owing to its departure from Jewish law and so its passage through the Knesset was not an easy one and it underwent many changes during that passage.

The Law provides that upon the death of a person his estate passes to his heirs according to law or his will. Every person alive at the date of the death of the decedent is capable of being an heir unless he was convicted of intentionally causing, or attempting to cause, the death of the decedent, or destroying, or forging, his last will or claiming under a forged will. If, however, the decedent has forgiven a person convicted of attempting to cause his death, either in writing or by making a will in his favour, that person will be capable of being his heir.

After the death of the decedent, and so long as his estate has not been distributed, an heir may, by written notice to the Court, withdraw from his share in an estate, in whole or in part, and if he does so, he will be deemed not to have been originally an heir to the extent to which he has withdrawn. Such a withdrawal will be void if it is conditional, and it cannot be in favour of any other person save the spouse, or children, of the decedent, while a minor or a person declared legally incompetent cannot withdraw without the confirmation of the Court.

The Law lays down rules for determining the rights to the estates of two or more persons who have died where it cannot be ascertained which of them died first. Where one of the claimants is an 'undoubted heir', who is defined as a person who will be an heir whether one or the other died first, and the other claimant is a 'doubtful heir', who is defined as a person who will be an heir only if one of them died first, preference is given to the undoubted heir. Where both claimants are doubtful heirs, preference is given to the claimant who is the spouse or relative of the decedent whose estate is being distributed. As between other claimants of the same degree of preference the estate will be distributed, in the absence of a will, according to the rules for distribution of an inheritance according to law.

The heirs according to law are: (1) the person who was the spouse of the decedent at the time of his death; (2) the children of the decedent and their descendants, his parents and their descendants, his grand-parents and their descendants (referred to in the Law as 'the relatives of the decedent').

The spouse of the decedent takes the movables which, customarily and in the circumstances, belong to the common household, and from the rest of the estate he or she takes: (1) one quarter, when the other heirs are children of the decedent from a previous marriage; (2) one half, when the other heirs are the children of the decedent otherwise than from a previous marriage, or their descendants, or the parents of the decedent; (3) two thirds, if the other heirs are brothers or sisters of the decedent, or grand-parents of the decedent; (4) five sixths, when the other heirs are heirs according to law other than those already mentioned; (5) the whole, in default of other heirs. But if at the time of the death of the decedent all the property of the spouses, or most of it according to its value, was in the joint ownership of both of them, the share of the surviving spouse in the estate of the decedent will be one quarter instead of one half when the other heirs are the children of the decedent otherwise than from a previous marriage.

Whatever is due to a spouse by reason of the matrimonial relationship, including what a wife receives under her Ketubah (marriage contract), will be deducted from the share of that spouse in the estate, without prejudice to the right of the spouse to receive from the estate what the decedent received by reason of the marriage on condition that he will return it when the marriage is dissolved.

The children of the decedent have preference over his parents, and his parents have preference over his grandparents, but if the decedent left children and parents, the parents take one sixth of the estate.

The children of the decedent share equally between them. If a child of the decedent dies before him and leaves children, his children will inherit in his stead, and the same will apply to the children of each of the relatives of the decedent who predecease him, and to a child or relative who is found incapable of inheriting, or who has withdrawn from the inheritance otherwise than in favour of the spouse or children of the decedent. In each of the above cases the children share equally between them.

A person who has been lawfully adopted inherits from his adopter as if he were his child, and his descendants will also inherit from the adopter, but the adopted person and his descendants will not inherit according to law from relatives of the adopter. The adopter will inherit from the adopted person as if he were his parent, but the relatives of the adopter will not inherit according to law from the adopted person. The adopted person and his descendants will inherit from his relatives, but his parents and grandparents and their descendants will not inherit from him.

In default of any of the abovementioned heirs the State will inherit as an heir according to law, and whatever it so inherits will serve the purposes of education, science, health and social welfare, but the Minister of Finance may grant out of the assets of the estate, or pay, within the limit of the value of the assets of the estate coming into the hands of the State after payment of the debts of the estate, a non-recurrent payment or recurrent payments to: (1) the person who immediately prior to the death of the decedent had his needs provided by the decedent; (2) the person who, or corporation which, immediately prior to the death of the decedent provided the needs of the decedent; (3) a member of the family of the decedent or of the spouse of the decedent who is not an heir according to law.

The Law provides for four categories of wills, namely, a holograph will, a will made before witnesses, a will made before an authority, and an oral will.

A holograph will must be written entirely by the hand of the testator, bear a date written by his hand and be signed by him. A will made before witnesses must be dated and signed by the hand of the testator before two witnesses after he has declared in their presence that that is his will. The witnesses must confirm on the same occasion by their signatures on the face of the will that the testator so declared and signed.

A person who has made a holograph will, or a will before witnesses, may deposit it in a District Court. The deposit will be effected by the delivery of the will by the testator himself to a Judge or Registrar of the Court or to the authority authorised by regulations made by the Minister of Justice to receive wills in order to transmit them to the Court. A will which has been so deposited and kept in deposit until the death of the testator will be prima facie evidence that the person stated therein as the testator made the will and that it was made at the latest on the date of its deposit. The testator may at any time get back the will which he has deposited.

A will made before an authority is made by the testator's stating the text of the will orally before a Judge or Registrar of a District Court or of a Magistrates' Court, or before a Judge of a Religious Court, or by the submission of the text of the will in writing, by the testator himself, to such a Judge or Registrar. The text of the will, as recorded by such Judge or Registrar, or as submitted to him, must be read out before the testator, who must declare it to be his will, and the Judge or Registrar must certify on the face of the will that it was so read out and that the testator so declared. If the will is written in a language which the testator does not know, it must be read out to him in a language which he knows, and the translator must certify that on the face of the will. Instead of the will or the translation thereof being read out before the testator the testator himself may read the will or the translation thereof. A will made before an authority may be deposited in a District Court, and it will be prima facie evidence that the person stated therein to be the testator made the will and that it was made on the date, and at the place, stated therein as the date on which, and the place at which, it was made.

A person who is dangerously ill and a person who considers himself, in circumstances which justify him, to be face to face with death, may make an oral will before two witnesses who understand his language. The words of the testator, with an indication of the date and the circumstances of the making of the will, must be recorded in a memorandum signed by the two witnesses and deposited by them in a District Court. Such recording, signature and deposit must be made as soon as possible. An oral will is void at the expiration of one month after the circumstances which justified its making have ceased and the testator is still alive.

A minor and a person declared to be legally incompetent are not capable of being witnesses to the making of any will.

If the Court has no doubt as to the authenticity of a will, it may confirm it notwithstanding any defect in the signature of the testator, or of the witnesses, or in the date of the will, or in the proceedings described above or in the capacity of the witnesses.

The Law enumerates the provisions of a will which will be void. They include a provision in any will, other than an oral will, which entitles the person who drafted the will, or was a witness to the making of the will, or otherwise took part in its drafting, and a provision which entitles the spouse of any of such persons.

A testator may revoke his will, either by express revocation in one of the ways for the making of a will, or by destroying the will. If a testator destroys the will he is presumed to have intended thereby to revoke it. A new will is deemed to revoke the previous will to the extent that the provisions of the new will are repugnant to the provisions of the previous will, even if there is no express revocation of the previous will, unless there is nothing in the new will except an addition to what is stated in the previous will.

No person may claim any rights under any will, and no document can be relied upon as a will, unless an order of confirmation has been made in respect thereof.

Where a man and a woman are living a family life in a joint household but are not married to each other, and one of them dies, and at the time of his or her death neither of them was married to any other person, the survivor is deemed to have had left to her or him by a will of the decedent what she or he would have inherited in accordance with law had they been married to each other, unless it is otherwise provided, expressly or by implication, in a will left by the decedent.

If the decedent leaves a spouse, children or parents and they are in need of maintenance, they are entitled to maintenance from the estate in accordance with the detailed provisions set out in the Law, whether there is an inheritance in accordance with law or a will, and the persons entitled to such maintenance, and the amount thereof, will be determined by the Court upon application made before the estate is distributed, or within six months after the distribution if the Court considers that the circumstances justify the making of the application after the distribution of the estate. The Court may also award maintenance even if no application is made therefor if it considers that the circumstances justify it in so doing.

Where the estate is not sufficient to provide maintenance for all the persons entitled thereto, the Court may treat as part of the estate what the decedent gave without adequate consideration within two years before his death, excluding presents and contributions usually given in the circumstances of the case, and it may require the recipient to return to the estate, or pay as maintenance, an amount equal to the value of what remains in his hands at the time of the death of the decedent, and if he did not receive it in good faith an amount equal to the value of what he received.

A provision in a will which deprives any person of any right to maintenance, or restricts that right, will be void.

Any person who has in his possession any will must deliver the original, or a certified copy thereof, to a District Court immediately after he has learned of the death of the decedent. If he fails to do so he will be liable to three months' imprisonment or a fine of Il. 1,000.

The sixth chapter of the Law contains detailed provisions regarding the administration and distribution of estates of decedents by administrators appointed by the Court or, in default of such administrators, by the heirs. If the decedent by his will appoints someone to execute his will, or administer his estate, the Court must appoint such person to administer the estate, unless he is unable or unwilling to accept the appointment or the Court is satisfied, for reasons to be recorded by it, that there are special reasons for not appointing him.

Special protection is given by the Law to a person who immediately prior to the death of the decedent was living with him in his dwelling house, whether owned or leased by the decedent. Such a person may continue to live there for three months, or if he is an heir, six months, after the death of the decedent, and he may, during that period, use the movables of the joint household to the extent to which he used them immediately prior to the death of the decedent. Furthermore, the Law provides that where the decedent immediately prior to his death owned a dwelling house and lived in it, his or her spouse, children and parents who were then living in the dwelling house with the decedent, may continue to live in it as tenants of the heirs entitled to the dwelling house, at such rent, for such period and upon such conditions as may be agreed upon by the persons remaining in the dwelling house and such heirs, or, in default of agreement, as may be fixed by the Court. The Court is empowered, upon application of such heirs, to decide that only those persons who have no other dwelling house to live in shall continue to live in the dwelling house of the decedent, and that those who remain in the dwelling house shall continue to live only in part of it, provided that such part contains the kitchen and service rooms, if any. If the deceased was the tenant of a dwelling house and was living in it immediately prior to his death, the tenancy rights, if under a contract not rescinded by the death of the decedent and not conferred by the Tenant Protection laws, will pass to the spouse, children and parents of the decedent who were living with the decedent in the dwelling house immediately prior to his or her death.

The seventh chapter of the Law contains rules of private international law relating to inheritance. For the purposes of that chapter, the expression 'domicil' of a person is defined as the place where the centre of his life is, and it is provided that the domicil of a minor or legally incompetent person is presumed to be the domicil of his representative within the meaning of the Legal Competence and Guardianship Law, 5722–1962 (see pp. 175–8.), so long as it is not proved that the centre of his life is elsewhere.

According to the Law, a Court in Israel is competent to deal with the inheritance of every person whose domicil at the time of his death is in Israel or who has left property in Israel. The law of the domicil of the decedent at the time of his death will apply to his inheritance, save that, as regards property which passes by inheritance only in accordance with the law of the place where such property is situated, such law will apply, and capacity to make a will will be determined by the law of the domicil of the testator at the time of the making of the will. Furthermore, a will will be valid in form if made according to Israel law, or the law of the place where it is made, or the law of the domicil of the testator, and if the testator was not a resident of Israel, also in accordance with his national law.

Notwithstanding anything contained in the Law, where the law of any particular state is applicable and that law refers to a foreign law, the reference must be ignored and the internal law of the particular state must be applied, but where the law of that particular state refers to Israel law, the reference must be acted upon and the internal Israel law must be applied. Where a foreign law is applicable it must not be applied in so far as it discriminates on the grounds of race, religion, or nation, or is contrary to public policy in Israel, while if a foreign law confers rights of inheritance according to law upon a person who is not related to the decedent by blood, marriage, or adoption, that law may not be applied save in so far as it recognises such rights of inheritance as are conferred by Israel law.

Among the miscellaneous provisions contained in the eighth chapter of the Law, which is the last chapter, the following provisions require special mention because of their great importance in the law of inheritance.

The first provision is that, for the purposes of inheritance, the special laws relating to land of the miri category are repealed, so that henceforth it will be possible to make a will as regards such land, a reform long overdue.

The second provision is that in matters of inheritance the provisions of Article 46 of the Palestine Orders-in-Council, 1922–1947 (see pp. 61–2) will not be applicable. Consequently, in the absence of a provision of statutory law applicable to any particular case the Israel Courts will not be obliged to apply the substance of the common law and the doctrines of equity in force in England as heretofore.

The third provision relates to a matter on which there was considerable controversy, namely, the jurisdiction of the Religious Courts, particularly the Rabbinical Courts in matters concerning inheritance, and the law to be applied by the Religious Courts in cases where they have jurisdiction in such matters.

The law provides that the Court which is competent to deal with matters of inheritance is a District Court, and that the provisions of the Law must be applied thereto, but it goes on to provide that nevertheless a Religious Court which had jurisdiction in matters of personal status of the decedent may make an order of inheritance or an order confirming a will and determine rights to maintenance from the estate, if all the parties concerned according to the Law have expressed in writing their consent thereto, and that where a matter is so brought before a Religious Court that Court may act according to the religious law applied by it, save that, if among the parties concerned there is a minor or a person who has been declared legally incompetent, his rights of inheritance, whether according to law or a will, and his rights to maintenance, may not be less than they would be under the Law.

Legal Competence and Guardianship

The Legal Competence and Guardianship Law, 5722–1962, was passed by the Knesset on the 8th August, 1962 and came into force three months later. Its first chapter deals with guardianship, the second with parents and minor children, the third with appointed guardians, and the fourth with miscellaneous matters. It forms part of the comprehensive draft Individual and Family Law prepared in the Ministry of Justice which is being brought piecemeal before the Knesset.

The first chapter of the Law opens with a general declaration that every person is capable of having rights and duties from the termination of his birth until his death, and that he is capable of performing legal acts, unless that capacity has been taken away from him or has been restricted by any law or by the judgment of a Court.

The Law for the first time prescribes the age of majority for all purposes, subject to the provisions of any special law, by providing that a person who has not completed 18 years is a minor, and that a person who has completed 18 years is an adult.

A legal act of a minor requires the consent of his representative, which may be given in advance, or retroactively, for a particular act, or a particular class of acts, and a representative of a minor may revoke his consent so long as the act has not been done.

A legal act of a minor done without the consent of his representative may be rescinded by his representative, or, if he has no representative, by the Attorney General within one month of his knowledge of the act, or by the minor himself within one month of his reaching his majority in the case where the act has not come to the knowledge of the representative or of the Attorney General.

A legal act of a minor which minors of his age are wont to do, and also a legal act between a minor and a person who did not have to know that he was a minor, cannot be rescinded even if done without the consent of his representative, unless it caused substantial damage to the minor or his property.

A legal act of a minor requires authorisation of the Court if it would have required such authorisation had it been done by his representative, and such act will have no effect so long as it has not been authorised by the Court.

All the above provisions will apply, *mutatis mutandis*, to a person who is legally incompetent, that is to say, a person who has been so declared by the Court, upon the application of his, or her,

spouse, or relative, or the Attorney General or his representative,
by reason of his being unable to look after his own affairs owing
to mental illness or mental deficiency.

The Law provides that a person's age shall be reckoned from
the day upon which he was born, unless otherwise provided
expressly or by implication, and that a day commences with the
setting of the sun on the previous day and ends with the setting
of the sun on that day. It also provides that where the year in
which a person was born is known but the day upon which he
was born is not known, there is a presumption that he was born
on the first day of Nissan in that year, and that where the month
in which a person was born is known but the day upon which
he was born is not known, there is a presumption that he was
born on the fifteenth day of that month.

The opening section of the second chapter of the Law provides
that the parents are the natural guardians of their minor children,
and the following section provides that the guardianship of
parents includes the duty and the right to care for the needs of the
minor, including its upbringing, education, training for work
and a vocation, and its religious worship, as well as preservation,
administration, and development, of its property, and linked
with it is the right to custody of the minor and the determination
of where it shall live and the authority to represent it.

In every matter of guardianship both parents have to act in
agreement, and the agreement of one of them to the act of the
other may be given in advance or retroactively, expressly or by
implication, for any particular matter, or generally, and there is
a presumption that one parent has agreed to an act of the other so
long as the contrary has not been proved, while in a matter which
cannot be delayed, each of the parents may act alone. Should
the parents not agree in a matter relating to the property of the
minor, either of them may apply to the Court, and the Court
will decide. Should the parents not agree on any other matter subject to their guardianship, they may jointly apply to the Court,
and the Court, if it cannot get them to agree and it considers
that it should decide, will itself decide or it will leave it to one
of the parents to decide.

The Law then goes on to specify the acts in which the parents may not represent the minor without the prior authorisation of the Court. Those acts fall into five categories. The first category comprises the transfer, charging, partition, or dissolution of an economic unit in agriculture, industry, trade or commerce or of dwelling. The second comprises an act the validity of which depends upon registration in a register which is kept in accordance with law. The third comprises the giving of gifts other than gifts given according to custom in the circumstances of the case. The fourth is the giving of a guarantee, and the fifth is a legal act between the minor and its parents, or the relatives of its parents, other than the acceptance of gifts given to the minor. As regards the last mentioned acts, they will be valid even in the absence of the required authorisation, if they were done as respects a person who did not know and did not have to know that they required authorisation.

Where the parents are not living together they may agree which of them shall have the guardianship, in whole or in part, which of them shall have custody of the minor, and what shall be the rights of access to the minor of the parent who does not have the custody. Such an agreement requires the authorisation of the Court. Should the parents not come to such an agreement, or should they come to such an agreement and such agreement be not carried out, then the Court may determine the matters upon which they could come to an agreement as it deems fit for the benefit of the minor, save that children up to the age of six years shall be with their mother unless there are special reasons for ordering otherwise.

Where one of the parents dies the other parent will have the guardianship of the minor, but the Court may appoint an additional guardian, either generally or for such matters as it may determine. The Court may also so act when one of the parents has been declared legally incompetent, or is unable to perform his or her duties as guardian or has been deprived of guardianship by the Court, and also in the case where one of the parents is unknown, or was not married to the other parent and did not recognize the minor as his or her child. The Court may not appoint such an additional guardian unless it considers that there is a special reason to do so for the benefit of the minor and after giving an opportunity to the parent to submit his or her arguments.

The third chapter of the Law contains detailed provisions regarding the appointment and dismissal of guardians of various classes of persons, including minors, legally incompetent persons and persons unable to look after their own affairs, persons who cannot be identified and embryos, and regarding their duties and responsibilities. An individual, a corporation, or the Administrator General, may be appointed as a guardian, and where the Court appoints a corporation to be a guardian it may appoint an individual to perform the duties of the guardian on behalf of the corporation. The Court is empowered to fix the remuneration of the guardian if it sees fit to do so in the circumstances of the case.

Where the Administrator General is appointed as a guardian under the Law certain specified provisions of the Law will not be applied.

The fourth and last chapter of the Law contains a number of miscellaneous provisions, including a provision that the Court referred to in the Law is a District Court, and that the Law does not add to, or derogate from, the jurisdiction of the Religious Courts.

The Law also provides that the Court may, at any time, upon the application of the Attorney General or his representative, or upon the application of an interested party, or even upon its own motion, take such temporary measures as it considers appropriate for the protection of the affairs of a minor, legally incompetent person, protected person, or a person in need of guardianship, either by the appointment of a temporary guardian or a guardian *ad litem*, or otherwise, and the Court may also do so if the minor, legally incompetent person, protected person or the person in need of guardianship himself applies to it. In addition, the Attorney General or his representative, if he is satisfied that the good of a minor, legally incompetent person, protected person or person in need of guardianship or the good of the public so requires, may institute any legal proceeding, including an appeal, under the Law and appear and plead in any such proceeding.

The Court may conduct proceedings under the Law in camera if it considers it necessary to do so for the protection of a minor, legally incompetent person or protected person, or for the protection of the spouse or relative of such person.

Finally, the Law repeals the provisions of certain Ottoman laws in force dealing with matters dealt with by the Law.

Reputed Spouse

Israel legislation confers certain rights upon reputed spouses. Thus, for the purposes of the laws under which benefits are payable to spouses of persons killed or disabled while serving in the Defence Army of Israel, the Police Force, the Prisons Service, or the Civil Defence Organisation, or in the war against the Nazis, or of border casualties, or of pensioners of the State Service, or of a former Head or Deputy Head of a local authority, spouse is defined as including a reputed spouse, in some cases whether male or female and in other cases only when a female. A spouse is also so defined for the purposes of the National Insurance Law, 5714–1953 (see p. 117), and the Tenant Protection Law, 5715–1955 (see p. 139).

Furthermore, under section 57(c) of the Inheritance Law, 5725–1965 (see pp. 171–2), where a man and a woman are living a family life in a joint household but are not married to each other, and one of them dies and at the date of his or her death neither is married to another person, the survivor is entitled for life to maintenance from the estate of the deceased person as if they were married to each other, while under section 2C of the Estate Tax Law, 5709–1949 (as amended by the Estate Tax (Amendment No. 3) Law, 5724–1964), for the purpose of calculating the amount of an estate on which the tax is payable, a deduction of Il. 25,000 is to be made in respect of a reputed spouse of the deceased who was residing with him at the time of his death if neither of them had at that time another spouse.

Protected Persons

The Protection of Protected Persons Law, 5726–1966, which came into force on the 28th July, 1966, makes provision for the protection of protected persons from exploitation by those responsible for them and for providing suitable treatment for them.

For the purposes of the Law, a 'protected person' is defined as 'a minor under the age of 14 years, or a person who, by reason of disability, defect of mind or old age, is not capable of looking after his needs' and a 'person responsible for a protected person' is defined as 'a parent, including a step-parent, adopter, guardian or person in whose custody or care the protected person is, or a person to whose influence the protected person is subject at the time'.

The Law confers certain powers on social welfare officers and Magistrates' Courts for giving effect to the purposes of the Law, and defines the cases in which persons responsible for protected persons will be guilty of a criminal offence by reason of acts or omissions done in circumstances likely to cause physical or mental harm to the protected persons.

Names

Until the Names Law, 5716–1956 came into force on the 3rd August, 1956, the only law in force with regard to names was a totally inadequate public notice of the 21st March, 1921, dealing only with the procedure for notification of a change of name. The new Law, substantially based upon the second chapter of the comprehensive draft Individual and Family Law prepared by the Legal Planning Department of the Ministry of Justice, requires every person to have a family name and at least one first name, and lays down rules for the giving of such names, and as to changes of name. It empowers the Minister of the Interior to give a name to a person who has not acquired one in one of the prescribed ways. A woman, upon marriage, receives her husband's family name, but she may, at any time, add to her husband's name her maiden name, or her former family name. She may also use only her maiden name or her former family name. Where the marriage of a woman who has received the name of her husband, alone or in addition to her maiden name or former family name, has been terminated, she may at any time resume her maiden name or former family name. Spouses may only change their family name together, and may only choose one family name for both of them, unless the Minister of the Interior has permitted a change of name of one of them or a choice of different names. Every choice, or change, of name must be published in *Reshumot*. A person who has changed his name may not change it again within seven years of the former change taking effect, save with the approval of the Minister of the Interior.

LABOUR LEGISLATION

Palestine Ordinances

UNTIL A DEPARTMENT OF LABOUR was established upon a statutory basis by the Department of Labour Ordinance, 1943, there was but little labour legislation in force in Palestine apart from the Workmen's Compensation Ordinance which was enacted in 1927 upon the model of the corresponding British legislation. That Department prepared a number of Ordinances which were duly enacted. They include the Accidents and Occupational Diseases (Notification) Ordinance, 1945, the Employment of Children and Young Persons Ordinance, 1945, the Employment of Women Ordinance, 1945, the Trade Boards Ordinance, 1945, the Factories Ordinance, 1946, the Industrial Courts Ordinance, 1947, the Trade Unions Ordinance, 1947 and the Workmen's Compensation Ordinance, 1947, modelled upon the corresponding British legislation with modifications to suit them to the needs of the inhabitants of Palestine. The first of those Ordinances and the Factories Ordinance, 1946, are in force in Israel, while the Workmen's Compensation Ordinance, 1947 was in force as amended by the Israel legislature to render it more suitable in view of the considerable rise in the cost of living, until its repeal by the National Insurance Law, 5714–1953 (see p. 117). On the other hand, effect has not been given in Israel to the Trade

Boards Ordinance, 1945, the Industrial Courts Ordinance, 1947, and the Trade Unions Ordinance, 1947.

Israel Laws

The Israel legislature, however, has added considerably to the volume of labour legislation in force in this country.

The first of the labour laws to be enacted by it, the Prohibition of Night Baking Law, 5711–1951, which came into force on the 1st April, 1951, prohibits baking at night, between 22.00 hours and 06.00 hours, save with a permit from the Minister of Labour.

The Hours of Work and Rest Law, 5711–1951, which came into force on the 28th September, 1951, provides for an eight hour working day, and a forty seven hour working week, and that every worker shall have at least 36 consecutive hours rest every week, including his weekly day of rest. It also regulates the hours of overtime work and the periods of break for those working more than six hours a day. The law applies also to State employees.

The Annual Leave Law, 5711–1951, which came into force on the 1st October, 1951, provides for annual leave with pay and empowers the Minister of Labour to set up a Leave Fund for each branch of work, on such conditions as he deems fit. According to an amendment to the Law which came into force on the 22nd July, 1965, the period of annual leave in respect of work with one employer or in one place of work for each year of work is 14 days for each of the first four years, 16 days for the fifth year, 18 days for the sixth year, 21 days for the seventh year, and for the eighth and each subsequent year, an additional day for each year of work up to leave for 28 days, and in the days of leave there will be included only one weekly day of rest for every seven days of leave, but the Minister of Labour is empowered, by regulations, to increase that period in respect of any particular work, if he considers it necessary to do so on health grounds or by reason of the circumstances of the work. The Law specifies the days which are not to be taken into account in calculating the days of leave, such as days of service with the Reserves under the Security Service Law, 5709–1949, days when the worker is unable to work by reason of accident or illness, and days of family mourning, and provides for leave pay, leave compensation and leave equivalent. The Law applies also to State employees and does not derogate from any right given to a worker by any law, collective agreement, labour agreement or custom.

The Employment of Children and Young Persons Ordinance, 1945, has been replaced by the Youth Labour Law, 5713–1953 the Employment of Women Ordinance 1945 has been replaced by the Women's Work Law, 5714–1954 (see pp. 187–8), and a comprehensive Apprentices Law, 5713–1953, has been enacted.

The Labor Inspection Organisation Law, 5714–1954 provides for the establishment of a Labour Inspection Service, defines its powers and functions, and also provides for the establishment of a Safety and Hygiene Institute, the object of which is to promote industrial hygiene and safety conditions at work.

The Factories Ordinance Amendment Law, 5723–1963, which came into force on the 1st January, 1963, increases the number of categories of undertakings to which the Factories Ordinance, 1946 will apply, and also provides that the Minister of Labour may, if he is of the opinion that the production, machinery, installation, plant, material, process, act or omission obtaining in an undertaking, or a particular place of work, even if it is not an undertaking within the meaning assigned to that expression in the Factories Ordinance, 1946, are likely to cause bodily injury, make regulations regarding safety and hygiene at work as he may deem fit for the prevention of such danger, but he may not make regulations regarding the use of material for destruction in agriculture without the consent of the Minister of Agriculture and the Minister of Health. In view of the extension of the scope of application of the Factories Ordinance, 1946 introduced by the amending law, the latter provides that the title of the Ordinance shall be changed to the Safety at Work Ordinance, 1946.

The Settlement of Labour Disputes Law, 5717–1957, and the Collective Agreements Law, 5717–1957, came into force on the 1st March, 1957. The former provides for the appointment of a Chief Labour Relations Officer, and Labour Relations Officers and prescribes their functions in relation to mediation and arbitration in labour disputes, provides for the appointment, and prescribes the functions, of Arbitration Boards, whose decisions are final, and provides for the appointment of a Labour Relations Council to advise the Minister of Labour in matters concerning labour relations. It repeals the Industrial Courts Ordinance, 1947 and the Ottoman Law of Strikes, 1909. The Collective Agreements Law defines the various classes of collective agreements to which it applies and the persons who are bound by such agreements, and provides for the submission of such agreements, which must be in writing, for registration by the Minister of Labour. It is provided that rights conferred upon a workman by the personal provisions of a collective agreement cannot be waived, and that a collective agreement may add to, but may not derogate from, any right conferred upon a workman by law.

Wage Protection

The Wage Protection Law, 5718–1958, which came into force on the 1st April, 1958, contains detailed provisions regarding the conditions of, and times for, payment of wages, restriction on attaching, transferring and charging wages, and compensation for delay in payment thereof, and provides for the appointment of Wage Collection Commissioners, and prescribes their functions.

As regards compensation for delay in payment, the Law provides that delayed wages shall be increased, in respect of the first week of delay or any fractional part thereof, by an amount equal to the twentieth part of the delayed wage, and in respect of every subsequent week of delay or a fractional part thereof, by an amount equal to the tenth part of the delayed wage, but a Wage Collection Commissioner is empowered in certain specified circumstances to reduce or cancel any wage delay compensation.

A Wage Collection Commissioner may, on the application of the employee or of a representative of an employees organization representing the employee, make an order for the payment of a delayed wage which for the purpose of execution, will have the effect of a final judgment of a Magistrates' Court in a civil case, unless it is rescinded by a Magistrates' Court upon the employer's application. The Law applies to the State as an employer as it applies to any other employer.

The Wage Protection (Amendment No. 3) Law, 5724–1963, which came into force on the 2nd January, 1964, adds a new provision to the principal Law whereunder the right to compensation for delay in payment of wages must be claimed in an action in Court or before the Wage Collection Commissioner within one year of the date on which the wage is deemed to be delayed, or within 14 days of the date on which the worker received the wage with which the compensation is connected, whichever is the earlier, but the Court or the Wage Collection Commissioner may extend the period of 14 days to a period of 30 days. Another amendment alters the power of the Wage Collection Commissioner to reduce or cancel the compensation for delay in payment of wages, and for the first time empowers the Court to reduce or cancel such compensation. Both the Wage Collection Commissioner and the Court are empowered to reduce or cancel the compensation for delay in payment of wages if he or it is satisfied that the wage was not paid in due time by reason of a genuine mistake, or some circumstance over which he had no control or a dispute as to the debt itself, which, in the opinion of the Wage Collection Commissioner, or the Court, as the case may be, is one of substance, provided that the amount which was not in dispute was paid in due time.

Under another new provision neither the Official Receiver, a trustee in bankruptcy, nor a liquidator of a company or a cooperative society is liable to pay compensation for delay in payment of wages for a period of time beginning six months before 'the prescribed date', that is, the date of the petition for a receiving order or an order for winding up by the Court, or the date of the making of an order for the winding up of a cooperative society, as the case may be. Furthermore, no order for payment may be made against the Official Receiver, a trustee in bankruptcy or a liquidator of a company or cooperative society. None of those provisions will apply to a voluntary winding up of a company, or to the wages which the Official Receiver, trustee in bankruptcy or liquidator of a company or cooperative society is under no obligation to pay after the prescribed date.

Finally, the amending law confers upon a Wage Collection Commissioner additional powers, such as the power to summon witnesses and fine them up to IL. 100 for refusing to give evidence, and empowers the Minister of Labour, in consultation with the Minister of Justice, to make regulations regarding the practice and procedure before a Wage Collection Commissioner.

The Equal Wage for Male and Female Worker Law, 5724–1964, which came into force nine months after its publication in *Reshumot* on the 5th August, 1964, provides that an employer shall pay to a female worker a wage equal to the wage of a male worker in the same place of work for the same work.

If any disputes arise as regards the wage to which a femal worker is entitled under that provision the female worker, the employer, or the workers' committee in the place of work, may apply to a Wage Collection Commissioner within the meaning of the Wage Protection Law, 5718–1958 (see pp. 185–7), and he will decide the matter in the manner prescribed by that law for the making of an order for payment of a wage the payment of which has been delayed and his decision will be treated for all purposes as a payment order, and the amount which an employer is obliged to pay in accordance with the decision of the Wage Collection Commissioner will be treated, for the purposes of payment of compensation for delay in payment, as a wage the payment of which has been delayed if it is not paid by the fifteenth day after the day upon which the decision of the Wage Collection Commissioner is given.

The above Law also applies to the State as an employer.

Women's Work

The Women's Work Law, 5714–1954, which came into force on the 12th August, 1954, prohibits the employment of women at night subject to certain specified exceptions, save with a permit issued by the Minister of Labour in accordance with the Law.

The Law also provides for maternity leave and imposes restrictions on the dismissal of a female worker.

For the purposes of the Law a State employee is to be treated like any other employee.

The Law does not derogate from any right conferred upon a worker by law, collective agreement, contract of employment or custom.

The Women's Work (Amendment No. 2) Law, 5724–1964, which came into force on the 5th August, 1964, makes a number of amendments to the principal law with regard to night work, absence from work and restrictions on dismissal.

The amending law empowers the Minister of Labour to permit the employment of a woman at night in an additional class of case, namely, in a place of work in which three shifts work if, in his opinion, the refusal of a permit would be likely to affect the possibilities of employment for women and the night work will not especially affect the health of the woman. A permit given under this new provision will be given for the period stated therein, not exceeding two years, but no such permit may be given after the 1st January 1967 save with the approval of the Labour Affairs Committee of the Knesset, which may be general or according to branches of work, classes of undertakings or areas.

As regards the right of a female worker to absent herself from work, the amending law adds a new provision whereunder if a female worker who has absented herself from work after having given birth to a child, reports for work, or expresses her desire to return to work before the termination of her maternity leave, her employer may not postpone her return to work more than four weeks from the day on which she reports for work or expresses her desire to return to work.

Under the principal law an employer may not dismiss a female employee who is pregnant but has not yet gone on maternity leave save with a permit from the Minister of Labour, and the Minister of Labour may not permit her dismissal if it is, in his opinion, connected with her pregnancy. The amending law provides that such provisions shall not apply to a casual or temporary female worker unless she has worked for the same employer or in the same place of work for at least six consecutive months.

Severance Pay

The Severance Pay Law, 5723–1963, which was passed by the Knesset on the 6th August, 1963 and came into force on the the 1st January, 1964, gave legislative effect to a custom which had been in force in this country for many years.

Under the Law, a person who has been employed continuously for one year or, in the case of a seasonal employee, has been employed for two seasons in two consecutive years, by the same employer or at the same place of employment and has been dismissed, is entitled to receive severance pay from the employer who has dismissed him. For the purposes of the Law, 'season' is defined as meaning three consecutive months, in any one year, during which the employee has been employed for not less than 60 days.

Employment is deemed to have been continuous despite the fact that there has been a break if the break is owing to military service; the day of weekly rest or a holiday on which no work is done, whether under any law or by custom or agreement, and the first day of May; annual leave; leave or vacation with pay, granted to the worker under any law or with the consent of the employer; leave or vacation without pay, granted to the worker under any law or with the consent of the employer; a strike or lock-out; an accident or illness; days of family mourning on which the employee did not work in deference to religion or custom; a temporary break not involving an interruption of the employee-employer relationship or a break involving an interruption of the employee-employer relationship or a break involving an interruption of the employee-employer relationship but not exceeding three months.

Dismissal shortly before the end of the first year of employment will, unless the contrary be proved, be deemed to have been intended to avoid the obligation to pay severance pay and will in that case not affect the right to such pay.

An employee whose employment has ceased owing to the death or bankruptcy of his employer or, where the employer is a corporation, owing to the winding-up or striking-off thereof, will be entitled to severance pay as if he had been dismissed.

Where an employee has died, the employer must pay severance pay to his survivors as defined in the Law as if the employee had been dismissed, and such severance pay will not be regarded as part of the estate of the deceased employee.

In certain specified cases the resignation of an employee is deemed to be a dismissal for the purposes of severance pay. For example, where an employee resigns by reason of his state of health, or the state of health of a member of his family, and, in view of the medical findings, the conditions of employment and the other circumstances of the case, there is sufficient reason for the resignation, or where a woman resigns from her employment within nine months after giving birth, in order to take care of her child, or where the resignation of an employee results from the transfer upon his marriage of his residence to a locality in Israel where his spouse had been living, subject to conditions prescribed by regulations made by the Minister of Labour with the approval of the Labour Affairs Committee of the Knesset, or the transfer of his residence to an agricultural settlement from a locality other than an agricultural settlement or to a locality in a development area from a locality other than a locality in a development area, subject to conditions prescribed by such regulations, or the transfer of his residence for other reasons designated by such regulations as justifying such transfer. Furthermore, where an employee resigns by reason of an appreciable deterioration of his conditions of employment, or in view of other matters of labour relations affecting him, and because of which he cannot be expected to continue in his employment, the resignation is deemed for the purposes of the Law to be a dismissal, and where a seasonal employee, after being employed at the same place of employment for not less than three consecutive seasons, resigns because continuous seasonal employment at that place of employment has not been assured to him, he will be deemed to have been dismissed.

Where an employee has been employed under a contract for a specific period and that period has come to an end, he will, for the purposes of the Law, be deemed to have been dismissed, unless the employer has offered to renew the contract. If the employee refuses to renew the contract he will, for the purposes of the Law, be deemed to have resigned. The employer's offer to renew the contract must be delivered to the employee not less than three months before the expiration of the period of the contract.

The rate of severance pay in the case of an employee the remuneration for whose work is mainly paid on the basis of a month or a longer period, called in the Law a 'salaried employee', who has been employed by the same employer or in the same place of employment, is one month's wages per year of employment, and in the case of any other employee, two weeks' wages per year of employment or such higher rate as the Minister of Labour may, after consultation with the Minister of Finance and with the approval of the Labour Affairs Committee of the Knesset, fix by regulations, either generally or according to branches of employment. Employment for a fraction of a year following a year of employment will entitle the employee to proportionate severance pay, and in the case of a seasonal employee, employment for a fraction of a year will entitle the employee to proportionate severance pay even if the periods of employment do not add up to one year. The Minister of Labour, with the approval of the Labour Affairs Committee of the Knesset, is to determine by regulations, generally or in respect of particular classes, such components of the total wage as shall be taken into account for the purposes of severance pay, the methods of calculating the wage on which the calculation of severance pay is to be based and such breaks in employment under certain specified circumstances as shall not be taken into account in fixing the amount of severance pay. In making such regulations, the Minister of Labour must have regard to the relevant provisions of the collective agreement applying to the greatest number of employees to which the regulations relate.

A payment to a provident fund, pension fund or any other similar fund, will not serve in lieu of severance pay except if and in so far as it is so provided in the collective agreement applying to the employer and the employee, or if and in so far as such payment has been approved by the Minister of Labour by order. On the other hand, where an employee or his survivor is entitled under any enactment to a benefit from the employer in consequence of the retirement of the employee from employment or for any other reason, such benefit will serve in lieu of severance pay under the Law.

An employee will not be entitled to severance pay, or will be entitled only to partial severance pay, as the case may be, if he is dismissed in circumstances which, under a collective agreement applying to the employer and the employee or, in the absence of such an agreement, under a collective agreement applying to the greatest number of employees in that branch of employment, justify dismissal without severance pay or with partial severance pay only.

In a branch of employment in which there is no collective agreement, the Court may rule that the dismissal of an employee occurred in circumstances justifying dismissal without severance pay or with such severance pay as it shall determine, and in dealing with such a matter the Court must be guided by the rules contained in the collective agreement applying to the greatest number of employees.

Where an employee has been dismissed by reason of a reduction in the volume of employment at the undertaking and the right of priority of reinstatement in employment at the undertaking, within a specified period, has been assured to him, the provisions of the collective agreement applying to the employee and the employer or, in the absence of a collective agreement in the matter, the provisions of a special agreement between those entitled to be parties to a collective agreement will apply to everything relating to severance pay, so long as the agreement in question does not contain a permanent waiver of severance pay.

A collective agreement may prescribe the modes and methods of paying severance pay, including the deposit thereof in favour of the employee, with a view to ensuring the accumulation thereof in his favour, and where those matters have been so prescribed, severance pay must be paid in accordance with the agreement.

With a view to ensuring the accumulation of the severance pay which employers are likely to have to pay to their employees under the Severance Pay Law, 5723–1963, that law empowers the Minister of Labour, after consultation with the Minister of Finance and with the approval of the Labour Affairs Committee of the Knesset, to direct employers, by order, known as a 'deposit order', to deposit in a benefit fund, within the meaning of section 47 of the Income Tax Ordinance, referred to in the Law as a 'benefit fund', amounts at a rate prescribed in the order. A deposit order must be published in *Reshumot* and it must indicate the classes of employers to which it relates, by branches of the economy or the size of the undertakings or by regions, and the date of its coming into force, which may not be prior to the date of publication.

The Minister of Labour may, with the approval of the Labour Affairs Committee of the Knesset, by regulations, make provisions for certain specified matters relating to deposits of moneys save in so far as other provisions have been made by rules made under section 47 of the Income Tax Ordinance.

Severance pay deposited under the provisions of a collective agreement or under a deposit order may not be charged, attached or transferred and will not form part of the assets of the employer in the event of death, bankruptcy or winding up, so long as the claims of employees under the Law have not been met. Furthermore, for the purposes of debts the discharge whereof, according to the Bankruptcy Ordinance, 1936, or the Companies Ordinance, takes precedence over the discharge of all other debts, severance pay is deemed to be wages payable in precedence to all other debts, but the amount of severance pay and wages so paid may not in the aggregate exceed 150 per cent of the maximum amount of wages which may be paid in precedence to all other debts under the said Ordinances, and severance pay will also be one of the debts the discharge whereof takes precedence over all other debts in the winding up of a cooperative society or of an association to which the Ottoman Law of Associations, 1909 applies.

An agreement between an employer and an employee which

specifies that severance pay is included in the wages and which
has been approved by the Minister of Labour, or a person empowered by him in that behalf, will, for the purposes of severance
pay, replace the provisions of the Law unless there is a collective
agreement applying to the employer and the employee and requiring the payment of severance pay.

No composition as to severance pay and no acknowledgment
of discharge will be valid unless it is drawn up in writing and
states expressly that it relates to severance pay.

The State as an employer has, for the purposes of the Law, the
same status as any other employer, save that certain modifications
are made in the provisions of the Law in so far as they apply to
a member of the Police Force or the Prisons Service.

The Law does not derogate from any right granted to an employee by any law, collective agreement, contract of employment or, for the purposes of the calculation of the rate of severance
pay, any custom, and in any negotiations as to rights in connection
with retirement from employment, it will not be construed as
dealing exhaustively with the rights of an employee.

The Minister of Labour is charged with the implementation
of the Law, and before making regulations he is required to
consult with the employees' organisation representing the greatest
number of employees in Israel and with representative national
organisations of employers which, in his opinion, are concerned
with the matter.

Employment Service

The Employment Service Law, 5719–1959, which came into
force on the 1st April, 1959, established, under the general
supervision of the Minister of Labour, a corporate body known
as the Employment Service, the functions of which are to cen-
tralise information regarding the state, and development trends,
of the labour market with a view to regulating it, to obtain
work for those seeking it and direct workers to those seeking
them, by means of labour exchanges set up by the Law, and
to cooperate with other bodies in matters of vocational training
and guidance in choosing a trade. Labour relations and con-

ditions of work are excluded from the scope of activity of the Employment Service, which is expressly forbidden to deal with such matters.

The supreme authority of the Employment Service is the Employment Service Council, composed of an equal number of representatives of employees and employers and also representatives of the Government not exceeding one third of the total number of members. All the members of the Council are appointed by the Minister of Labour who, or whose representative, is the chairman of the Council. The administrative and executive authority of the Employment Service is the Employment Service Administration, headed by a Director appointed by the Minister of Labour, and composed of such other officials as the Minister fixes after consultation with the Council.

The Minister of Labour, upon the recommendation of, or after consultation with, the Employment Service Administration, is to establish Employment Service Labour Exchanges and fix the scope of their jurisdiction.

In the trades and classes of work specified in the Law, which the Minister of Labour may vary, no person may accept an employee, and no person may begin to work for an employer, unless the employee has been sent by the Labour Exchange and it has given a written confirmation in that behalf, unless the employee is engaged in an executive capacity, or higher education or a special degree of personal training is required for the work, or he is an employee prescribed by regulations under certain conditions, or is a member of the family of the employer or the employer's spouse. Provisions as to registration of employees by Labour Exchanges are to be prescribed by regulations and Labour Exchanges must send employees to work in accordance with those provisions. Special provisions may be made with regard to discharged soldiers, disabled persons, aged persons and other classes of persons whose special condition justifies such provisions, but there must be no discrimination by reason of age, sex, race, religion, nationality, country of origin, outlook, or political party, and no person in need of an employee may refuse to accept a person for work on any of those grounds, but there is deemed to be no discrimination when the character or nature of the work or State security prevents the sending, or the acceptance, of the person for any particular work. Persons considering themselves aggrieved may submit an objection to an Objections Tribunal appointed by the Council of the Labour Exchange, and from its decision an objection may be made to a Supreme Objections Tribunal appointed by the Employment Service Council and presided over by a District Court Judge appointed by the Minister of Justice.

The provisions regarding applications to a Labour Exchange will not apply to an employer whose employees are on strike or have been locked out, or to employees so long as they are on strike or are locked out. A Labour Exchange may not send employees to a place of work where there is a strike or lock-out, or send employees on strike to any work, so long as the strike or lock-out continues. An employer who employs employees who are on strike or are locked out, and employees working in an undertaking where there is a strike or lockout, will not be prosecuted.

The Law also provides for the appointment by the Minister of Labour of trade committees which may recommend the issue of certificates as to vocational qualifications and their standard and category which employees are required to produce to a Labour Exchange when applying for registration, and, for that purpose, the Law empowers them to conduct examinations in accordance with a scheme approved by the Minister of Labour so long as no scheme is prescribed by regulations.

No person may without a licence from the Minister of Labour conduct, or establish, a private employment bureau. The Minister of Labour may not issue such a licence in respect of those branches of work, trades and works in respect of which employment must, or may, in his opinion, be through the Employment Service. A private employment bureau may not act as an agent for work to be done abroad, or to persons abroad, save under, and in accordance with, a permit from the Minister of Labour. In a licence or permit issued by him the Minister of Labour must prescribe whether the private employment bureau may receive a commission or other consideration, or expenses, and from which party to the employment it may receive them, and no private employment bureau may receive any payment or other material benefit, save in accordance with the tariff prescribed, or approved, by the Minister of Labour.

The expenditure of the Employment Service, as provided for by the annual budget approved by the Knesset, will be met by the State Treasury, and the Employment Service may not demand any payment from those resorting to it.

The Law applies to the State as an employer with such modifications as may be prescribed by regulations made by the Minister of Labour, who is charged with its implementation.

COURTS

THE COURTS in Israel are either civil or religious courts, apart from the courts martial.

Civil Courts

The following are the civil courts:

Municipal Courts established under the Municipal Courts Ordinance (of 1928) in certain municipal areas, having criminal jurisdiction over any offences against municipal regulations and by-laws and certain other offences committed within the municipal area. The maximum sentence which such courts may impose is a fine of IL.750 or 15 days' imprisonment or both such penalties in respect of any one offence. The members are laymen appointed by the Minister of Justice save for the two Stipendiary Magistrates in Tel Aviv, one in Jerusalem, one in Petah Tiqva, one in Ramat Gan and one in Haifa, who are also appointed by the Minister of Justice.

Under amendments to the Municipal Courts Ordinance passed by the Knesset on the 29th November, 1954 and 13th January, 1958, the Minister of Justice may, by order, establish a municipal court for the area of a local council or of several local councils or of several local authorities.

Magistrates' Courts, established in each district and subdistrict, having limited jurisdiction in both civil and criminal matters. In exercising their criminal jurisdiction they may try offences which are contraventions or misdemeanours, that is, offences punishable with not more than 3 years' imprisonment.

In exercising their civil jurisdiction they may try actions concerning possession or use of immovable property or the partition thereof or of the use thereof, including claims involved therein the subject matter of which is the partition or use of movable property, whatever may be the value of the subject matter of the action. They may also try other civil actions, other than those concerning immovable property, where the amount of the claim or the value of the subject matter does not exceed IL. 3,000, and counter-claims to a civil claim in respect of the same subject-matter or arising from the same circumstances, whatever may be the value of the subject-matter of the counter-claim. An appeal from a judgment of a Magistrates' Court lies to the District Court. There are 25 Magistrates' Courts in which 73 Judges, including 7 Chief Judges, sit.

A Magistrates' Court is normally composed of one Judge, but a Judge trying a case, or a Chief Judge, may direct that any particular case shall be tried by a bench of three Judges chosen by the Chief Judge.

District Courts, having unlimited jurisdiction as Courts of first instance in all civil and criminal matters not within the jurisdiction of a Magistrates' Court, and also in respect of counter-claims in civil actions although the matter or claim is within the jurisdiction of a Magistrates' Court; all matters not within the exclusive jurisdiction of any other Court or tribunal, so long as such Court or tribunal does not deal with them; appeals from judgments and decisions of Magistrates' Courts and judgments of Municipal Courts and various administrative tribunals.

Judgments of Districts Courts sitting in first instance are appealable to the Supreme Court, and other decisions of a District Court in civil matters and judgments of a District Court sitting as an appellate Court are appealable to the Supreme Court, if leave to appeal has been given in the decision or judgment or by the President or other Justice of the Supreme Court chosen by the President, or by the Supreme Court.

The District Courts will be composed of three Judges when trying any criminal offence for which the maximum punishment is death or imprisonment for ten years or more, appeals from judgments of Courts and tribunals in which a Judge of a Magistrates' Court sits, other than applications for interim orders, temporary orders and other interim decisions in appeals, and every matter which the President or a Relieving President of the Court directs shall be tried by three Judges. In every other matter the Court will be composed of one Judge.

Under the Courts (Offences Punishable with Death) Law, 5721–1961, which came into force on the 6th February, 1961, notwithstanding anything contained in any other law, when a District Court is trying any person for any offences punishable with death, whether or not death is the only punishment which may be imposed for such offences or there are included in the information only such offences, or other offences are also included therein, the District Court will be composed of a Justice of the Supreme Court chosen by the President of the Supreme Court, as Presiding Judge, and two District Court Judges chosen by the President, or a Relieving President, of the District Court under the Courts Law, 5717–1957.

There are four District Courts: in Jerusalem, having jurisdiction in the Jerusalem District, in Tel Aviv-Jaffa, having jurisdiction in the Tel Aviv and Central Districts, in Haifa, having jurisdiction in the Haifa and Northern Districts, and in Beersheba, having jurisdiction in the Southern District. 4 Presidents, 6 Relieving Presidents and 40 other Judges sit in those Courts.

The *Supreme Court*, the highest Court in Israel, having jurisdiction as an appellate Court from the District Courts in all matters, both civil and criminal (sitting as a Court of Civil Appeal or as a Court of Criminal Appeal) and as a Court of first instance (sitting as a High Court of Justice) in matters in which it considers it necessary to grant relief in the interests of justice

and which are not within the jurisdiction of any other Court
or tribunal, and, in particular, but without prejudice to the
generality of the foregoing, it has jurisdiction (1) to make orders
for the release of persons detained or imprisoned unlawfully;
(2) to make orders directed to State authorities, local authorities
and their officials and to other bodies and persons performing
public functions under the law, requiring them to do or refrain
from doing any act in the performance of their functions according to law, and, if they were unlawfully elected or appointed,
to refrain from acting; (3) to make orders directed to Courts,
tribunals and bodies of persons having judicial or quasi-judicial
powers under the law, other than Courts to which the Courts
Law, 5717–1957 applies and Religious Courts, to adjudicate in
any particular matter or to continue to adjudicate in any particular
matter, and to set aside any proceeding held, or decision given,
unlawfully; (4) to make orders directed to Religious Courts
to deal with any particular matter within their jurisdiction or
to refrain from dealing with any particular matter not within
their jurisdiction, but it may not entertain any application with
respect to such matters if the applicant did not raise the question
of jurisdiction at the first available opportunity, while if the
applicant had no reasonable opportunity to raise the question
until a decision was given by the Religious Court, the High Court
may set aside the proceeding which took place or the decision
which was given by the Religious Court without jurisdiction.

In any matter which is decided by the Supreme Court when
composed of three Justices, it may decide, when giving judgment, that the Supreme Court shall deal with the matter at a
further hearing when composed of five or more Justices of the
Supreme Court. If the Supreme Court does not decide to do
so, any party may apply for such a further hearing, and the
President of the Supreme Court, or a Justice or Justices appointed in that behalf, may grant the application if, by reason
of the importance, difficulty or novelty of the rule laid down
in the matter, in his or their opinion, there should be a further
hearing. The provisions for such a further hearing are among
the innovations introduced by the Courts Law, 5717–1957,

the provisions of which, other than those for a re-trial, came
into force on the 28th August, 1957

Another innovation introduced by that Law is the provision
for a re-trial by the Supreme Court or a District Court of a
criminal matter finally decided upon. Such a re-hearing may be
ordered by the President, or permanent Deputy President, of
the Supreme Court in the following cases: (1) if a Court has
held that certain evidence produced in the matter in question
was false or forged, and there is reason to assume that without such evidence the result of the case would have been changed
in favour of the convicted person, (2) new facts or new evidence
have come to light, which either alone or together with the
material which was originally before the Court, are, or is, capable
of changing the result of the case in favour of the convicted
person, and could not have been known to it at the time of
the trial of the case,   (3) if in the meantime some other person
has been convicted of the same offence, and, from the circumstances revealed in the trial of such other person, it appears that
the person who was originally convicted of the offence did not
commit it.

Both the convicted person and the Attorney General have
a right to request a retrial, and if the convicted person is dead,
his spouse, each of his descendants, parents, brothers and sisters
may exercise such right.

On a retrial the Court may not increase the punishment.

When an application is made to the President of the State
for a pardon or a reduction of sentence, and there arises a question
which, in the opinion of the Minister of Justice, is worthy of
decision by the Supreme Court and cannot serve as a ground
for a retrial, the Minister of Justice may refer the question to
the Supreme Court, and that Court, if it decides to deal with
the question, will do so as if the President thereof had directed
that there should be a retrial.

The Supreme Court sits in Jerusalem, and is composed of such
number of members as the Knesset, by resolution, determines.
At present it is composed of a President, a permanent Deputy
President and eight other members. It is normally constituted

of three members, unless, before any particular proceeding is commenced, the President, or permanent Deputy President has directed that for that proceeding there shall be an uneven number of members exceeding three, or, after the commencement of any particular proceeding, the Court decides that the hearing shall be continued before an uneven number of members, exceeding three, including themselves, or if there is an application for an interim order or temporary order or other interim decision or an order nisi, in which case the application may be heard by one member of the Court sitting alone, but one member may not refuse an order nisi or grant such an order in respect of some only of the grounds of the application.

The Courts Law, 5717–1957 also contains a number of provisions of general application.

When a Court is composed of three or more members, and there is a difference of opinion among them, the majority opinion will prevail. If there is no majority for any particular opinion, the opinion of the presiding member will prevail, while in a criminal matter that opinion which, in the opinion of the presiding member, is most favourable to the accused will prevail.

Every Court will be guided by a rule laid down by a higher Court, while a rule laid down by the Supreme Court will bind every Court except itself.

Where any Court finds that it cannot deal with any matter before it for want of local or material jurisdiction but that such matter is within the jurisdiction of some other Court or tribunal, it may transfer the matter to such other Court or tribunal and that Court or tribunal must deal therewith as if the matter had originally been brought before it, and may deal therewith from the stage which the previous Court had reached, but it may not transfer the matter further.

Every Court must conduct a trial in public, but it may deal with any particular matter, wholly or partially, in camera, if it deems it necessary to do so for the preservation of the security of the State, the protection of morality or the protection of the safety of a minor. If it is decided to conduct a trial in camera, no appeal will lie against its decision, but it may permit any particular person, or class of persons, to be present during the whole, or part, of the trial.

A Court may forbid a minor to be present in Court during a trial and may order his removal, and no appeal will lie from its decision.

No person may publish anything about a trial which has been held in camera, save with the leave of the Court, and no person may photograph in the Court room or publish any such photograph, save with the leave of the Court.

No person may, without the leave of the Court, publish the name, photograph, address, or other particulars likely to reveal the identity, of any minor under the age of sixteen who is an accused person, or a witness in a criminal case, or a complainant, or the victim of an offence against morality.

A Court may prohibit any publication in connection with the proceedings of the Court to such extent as it deems necessary for the protection of the safety of a litigant, witness or other person whose name is mentioned in the proceedings. Any person contravening the above provisions as to publication will be liable to imprisonment for six months or a fine of IL. 1,000.

No person may publish anything regarding a matter which is pending in any Court if such publication is likely to influence the course or result of the trial, but such prohibition will not apply to the publication in good faith of any information about anything which was said, or which occurred, at a public hearing by the Court. Any person contravening any such provision will be liable to one year's imprisonment or a fine of IL. 2,000.

Where a person disturbs the proceedings of the Court in its presence, or near the place of the proceedings, the Court may order his removal or compel him, by imprisonment or fine, to conduct himself properly, and no appeal will lie from its decision, but written notice of an order for imprisonment or a fine must be given immediately to the President of the Supreme Court, and he may annul or mitigate the order. Such provisions add to the powers of the Court under any other law, but a person may not be punished for conduct for which imprisonment or a fine has been imposed on him under those provisions.

The Law vests in the Minister of Justice all the administrative powers and the power to make rules of Court vested in the Chief Justice by the law in force in Palestine on the eve of the establishment of the State of Israel, and in the President and permanent Deputy President of the Supreme Court the judicial powers vested in the Chief Justice by that law.

The Minister of Justice is also authorised to make rules regarding the publication of judgments of the Courts.

The judgments of the Supreme Court are published regularly by the Ministry of Justice, while judgments of the District Courts, with annotations, are published regularly by the Israel Chamber of Advocates, and judgments of a number of tribunals, such as National Insurance Tribunals and Rent Tribunals, are also published from time to time. A selection of judgments of the Supreme Court in English translation is published by the Ministry of Justice.

The Judges Law, 5713–1953, of the 28th August, 1953, prescribes the qualifications, manner of appointment, term of office, salaries and other emoluments of the Civil Judiciary composed of Justices of the Supreme Court, Judges of the District Courts and Judges of the Magistrates' Courts, and provides for the establishment of a Disciplinary Tribunal appointed by the Justices of the Supreme Court, who will form the majority of its members, to deal with complaints against members of that Judiciary.

The members of the Civil Judiciary are appointed by the President of the State upon the recommendation of a Nominations Committee submitted to him by the Minister of Justice, who is the chairman of the Committee. The Nominations Committee is composed of the following nine members: the President of the Supreme Court, and two Supreme Court Justices elected by the Justices of that court, the Minister of Justice and one other member of the Government selected by it; two members of the Knesset elected by that body in a secret ballot; and two practising advocates elected by the Chamber of Advocates.

Candidates for appointment to the Judiciary may be proposed by the Minister of Justice, by the President of the Supreme

Court, or jointly by three members of the Nominations Committee, and recommendations of the Committee will be decided upon by a majority vote of members of the Committee participating in the voting.

The following persons are qualified to be appointed Justices of the Supreme Court:(1) a person who has held office as a Judge of a District Court for a period of five years; (2) a person who is inscribed, or entitled to be inscribed, in the Roll of Advocates in Israel and who, continuously or intermittently, for not less than ten years, including at least five years in this country, has been engaged in one or several of the following: (a) the profession of an advocate; (b) a judicial or other legal function, in the service of the State of Israel or another service approved by the Minister of Justice, by regulations, for the purposes of this section; (c) the teaching of law at a university or law school approved by the Minister of Justice, by regulations, for the purposes of this section; (d) an eminent jurist.

The following persons are qualified to be appointed Judges of a District Court: (1) a person who has held office as a Judge of a Magistrates' Court for a period of four years; (2) a person who is inscribed, or entitled to be inscribed, in the Roll of Advocates in Israel and who, continuously or intermittently, for not less than six years, including at least three years in this country, has been engaged in one or several of the occupations enumerated in paragraph (2) above.

A person who is inscribed, or entitled to be inscribed, in the Roll of Advocates in Israel and who, continuously or intermittently, for not less than three years, including at least one year in this country, has been engaged in one or several of the occupations enumerated in paragraph (2) above, is qualified to be appointed as a Judge of a Magistrates' Court.

A person may not be appointed as a Judge if he is not an Israel citizen, and if a candidate for appointment also possesses another nationality and the laws of the state of which he is a national enable him to free himself from such nationality, he may not be appointed until after he has done all that is necessary on his part in order to free himself therefrom.

A Judge must retire on pension upon attaining the age of seventy years or, if the Nominations Committee, on the basis of a medical opinion in conformity with rules prescribed by the Committee, establishes that by reason of the state of his health he is unable to carry out his functions.

A Judge may retire on pension: (1) if he has attained the age of sixty years after holding office for twenty years; (2) if he has attained the age of sixty five years after holding office for fifteen years; (3) if he so requests and his request is approved by the Nominations Committee.

In calculating the period of tenure of a Judge for the purposes of such premature retirement there must be added to the period of his tenure as a Judge the whole or part of the period of his service in the State Service or in another institution approved for the purpose by the Finance Committee of the Knesset as the Finance Committee may, by rules, determine.

Only the Minister of Justice may lodge a complaint against a Judge with the Disciplinary Tribunal, and he may do so only if: (1) the Judge has acted improperly in carrying out his functions; (2) the Judge has behaved in a manner unbefitting his status as a Judge in Israel; (3) the Judge has been convicted of an offence which, in the circumstances of the case, involves moral turpitude; (4) the Nominations Committee has found that the Judge obtained his appointment unlawfully.

The Disciplinary Tribunal must submit its findings, whether favourable or unfavourable, to the Minister of Justice. If it finds that the Judge is not worthy to continue in his function, the Minister of Justice must submit its findings to the President of the State, who must remove the Judge from office.

If a complaint is lodged with the Disciplinary Tribunal or a criminal case is brought against a Judge, the President of the Supreme Court may suspend the Judge from office for such period as he may think fit, but the Disciplinary Tribunal may, upon the application of the Judge, rescind his suspension.

Only the Attorney General may file a criminal charge against a Judge, and such a charge will be tried only by a District Court composed of three Judges.

The independence of the Judiciary is guaranteed by the provision that in the discharge of his judicial functions a Judge is subject only to the law, and his term of office will be terminated only by death, resignation, retirement on pension or dismissal in accordance with the provisions of the Judges Law. Furthermore, the Minister of Justice may not transfer a Judge permanently from one Court to another for administrative reasons, save with the prior approval of the President of the Supreme Court. The Minister of Justice is responsible for the administration of the Courts, but this is actually carried out by a member of the Judiciary (of the rank of a Relieving President of a District Court), who is responsible to him, assisted by another member of the Judiciary (of the rank of a Chief Judge of a Magistrates' Court).

In addition to the abovementioned civil courts there are *Tribal Courts*, for the sub-district of Beersheba, composed of sheikhs appointed by the Minister of Justice, which may apply tribal custom, so far as it is not repugnant to natural justice or morality, and various tribunals for special classes of cases such as the Rent Tribunals and National Insurance Tribunals, while under the Road Transport Ordinance, provision is made for the appointment of Traffic Magistrates for a limited period not less than one year and not more than three years, to try traffic offences, that is, offences under the Road Transport Ordinance or any rules or by-laws made thereunder. There are 11 such Traffic Magistrates, seven of whom sit in Tel Aviv.

Religious Courts

The Religious Courts are: Rabbinical Courts, Moslem Religious Courts, Christian Religious Courts, and Druze Religious Courts.

The *Rabbinical Courts*, under the Rabbinical Courts' Jurisdiction (Marriage and Divorce) Law, 5713–1953, which came into force on the 4th September, 1953 and enlarged their jurisdiction compared with what it was during the Mandatory regime, have exclusive jurisdiction in matters of marriage and divorce of Jews in Israel who are citizens of the State or residents, in every matter connected with a claim for divorce filed in a Rabbinical Court by a Jew or Jewess against his or her spouse, including alimony or maintenance for the wife or children, and in respect of claims by Jewesses for *Halitza* against their brothers-in-law, including maintenance until the release is given. Furthermore, if a Jewess files a claim for alimony unconnected with divorce, against her Jewish husband or against his estate, the defendant may not plead that the Rabbinical Court has no jurisdiction in the matter. In matters of personal status (see p. 159) of Jews in which the Rabbinical Court has not exclusive jurisdiction, e.g. guardianship or the administration of the property of absent persons, it will have jurisdiction with the consent of all the parties concerned. They have also jurisdiction under the Adoption of Children Law, 5720–1960 (see p. 163) and under the Inheritance Law, 5725–1965 (see p. 175).

The Dayanim Law, 5715–1955, of the 25th May, 1955, prescribes the qualifications, manner of appointment, term of office, salaries and other emoluments of the Dayanim (Judges) of the Rabbinical Courts and the Rabbinical Court of Appeal. Its provisions, *mutatis mutandis*, follow closely those of the Judges Law, 5713–1953 (see pp. 204–7).

The *Moslem Religious Courts* have exclusive jurisdiction in all matters of personal status over Moslems who are not foreigners, and over Moslems who are foreigners, if under the law of their nationality they are subject in such matters to the jurisdiction of Moslem Religious Courts (Article 52 of the Palestine Orders-in-Council, 1922–47). They have also jurisdiction under the Adoption of Children Law, 5720–1960 (see p. 163) and under the Inheritance Law, 5725–1965 (see p. 175).

The Qadis Law, 5721–1961, of the 31st May, 1961, prescribes the qualifications, manner of appointment, term of office, salaries and other emoluments of the Qadis (Judges) of the Moslem Religious Courts and the Moslem Religious Court of Appeal. Its provisions, *mutatis mutandis*, follow closely those of the Judges Law, 5713–1953 (see pp. 204–7).

The *Christian Religious Courts* of the several recognised Christian communities (see p. 160) have exclusive jurisdiction in matters of marriage, divorce, and alimony of members of their community other than foreigners, and concurrent jurisdiction with the Civil Courts in such matters of members of their community who are foreigners, if they consent to the jurisdiction and in all other matters of personal status of all members of their community, whether foreigners or not, with the consent of all parties to the action, save that such Courts may not grant a decree of dissolution of marriage to a foreign subject (Article 54 of the said Orders-in-Council). They have also jurisdiction under the Adoption of Children Law, 5720–1960 (see p. 163) and under the Inheritance Law, 5725–1965 (see p. 175).

The *Druze Religious Courts* established by the Druze Religious Courts Law, 5723–1962, of the 3rd of January, 1963, have exclusive jurisdiction in matters of marriage and divorce of Druze in Israel who are citizens of the State or residents, and in matters of personal status of Druze in which they do not have exclusive jurisdiction they will have jurisdiction with the consent of the parties concerned. They also have jurisdiction under the Inheritance Law, 5725–1965 (see p. 175).

The Druze Religious Courts Law, 5723–1962 also prescribes the qualifications, manner of appointment, term of office, salaries and other emoluments of the Judges of the Druze Religious Courts and the Druze Religious Court of Appeal. Its provisions regarding those matters, *mutatis mutandis*, follow closely those of the Judges Law, 5713–1953 (see pp. 204–7).

Where any action of personal status involves persons of different religious communities, the President of the Supreme Court will decide which court shall have jurisdiction, and whenever a question arises as to whether or not a case is one of personal status within the exclusive jurisdiction of a Religious Court, the matter must be referred to a Special Tribunal composed of two judges of the Supreme Court and the president of the highest court of the religious community concerned in Israel (Article 55 of the said Orders-in-Council).

The judgments of the religious courts are executed by the process and offices of the civil courts (Article 56 of the said Orders-in-Council). The chief execution officer of the competent civil court will refuse to execute a judgment of a religious court given in excess of its jurisdiction or contrary to natural justice, but the validity of his refusal can be tested in the Supreme Court sitting as a High Court of Justice. As from the 1st September, 1968, when the Execution Law, 5727–1967, will come into force the judgments of the Religious Courts will be executed thereunder just as the judgments of the Civil Courts are executed thereunder.

In addition, under the Rabbinical Courts' Jurisdiction (Marriage and Divorce) Law, 5713–1953, where by a final judgment of a Rabbinical Court a husband is ordered to give a *Get* (Bill of Divorcement) to his wife, or a wife is ordered to accept a *Get* (Bill of Divorcement) from her husband, or a man is ordered to grant *Halitza* to his brother's widow, a District Court, upon the application of the Attorney General, may enforce the order by imprisonment.

The Religious Courts (Summons to Court) Law, 5716–1956, which came into force on the 22nd March, 1956, empowers the Religious Courts to summon parties and witnesses to appear before them and to compel their attendance by means of a warrant of arrest. It also obliges persons summoned to appear and give evidence and empowers the Religious Courts to fine up to IL. 75 persons refusing to do so, or to order them to pay the expenses incurred as a result of their refusal.

Under the Religious Courts (Prevention of Disturbance) Law, 5725–1965, which came into force on the 18th March, 1965, where a person disturbs the proceedings of a Religious Court in its presence or near the place of the proceedings, such Court may order his removal, or compel him to behave properly, by imposing upon him a fine not exceeding 200 pounds and if he disturbs the proceedings again a fine not exceeding 400 pounds without prejudice to any criminal proceedings for his act, with the consent of the District Attorney. Written notice of the imposition of the said fine must be given immediately to the President of the Supreme Court who may annul or mitigate it.

The Minister for Religious Affairs is responsible for the administration of the Religious Courts. Upon his initiative and with his assistance, Rabbinical Court judgements are published regularly.

Civil Procedure

With the exception of a few articles of the Ottoman Magistrates Law of 1913, dealing with the restitution of possession of immovable property, and a few articles of the Ottoman Code of Civil Procedure, 1879, dealing with provisional attachment of property prior to the commencement of an action, the provisions of the Ottoman Law relating to procedure in civil proceedings were replaced by Palestine legislation based substantially upon the corresponding provisions of the English law, although there is no provision for trial by jury.

The Civil Procedure Rules, 1938, made by the Chief Justice of Palestine with the concurrence of the High Commissioner for Palestine, replaced the relevant Ottoman Law by provisions based on the corresponding English rules of court. Subsequently they were replaced by Civil Procedure Rules made by the Minister of Justice but essentially the same system has been retained. Such rules contain, *inter alia*, provisions relating to attachment in replacement of those of the Ottoman Law. They also make provision for pre-trial and the appointment of medical experts by the Courts.

Under the Crown Actions Ordinance (of 1926) no claim against the Government could be entertained in any court in Palestine unless it was a claim for obtaining relief, other than relief in the nature of specific performance or injunction, against the Government in respect of the restitution of any movable property or compensation to the value thereof, or of the payment of money or damages in respect of any contract lawfully entered into on behalf of the Government, or of the possession or restitution of any immovable property or compensation to the value thereof, the written consent of the High Commissioner authorising the bringing of the action was required, and the action had to be commenced by the filing of a petition in a District Court or Land Court.

By the Courts (Transitional Provisions) Ordinance, 5708–1948, the provision requiring consent to the bringing of such an action was repealed, by the Civil Wrongs (State Liability)

Law, 5712–1952, with certain exceptions (see p. 98), the State was placed on an equal footing with a corporate body with regard to liability for torts, while the sections of the Crown Actions Ordinance limiting the classes of action which may be brought against the State, and the Courts in which they may be brought, were repealed by the Crown Actions Ordinance Amendment Law, 5718–1958. Finally, the Crown Actions Ordinance was repealed by the Civil Procedure Amendment (State as Party) Law, 5718–1958, of the 6th April, 1958, and it was provided by that law that the State is to be treated in civil proceedings as any person with certain specified modifications, among them, that no remedy by way of injunction or specific performance may be given against the State in the absence of statutory provision therefor.

It must be remembered, however, that section 42 of the Interpretation Ordinance, providing that, save as may be otherwise expressly provided, no enactment shall affect any right of, or impose any obligation upon, the State, is still in force. Such an express provision is contained in several Palestine Ordinances and in many Knesset laws, some of which have already been mentioned (see pp. 100, 109, 112, 140, 187, 188, 194, 197).

The Ottoman laws relating to the execution of judgments (1914) and to Notaries Public (1913) (see pp. 244-5) are still in force, but the former will be replaced as from the 1st September, 1968 by the Execution Law, 5727–1967.

The Limitation Law, 5718–1958, which came into force on the 6th April, 1958, repeals and replaces, or amends, a number of provisions of Ottoman, Palestine and Israel legislation relating to the limitation of actions, and provides that the period of limitation for claims not relating to land shall be seven years and for claims relating to land shall be fifteen years, or, if the land has been registered in the Land Register after settlement under the Land (Settlement of Title) Ordinance, twenty five years. The Law also contains rules for calculating the period of limitation in special cases such as minority, mental illness, guardianship, marriage, absence from Israel, and closure of the Courts. It also provides that the parties may, by a separate written agreement, agree upon a longer period of limitation than that prescribed by the Law, and, in the case of a claim not relating to land, also upon a shorter period, so long as it is not shorter than six months. The Law also provides a period of limitation of twenty five years for the execution of judgments.

The provisions of the Law also apply to the State, and the Minister of Justice is empowered to make, *inter alia*, regulations giving effect to the provisions as to the calculation and length of periods of limitation contained in any agreement between Israel and a foreign State, or in any international convention to which Israel is a party, notwithstanding that the provisions of such agreement or convention may be repugnant to the provisions of the Law.

Criminal Procedure

With the exception of a few articles, the Ottoman Code of Criminal Procedure, 1879, was replaced by Palestine legislation based upon the corresponding provisions of English law. One important feature of the English criminal procedure— trial by jury—was not adopted. Two of those articles of that Code which remained in force were replaced by the Criminal Law Amendment (Crimes Committed Abroad) Law, 5716– 1956, which conferred jurisdiction upon the Courts of Israel to try certain offences committed outside of Israel. Such jurisdiction will be exercisable in respect of two classes of persons, namely, every person, whether he owes allegiance to the State of Israel or not, if the offence he committed is a specified offence against the State of Israel as a sovereign State, and Israel citizens or residents or public officers, if their offence is an offence under the Criminal Law Amendment (Bribery Offences) Law, 5712– 1952, or any other specified offence which affects the property or rights of the State or of certain specified bodies. The remaining articles of the said Code ceased to have effect in Israel upon the coming into force of the Criminal Procedure Law, 5725–1965 (see pp. 214–9).

The Area of Jurisdiction and Powers Ordinance Amendment Law, 5716–1956 provides that, for the purposes of jurisdiction of the Courts, every vessel or aircraft registered in Israel, wherever it may be, shall be deemed to be part of the territory of the State of Israel.

The Criminal Procedure Law, 5725–1965, which came into force six months after its publication in *Reshumot* on the 15th July, 1965, repealed and replaced with modification nearly all the existing provisions of the law with regard to criminal procedure, whether Ottoman, Palestinian or Israeli. Generally speaking, the existing system has been retained, although a number of important changes have been made, as will appear from what follows.

Since the replacement of the Ottoman Criminal Code by the Criminal Code Ordinance, 1936 on the 1st January, 1937, there had been doubts as to how the provisions of the Ottoman Criminal Procedure Code should be applied as regards limitation of offences and penalties owing to the changes in the classification of offences introduced by the Criminal Code Ordinance, 1936. Such doubts no longer arise as the new Law uses the same classification of offences as in the Criminal Code Ordinance, 1936, namely, felonies, misdemeanours and contraventions, and at the same time it changes the provisions regarding the periods of limitation. Under the new Law, in the absence of any contrary provision in any other law, a person may not be prosecuted for any offence after the lapse of the following periods after its commission: in the case of a felony punishable with death or life imprisonment—20 years; in the case of any other felony—10 years; in the case of a misdemeanour—5 years; and in the case of a contravention—1 year. A sentence may not be carried out if, from the day when the period for appeal expired, or the last judgment on appeal was given, twenty years have elapsed in the case of a felony, ten years in the case of a misdemeanour and three years in the case of a contravention.

The new Law increases considerably the number of cases in which an accused person will be defended at the expense of the State. It provides that if an accused person has no defending advocate the Court must appoint one for him in each of the following cases: (1) if he is accused of murder or of an offence punishable with death, life imprisonment or imprisonment for ten years or more; (2) if he has not reached the age of sixteen years and he is not brought for trial before a Juvenile Court; (3) if he is dumb, blind or deaf. If the accused person is without means, or it is apprehended that he is mentally ill, and he has no defending advocate, the Court may, at the request of a party or of its own motion, appoint a defending advocate for him. The expenses of the defence, including the expenses and fees of the defending advocate and the witnesses, as prescribed by regulations made by the Minister of Justice, will be borne by the State if the Court appoints a defending advocate for the accused person. A defending advocate appointed by the Court may not accept from the accused person or any other person, any fee, compensation, gift or other benefit, and if he does so he will be liable to three months' imprisonment.

There are also new provisions with regard to detention which are in addition to the existing provisions. The new Law provides that every person who is detained, whether an information has been filed against him or has not yet been filed, is entitled, at his request, to have notice of his detention given as soon as possible to a person close to him, in so far as his whereabouts are known, and also to an advocate named by the person detained. A District Court Judge may, however, give permission that no notice be given of the detention of a person detained for a felony, or that the notice be given only to the person specified by him, if the Minister of Defence has certified in writing that the security of the State requires secrecy regarding the detention, or if the Inspector General of Police has certified in writing that the interests of the inquiry require secrecy regarding the detention. Such permission will be for a period not exceeding forty eight hours, but it may be extended from time to time, provided that the total of all the periods does not exceed seven days.

With a view to expediting the trial of offenders, the new Law provides that if a suspected person is detained and no information against him is filed within ninety days after his detention, or if an accused person is detained and his trial is not begun within sixty days after the information against him is filed, or if the trial in first instance of an accused person who is detained is not terminated by the delivery of judgment within one year after the information against him has been filed, he must be released from detention, unless he is being detained for some other act or upon order of an appellate Court pending an appeal by the prosecutor. A Supreme Court Justice, however, may order an extension of the detention, or that the released person be detained anew, for a period not exceeding three months, and he may make such an order from time to time.

The new Law, just as the existing law, provides for the commencement of criminal proceedings in Court by the filing of an information by a prosecutor, who is the Attorney General or his representative, or of a complaint by a private complainant, but unlike the existing law contains no provisions for the holding of a preliminary enquiry. Where the proceedings are commenced by the Attorney General or his representative they are taken in the name of the State of Israel as accuser and not in the name of the Attorney General as accuser as was previously done.

Another innovation in the new Law is the provision that before commencement of his trial an accused person may, by notice in writing to the Court, admit all or any of the facts alleged in the information, and also allege additional facts. A copy of the admission must be served by the Court on the prosecutor. An admission in writing will not preclude the accused person from raising any preliminary objection, or admitting facts, or alleging additional facts, during the course of the trial.

The new Law extends the possibility of departing from the general rule that the accused may not be tried in his absence. It provides that where the accused person has been originally summoned for his trial and does not appear, he may be tried in his absence if he was charged with a contravention or a misdemeanour and he admitted in a written admission all the facts alleged in the information, and he did not allege any additional facts which are prima facie liable to change the result of the trial, or if he has requested to be tried in his absence and he is represented at the trial by his defending advocate, and the Court is of the opinion that no injustice will be done to the accused person by trying him in his absence, but the Court may, at any stage of the trial, order the accused to appear before it. Where a person is tried in his absence, the Court may not impose upon him a sentence of imprisonment, other than imprisonment for non-payment of a fine, unless he has been previously given an opportunity to make his submissions regarding the sentence.

As regards the record of the proceedings, the new Law contains a provision first introduced into the law for the Eichmann case. Under that provision, the proceedings must be recorded in writing by the Judge, a person appointed by the Court to record them, a recording instrument or other mechanical means or an official of the Court approved as a shorthand writer by the President thereof or the Chief Judge of a Magistrates' Court, as the case may be, as the Court may determine, and the Court may, at the request of a party, permit the recording of the proceedings by another shorthand writer. Under the existing law, as a general rule, the proceedings must be recorded by the presiding Judge in his own handwriting.

The new Law makes an important change in the manner of pleading to the information. Under the existing law, after the information has been read to him at the commencement of the trial, the accused person is asked whether he pleads "guilty" or "not guilty", but under the new Law the Court must ask the accused person what is his answer to the information and he need not answer, while if he answers to it, he may admit all or any of the facts alleged in the information, or he may deny them, or he may allege additional facts, whether he admitted the alleged facts or not. The defending advocate may reply on behalf of the accused person.

The accused person may at any stage of the trial before judgment with leave of the Court withdraw his admission of facts, in whole or in part. If he does not do so, any fact admitted by him will be taken as proved against him unless the Court decides not to accept his admission as evidence.

Ever since the amendment of the law in 1954 which empowered the Court to require a probation officer to submit a report to it before it passes sentence, and in some cases required the Court to call for such a report, there has been a controversy as to whether the prosecutor, the accused and his defending advocate, or any of them, should be entitled or allowed to see the report of the probation officer. The new Law provides in that regard, that a copy of the report of the probation officer shall be delivered to the prosecutor and to the defending advocate of the accused, if there is one, and the Court must hear any submissions there are as respects the contents of the report, but the Court may order that a copy of the report shall also be delivered to the accused person, and it may, upon a reasoned proposal of the probation officer or of its own motion, order, for special reasons, that the contents of the report shall not be disclosed, in whole or in part, to the parties.

The Court is also empowered, after having given the accused person an opportunity to make his submissions in the matter, to order that the accused person be examined by a doctor or other expert, and it may order such other inquiries to be made as appear to it to be useful for the determination of the sentence. The above provisions as regards reports of probation officers will apply to the results of such examinations and inquiries.

As regards appeals, the new Law makes a number of changes. They include the restoration of the automatic appeal in cases in which a sentence of death has been passed. Such an appeal was abolished in 1939. It also deprives the appellate Court of its power under the existing law of increasing the sentence despite the fact that the prosecutor has not appealed against the lightness of the sentence imposed by the lower Court.

Another innovation as regards appeals is the provision that where the notice of appeal does not specify the grounds of appeal, or does not specify them in sufficient detail, the Court may order the appellant to submit grounds of appeal, or more detailed grounds of appeal, within the period fixed by it, and if the appellant does not do so the Court may, at the commencement of the hearing of the appeal, dismiss the appeal for lack of grounds of appeal.

The appellate court may also take further evidence, or order the lower Court to do so, if it considers it necessary in order to do justice.

The new Law also increases to 45 days the period for filing an appeal.

Just as under the existing law, so too under the new Law, the Attorney General is given power to stay any proceedings at any time after the filing of an information but before judgment, but the new Law requires him to give to the Court a reasoned notice of stay of proceedings, and when he has done so the Court must stay the proceedings in the case. It also limits the time within which the Attorney General can renew proceedings which have been stayed; in the case of a felony the time is 5 years from the date of the stay, and in the case of a misdemeanour it is one year. If the proceedings are stayed after they have been renewed they may not be renewed any more.

Finally, mention must be made of two further important innovations introduced by the new Law. The first is the provision that a civil claim may not be joined to a criminal case, and the other is that in any matter of procedure for which there is no provision in any enactment, the Court may act in such manner as appears to it to be best for doing justice.

Under the Law of Procedure (Amendment) Ordinance, 1934, if it appears to the Attorney General that any right of the State of Israel or any public right or interest is, or may be, affected or involved by or in any proceedings in any civil or criminal Court, or before a Settlement Officer or under the Land (Settlement of Title) Ordinance, the Attorney General may at his discretion appear in such proceedings or specially authorise his representative to appear on his behalf in any such proceedings, and he, or his representative, as the case may be, will be entitled to be heard therein.

The Ordinance also provides that where any public officer or any Board, Commission, Committee, Tribunal or other similar body of persons, which is established or constituted by or under any Ordinance or Law, is a party to any proceedings in any Court in his or its capacity as such, he or it may be represented in such proceedings by the Attorney General or the Attorney General's representative.

Coroners

The Coroners Ordinance, of the 1st September, 1926, made provisions for the regulation of the powers and duties of coroners. It empowered the High Commissioner for Palestine from time to time to appoint one or more administrative officers of the Government in each District to be coroners for the District, specified the cases in which a coroner was required to hold an inquest or could dispense therewith and in which he could direct that a post mortem examination should be carried out. It also provided for the adjournment of an inquest where criminal proceedings had been begun arising out of the death of the deceased, which was the subject of the inquest. In 1946 the Ordinance was amended so that any person, and not only an administrative officer, could be appointed a coroner and in Israel it became the practice to appoint Magistrates as coroners. That Ordinance was in force until replaced by the Criminal Procedure Amendment (Investigation of Felonies and Causes of Death) Law, 5718—1958, which came into force on the 21st February, 1958, and was re-entitled the Investigation of Causes of Death Law, 5718–1958 by the Criminal Procedure Law, 5725–1965 (see pp. 214-9).

Under the Investigation of Causes of Death Law, 5718–1958, where upon the death of any person there are reasonable grounds for suspecting that the cause of death was not a natural one, or that the death was caused by an offence, or where a person has died while under arrest or imprisonment or while an inmate of a mental hospital or a closed institution for backward children, the Attorney General or his representative, an officer of police, a physician or any interested person may request a Judge of a Magistrates' Court in the area of jurisdiction of which the death occurred or the body is situated, known as an Investigating Judge, to investigate the cause of death and the Judge must comply with such request. An interested person is defined as meaning a spouse, parent, grandparent, descendant, brother or sister of the deceased person.

The circumstances in which an Investigating Judge is required to investigate the cause of death are substantially the same as those in which a coroner was required to hold an inquest, but the said Law contains several new provisions as compared with the Coroners Ordinance

The new Law expressly provides that the Investigating Judge may hold the investigation in public or in camera, or partly in public and partly in camera, and that he may prohibit any publication of proceedings in an investigation of the cause of a death held in public, and may permit a publication concerning an investigation of the cause of a death held in camera, and that a person who publishes anything concerning an investigation of the cause of death in contravention of a prohibition or without permission under the Law is liable to imprisonment for a term of six months.

The new Law also provides that where it appears to an Investigating Judge that the evidence produced to him affords prima facie proof that an offence has been committed by a particular person, he may order that a District Attorney charge such person with such offence before a Court and the District Attorney must then file an information in the Court, but the Investigating Judge may not make such an order unless he has given such person an opportunity to set forth his contentions and produce his evidence to him. Such an order will also have the effect of a warrant for the arrest of such person until after his trial, but without derogating from the provisions of the Criminal Procedure (Arrest and Searches) Ordinance, the Criminal Procedure Law, 5725–1965, or any other law.

An Investigating Judge may, if it is necessary so to do in order to ascertain the cause of death in an investigation, order the examination or autopsy of the body by a physician or other expert and the postponement of the burial until after the examination or autopsy, or the opening of the grave and the exhumation of the body for the purpose of carrying out the examination or autopsy, but an interested person and a recognised body, within the meaning of the Anatomy and Pathology Regulations, 5714–1954, may appeal to the District Court against an order for the opening of a grave.

It was expressly provided in the Anatomy and Pathology Law, 5713–1953, of the 4th September, 1953, that that Law should not affect the provisions of the Coroners Ordinance, but section 28 of the Investigation of Causes of Death Law, 5718–1958 provides that the provisions of the Anatomy and Pathology Law, 5713–1953 shall apply *mutatis mutandis* to an examination or autopsy ordered by an Investigating Judge.

Section 2 of the Anatomy and Pathology Law, 5713–1953 provides that the body of a deceased person who consented in writing that it should be used for scientific purposes, and the body of a deceased person which the person entitled to claim it under the regulations made by the Minister of Health has not claimed within the time and in the manner prescribed by the regulations, may be dissected at a medical school for purposes of study and research. A person who has in his possession such a body must notify such fact to a medical school and must hand over the body to it on its demand, within the time and in the manner prescribed by the regulations, but such provision will not apply to a person to whom the body has been handed over for burial only.

Not later than one year from the day on which it is received by the medical school, the body and its dissected parts must be buried in accordance with the law of the religious community to which the deceased belonged and the entire cost of the burial must be borne by the medical school, but the medical school may retain the body or parts thereof if the deceased consented thereto in writing or if the person entitled to claim the body under the regulations has not objected thereto within the time and in the manner prescribed by the regulations.

The Law goes on to provide that a physician may operate on a body in order to ascertain the cause of death or to use a part thereof for the curative treatment of a person if it has been confirmed by a certificate signed by three physicians authorised in that behalf in accordance with the regulations that the operation serves one of the said purposes. A person who operates on a body otherwise than in accordance with those provisions will be liable to imprisonment for a term of three years or to a fine of IL. 7500 or to both such penalties, as will a person who hands over to a medical school a body in respect of which the requirements of section 2 are not fulfilled or who dissects a body not in the possession of a medical school.

Evidence

The Evidence Ordinance, which came into force on the 18th April, 1924, is, according to its long title, an Ordinance the objects of which are, *inter alia*, to declare the law of evidence on certain points and to amend the law on other points. In so far as that Ordinance may be defective, and there is no provision in any other Ordinance, or the Ottoman or Israel legislation, English common law is applied with such modifications as may be required.

Part 1 of the Evidence Ordinance contains general provisions which are to be applied in all proceedings before the Civil Courts in this country. With the one exception hereinafter mentioned, which relates to corroboration in criminal cases, those provisions have remained in force unaltered since the Ordinance was enacted, although two new provisions hereinafter described (see pp. 225, 226) have been added thereto by the Criminal Procedure Law, 5725–1965.

Section 3 of the Ordinance provides that all persons are competent to give evidence in all cases, and no person shall be considered incompetent to give evidence in any case by reason of his being a party to a civil action or a complainant or accused in a criminal case, or by reason of his being a master or servant, husband, wife or relative, of the plaintiff or complainant or of the defendant or accused, or by reason of his having been convicted of, or being under sentence for, any crime: Provided that in all criminal cases, except as provided in section 5, a wife shall not be competent to give evidence against her husband, nor compellable to give evidence against any person jointly accused with him in the same information, nor shall a husband be competent to give evidence against his wife, nor compellable to give evidence against any person accused jointly with her in the same information and that a parent shall not be competent to give evidence against a child nor compellable to give evidence against any person jointly accused with the child in the same information, nor a child competent to give evidence against a parent, nor compellable to give evidence against any person jointly accused with the parent in the same information

If a husband is called to give evidence in defence of his wife, or a wife is called to give evidence in defence of her husband, or if a parent or child is called to give evidence in defence of the other, the evidence so given, whether in examination in chief or obtained by cross-examination on behalf of the prosecution, may be used in proof of the guilt of the accused person, whether husband or wife or parent or child. (Section 4).

Section 5 of the Ordinance provides that in criminal proceedings against a husband or wife for any bodily injury or violence inflicted upon his or her wife or husband or child, and in proceedings in respect of adultery, the wife is competent to give evidence against her husband and the husband against his wife, and in criminal proceedings against a parent or child for any bodily injury or violence inflicted upon his or her child or parent, as the case may be, the parent is competent to give evidence against the child and the child against the parent.

Section 33 (1) of the Adoption of Children Law, 5720–1960 (see pp. 161–4), provides that the word 'child' is deemed to include an adopted child, and the word 'parent' is deemed to include an adopter, for the purposes of sections 3, 4 and 5 of the Evidence Ordinance.

Section 6 of the Evidence Ordinance originally provided that 'no judgment shall be given in any case on the evidence of a single witness unless such evidence is, in a civil case, uncontradicted or, in a criminal case, is admitted by the accused person or, whether in a civil or criminal case, is corroborated by some other material evidence which in the opinion of the court, is sufficient to establish the truth of it.'

That section was suspended, and the following section was substituted therefor by section 3 of the Law of Evidence Amendment Ordinance, 1936, during the continuance in operation of that Ordinance:

'No judgment shall be given in any civil case on the evidence of a single witness unless such evidence is uncontradicted or is corroborated by some other material evidence which, in the opinion of the Court, is sufficient to establish its truth.'

The Law of Evidence Amendment Ordinance, 1936, was passed by reason of the situation created in the country by what were known as the disturbances which began on the 19th April 1936, but it is still in operation, so that there is no provision in the Evidence Ordinance requiring corroboration in a criminal case, although both the Palestine Courts and the Israel Courts require corroboration in certain criminal cases, (e.g. where the accused is charged with a sexual offence or the sole prosecution witness is an accomplice of the accused) while the Israel Courts have laid down a rule that when a Judge convicts upon the evidence of a single witness he must make it clear that he is aware of the dangers of so doing but that nevertheless he is satisfied that he is justified in the particular case in so doing. Furthermore, Section 221 of the Criminal Procedure Law, 5725–1965 inserts in the Evidence Ordinance a new section, Section 6A, whereunder an accused person may not be convicted upon the evidence of a minor which has not been received on oath, unless there is corroboration thereof.

Section 7 of the Evidence Ordinance provides that evidence of a statement made at the time when, or shortly before, or after, an offence is alleged to have been committed and directly relating to a fact or facts relevant in the case is admissible if made by a person who is himself also a witness.

The admissibility of statements by victims of violence is dealt with by Section 8 of the Ordinance, which provides that evidence of a statement made by a person on whom an act of violence is alleged to have been committed and relating to such an act of violence or attendant circumstances is admissible if made at the time, or shortly after, the act of violence was committed, or so soon after as he had an opportunity of complaining of it, or so related to it in the sequence of events as to be part of the train of circumstances directly connected with the commission of the offence, or made when the person was, or believed himself to be, dying as a direct consequence of the act of violence, is admissible although the person who made the statement is not present as a witness and cannot be produced at the trial because of his death, infirmity or sickness, or absence from Israel.

Section 9 of the Ordinance provides that evidence of confession by the accused that he has committed an offence is admissible only when the prosecution has given evidence of the circumstances in which it was made and the court is satisfied that it was free and voluntary.

A new section, Section 9A, added by Section 221 of the Criminal Procedure Law, 5725-1965, provides that a statement made by an accused person may be proved by the evidence of a person who heard the statement, and that where the statement has been recorded in writing and the accuded person has signed it or has confirmed it in some other way it may be proved by evidence thereof from a person who was present on the same occasion.

The effect of wrongly admitted evidence is dealt with by Section 10 of the Ordinance, which provides that, when evidence which is not admissible in proof of a criminal charge has been admitted by error or inadvertence, such evidence shall not be used in proof of the charge nor shall any judgment be based thereon; nevertheless, the fact that such evidence has been heard by the court shall not be held to invalidate the judgment unless, in the opinion of the court, the accused would not have been convicted if such evidence had not been given or there was no other sufficient evidence to support the conviction apart from that evidence.

Contradictions in the evidence of witnesses do not, in themselves, prevent the court from finding facts in respect of which the contradictions occur (Section 11).

The value of oral evidence and the credibility of witnesses are questions for the court to decide according to the demeanour of the witnesses, the circumstances of the case and such indication of the truth as may appear during the trial; it shall not be the duty of the court to make enquiry as to their credibility either through verbal testimony or by private inquistion; (Section 12).

Subject to the provisions of the Ordinance, any person may be summoned to give evidence which is admissible and relevant to the case, subject to the discretion of the court to refuse to issue a summons which may be unnecessary or which may appear to be demanded for some other purpose than the elucidation of the truth. (Section 13).

In a civil case, either party may give evidence on his own behalf or be summoned to give evidence for the other party. (Section 14).

The other parts of the Ordinance contain provisions regarding bankers' books (Part IA), evidence on commission (Part II), admissibility of evidence taken abroad (Part III), proof of foreign documents (Part IV), proof of public documents (Part V), miscellaneous (Part VI), evidence of experts (Part VII) certificates of public officials (Part VIII), declarations as evidence (Part IX).

Part VII, which was added by the Evidence Ordinance Amendment Law, 5714–1954, provides that the Court may, unless it apprehends that a miscarriage of justice may result, receive in evidence, in writing, the opinion of an expert as to a matter of science, research, art or professional knowledge and a certificate of a medical practitioner as to the state of health of a person, each of which must be in the prescribed form and will be treated as evidence on oath for the purposes of Section 117 of the Criminal Code Ordinance, 1936, which deals with perjury and subornation of perjury. The Court, however, may order the expert or medical practitioner to be examined in Court and it must do so if requested by one of the parties.

The Evidence Law Amendment (Protection of Children) Law, 5715-1955, of the 20th September, 1955, provides that no child under the age of fourteen years may be called to give evidence in court regarding any offence against morality, committed on its person or in its presence, or which it is suspected of having committed, and no statement of such a child may be received in evidence, save with the permission of a Youth Interrogator appointed by the Minister of Justice. It also provides for the taking and submission to the Court of such evidence by Youth Interrogators, but no person may be convicted upon such evidence unless it is corroborated by other evidence.

Extradition

The Extradition Law, 5714-1954, which came into force on the 1st September, 1954, replaced the provisions of the Extradition Ordinance (of 1926) with regard to the extradition of criminals. It provides that a person who is in Israel shall not be extradited to another state except thereunder, and that he may be extradited if (1) an agreement providing for reciprocity as to the extradition of offenders exists between Israel and the state requesting his extradition (known as 'the requesting state') and (2) he is accused, or has been convicted, in the requesting state of an offence of a non-political character and which, had it been committed in Israel, would be one of the offences set out in the Schedule to the Law (known as 'extradition offences'), which are offences punishable with death or imprisonment for more than three years, with certain specified exceptions, and offences punishable with a lighter penalty which are offences under the Criminal Law Amendment (Bribery) Law, 5712–1952, (see p. 75) or under any of twenty five specified sections of the Criminal Code Ordinance, 1936.

Where a request has been submitted by a foreign state for the extradition of a person accused, or convicted, in that state of an extradition offence (known as a 'wanted person'), the Minister of Justice may direct that he be brought before a District Court in order to determine whether he is subject to extradition, and, if he so directs, the Attorney General or his representative must submit to the District Court a petition to declare the wanted person subject to extradition. The District Court must dismiss such a petition (1) if the wanted person has been tried in Israel for the criminal act for which his extradition is requested, and has been acquitted or convicted, or if he has undergone his punishment for it abroad, or (2) if, according to the laws of the requesting state, or the State of Israel, the offence is no longer liable to prosecution, or the punishment imposed for it is no longer enforceable, owing to lapse of time, or (3) if the wanted person had been pardoned, or has had his punishment remitted in the requesting state in respect of the criminal act in question.

If, at the hearing of a petition, it is proved that the wanted person has been convicted of an extradition offence in the requesting state, or that there is evidence which would be sufficient for committing him for trial for such an offence in Israel, and that the other conditions laid down by law for his extradition are fulfilled, the Court must declare the wanted person subject to extradition, but it may not so declare if it finds that there are reasonable grounds for assuming that (1) the accusation or the request for extradition arises from racial or religious discrimination, or (2) the request for extradition aims at prosecuting, or punishing, him for an offence of a political character, although *prima facie* it is not made in connection with such an offence.

A wanted person may not be extradited for an offence punishable with death in the requesting state, but not so punishable in Israel, unless the requesting state gives an undertaking that the death penalty will not be imposed on him, or that the death penalty which has been, or may be, imposed on him will be commuted, nor may a wanted person be extradited unless it has been ensured, by an agreement with the requesting state, that he will not be detained, tried, or punished, in that state for another offence committed prior to his extradition, unless he left the requesting state after his extradition and voluntarily returned to it, or if he has not left the requesting state within 60 days after his being given an opportunity to do so, or if the State of Israel has consented in writing to such an act against the wanted person. Such consent may not be given unless the person in question has, in his absence, been declared subject to extradition also in respect of the other offence after he has been given an opportunity to be represented in the proceeding for obtaining such a declaration.

The Minister of Justice may order the carrying out of the extradition of a wanted person whose declaration as subject to extradition has become final, and the wanted person may thereupon be surrendered to the requesting state and be transferred outside the boundaries of Israel. If a wanted person is not extradited or transferred outside the boundaries of Israel within 60 days from the day on which his declaration as subject to extradition becomes final, the declaration will expire, unless its effect is extended by the Court owing to special circumstances delaying the carrying out of the extradition.

Certain specified provisions of the Law may be modified by an extradition agreement between Israel and a foreign state.

Where a person has been extradited to Israel by a foreign state, he may not be detained, or tried, for another offence, or extradited to another state for any offence, committed before his extradition, unless the foreign state consent in writing to such an act, or he has not left Israel within sixty days after being given an opportunity, subsequent to his extradition, so to do, or he left Israel after his extradition and has voluntarily returned to it.

Legal Assistance to Foreign States

Replacing certain British legislation in force here, the Legal Assistance to Foreign States Law, 5716-1956, which came into force on the 27th July, 1956, prescribes the arrangements to be made for the submission of documents, taking of evidence and production of documents, upon the request of legal authorities in foreign states, and empowers the Government to conclude international agreements in other matters of legal assistance on a basis of reciprocity, giving such agreements the force of law.

Enforcement of Foreign Judgments

Replacing the relevant Palestine legislation, the Enforcement of Foreign Judgments Law, 5718-1958, which came into force on the 20th February, 1958, provides that no foreign judgment shall be enforced in Israel save thereunder. A foreign judgment is defined as meaning a judgment given by a Court in a foreign State in a civil matter, including a judgment for the payment of compensation or damages to an injured party, even if not given in a civil matter.

The Law empowers the District Court, Jerusalem, and only that Court, to declare a foreign judgment enforceable if the following conditions are fulfilled: (1) the judgment was given in a State according to the laws whereof its Courts were competent to to give it; (2) the judgment is no longer appealable; (3)   the contents of the judgment are not in conflict with the laws of the State of Israel or public policy in Israel; (4) the judgment is executable in the State in which it was given.   But a foreign judgment may not be declared enforceable if it was given in a State according to the laws whereof judgments of the Israel Courts are not enforced, unless the Attorney General requests the Court to enforce it.

The Court may not entertain an application to enforce a foreign judgment which is made after the expiration of five years from the date when the judgment was given, save where another period has been agreed upon between Israel and the State in which the judgment was given, or the Courts finds special reasons justifying the delay.

Furthermore, a foreign judgment may not be declared enforceable if (1) the judgment was obtained by fraud (2) the opportunity given to the defendant to submit his arguments and adduce evidence before the judgment was given was not, in the opinion of the Court, a reasonable one (3) the judgment was given by a Court which was not competent to give it (4) the judgment is contrary to another judgment given in the same matter between the same parties which is still in force, or(5) at the time of the lodging of the claim in the Court in the foreign State there was an action pending in the same matter and between the same parties, in a Court or tribunal in Israel. In addition, a foreign judgment may not be declared enforceable if its enforcement is likely to affect the sovereignty or security of Israel.

The Court may, if it considers that it is justifiable so to do in the circumstances of the case, enforce a temporary judgment or interim order in matters of maintenance, despite the fact that it is still subject to appeal, if the rest of the conditions prescribed by the Law are complied with.

When a foreign judgment has been declared to be enforceable, it is to be treated for the purposes of execution as if it were a judgment duly given in Israel.

Any Court or tribunal may, in the course of trying any matter within its jurisdiction, recognize a foreign judgment, for the purposes of such matter, if it considers it just and lawful to do so.

LEGAL PROFESSION

UNTIL THE Chamber of Advocates Law, 5721-1961, came into force, advocates, some of whom were also notaries for foreign documents, were under the control and supervision of a Law Council, composed of Judges and advocates, both State and private, appointed as members by the Minister of Justice, and presided over by the Attorney General who was *ex officio* its chairman, and membership of the Israel Bar Association was voluntary.

Advocates

The Chamber of Advocates Law, 5721-1961, which was passed by the Knesset on the 13th June, 1961 and came into force nine months later, established for the first time in this country a Chamber of Advocates which will comprise all the advocates in the country. Its function is to take care of the standard and integrity of the profession, and for that purpose it is charged with the registration, control and examination, of law apprentices, the authorisation of persons to practise as advocates by accepting them as members of the Chamber of Advocates, and the maintenance of disciplinary tribunals for advocates and law apprentices.

The Chamber is a corporation with capacity to enter into any obligation, acquire any right and do any legal act, and it is subject to inspection by the State Comptroller. Among other things, it may do the following: give an opinion upon any draft law regarding matters of Courts and legal procedure, provide legal aid for persons of limited means, act as arbitrator and appoint arbitrators, act for the protection of the professional interests of the members of the Chamber, establish insurance funds, pension funds and other institutions for mutual aid for the members of the Chamber, promote activities and projects for legal research in general, and research in Jewish law in particular, participate in such activities and projects, and engage in the publication of legal literature.

The organs of the Chamber are the National Conference, the

National Council, the Central Committee, the District Committees, the National Disciplinary Tribunal, and the District Disciplinary Tribunals.

The National Conference is elected by the members of the Chamber once every two years in elections which are general, equal, proportional, secret, direct and national, and so long as the National Conference has not fixed any other number, the number of delegates to the Conference will be ten per cent of the total number of members of the Chamber at the time the elections are held. The National Conference elects one of the members of the Chamber as President.

The National Council is composed of the President of the Chamber, twenty members of the Chamber elected by the National Conference in proportional and secret elections, four members of the Chamber from each District Committee, namely, the chairman of the District Committee, and three other members chosen by the District Committee, and six other persons appointed by the Minister of Justice. The six persons appointed by the Minister of Justice to the first National Council were the Dean of the Law Faculty of the Hebrew University, the Chief Military Advocate, the Director General of the Ministry of Justice, the State Attorney, and two private practising advocates.

The Central Committee is the executive organ of the Chamber, and it has all the powers of the Chamber which are not vested in any other of the institutions of the Chamber. It is composed of the President of the Chamber and such number of other members, not exceeding fourteen, as may be fixed by the National Council, elected by the National Council from among its members in equal, secret and proportional elections.

There will be a District Committee for each of the districts in which a District Court has jurisdiction. The members of each District Committee will be elected by the members whose principal place of business is in the district of the Committee, in general, equal, proportional, secret and direct elections, and the District Committee will choose one of its members as its chairman.

The members of the National Disciplinary Tribunal will be chosen by the National Council from among the qualified members of the Chamber, while the members of each District Disciplinary Tribunal will be chosen by the members of the Chamber in the district qualified therefor. Members of the National Disciplinary Tribunal must have been members of the Chamber for at least eight years, while members of a District Disciplinary Tribunal must have been members of the Chamber for at least five years, but members of the National Council and members of the District Committees may not be members of any Disciplinary Tribunal. Any three members of a Disciplinary Tribunal will constitute the tribunal.

The law defines the acts which fall within the scope of the profession of an advocate and prohibits the doing of any of those acts by way of his occupation, or for remuneration if not by way of his occupation, by any person who is not an advocate.

The following are the acts which are within the scope of the profession: (1) representation of another person and any pleading or other act in his name before any Court, tribunal, arbitrator or person or body of persons having judicial or quasi-judicial powers; (2) representation of another person and doing any other act in his name before the Execution Office, the Land Registry, the authorised officer for the purposes of the Cooperative Houses Law, 5713-1953, the Registrar of Companies, the Registrar of Cooperative Societies, the Registrar of Partnerships, the Registrar of Patents and Designs, the Registrar of Trade Marks, any Assessing Officer or the Commissioner of Income Tax for the purposes of the Income Tax Ordinance, the Director for the purposes of the Land Betterment Tax Law, 5713-1952, the Director of Estate Tax for the purposes of the Estate Tax Law, 5709-1949; (3) the drafting of documents of a legal nature for another person, including the representation of another person in negotiations leading to the drafting of such a document; (4) giving of legal advice and legal opinions.

Those provisions are not to affect: (1) the powers of the Attorney General to the Government and his representatives; (2) representation before Religious Courts and Courts Martial; (3) representation before any Court, tribunal, body of persons or other person the representation before which or whom is regulated by any enactment, including the provisions of S.236 of the Income Tax Ordinance; (4) the powers of a patent agent under the Patents and Designs Ordinance and the Trade Marks Ordinance, 1938; (5) the right of auditors to perform functions permitted to them by any law; (6) representation of any organisation of employees or employers or any member thereof by the representative of the organisation, in any arbitration in labour matters or in connection with a labour agreement; (7) the giving of a legal opinion by a person requested to give it by an advocate or by one of the authorities of the State.

Any person who has given a power of attorney to an advocate is entitled to be represented by him before all State authorities, local authorities and other persons, or bodies of persons, performing public functions according to law.

The Law also incorporates the special provisions enacted prior to the commencement of the trial of Adolf Eichmann to enable him to be represented in the Israel Courts by Dr. Servatius, a German lawyer. It provides that where a person who is not an Israel citizen is charged with an offence punishable with death, or where any investigation is being carried out against him for such an offence, he may appoint for himself, with the approval of the Minister of Justice, a defending counsel who is not an advocate within the meaning of the Chamber of Advocates Law, 5721-1961, if such person is qualified as an advocate abroad, and it empowers the Minister of Justice to approve the appointment in special circumstances and after consultation with the National Council of the Chamber. When the appointment of a defending counsel has been so approved, he will be treated for that purpose as if he were an advocate within the meaning of the said law. The Minister of Justice may, in special circumstances, and with the consent of the President of the Supreme Court, or if the accused has been committed for trial, with the consent of the presiding Judge of the Court before which he has been committed for trial, revoke the approval and then the appointment will become void.

The fourth chapter of the Law deals with professional qualifications. In order to become an advocate a person must have had the necessary legal education, have served the necessary period of apprenticeship, and have passed the prescribed examinations of the Chamber of Advocates.

A person will have had the necessary legal education if (1) he is a graduate of the Law Faculty of an institution in Israel recognised as an institution of higher learning under the Council for Higher Learning Law, 5718–1958, or (2) is a graduate in law of an institution abroad recognised for that purpose by the Hebrew University, Jerusalem, as an institution of higher learning, or (3) has been qualified abroad as an advocate and has practised abroad for at least two years as an advocate or served in a judicial function or has served abroad for at least two years in a judicial function for which only a person with legal education is qualified.

A person may not be registered as a law apprentice unless (1) he has received a degree from a Law Faculty mentioned above or is certified as having complied with its requirements for such a degree or has received a certificate that he has completed the period of his studies in the Faculty or that he is entitled to pass on to the last year of his studies and has passed all the examinations of the previous years. (2) he is a graduate in law of a foreign institution mentioned above, and has proved that he has sufficient knowledge of Hebrew and has passed the examinations of the Chamber in the laws of the State of Israel, except those examinations from which he has been exempt in accordance with regulations made by the Minister of Justice, although he may be registered as a law apprentice also if he has still to pass two of the examinations (3) if he is in the third category of persons having the necessary legal education and has proved that he has sufficient knowledge of Hebrew. Such a person will have to pass the examination of the Chamber in the laws of the State of Israel except those examinations from which he has been exempted in accordance with regulations made by the Minister of Justice, but his registration as a law apprentice is not dependent on his passing the said examinations or any of them. The Chamber, however, is empowered, after giving the candidate an opportunity of presenting his case before it, to refrain from registering him as a law apprentice despite his being duly qualified, if facts are revealed in view of which the Chamber is of the opinion that the candidate is not fit to be an advocate. An appeal against such a decision of the Chamber will lie to the Supreme Court.

The persons who are qualified to act as principals to law apprentices are: (1) a Justice of the Supreme Court and a District Court Judge; (2) a Judge of a Magistrates' Court of at least five years standing as a member of the Chamber and as a Judge together; (3) a Court Martial Judge who is a jurist within the meaning of the Military Justice Law, 5715-1955, of at least five years standing as a member of the Chamber and as a Judge together; (4) a member of the Chamber of five years standing who is approved by the Chamber as fit to be a principal; (5) a member of the Chamber of five years standing in one of the posts in the Legal Service prescribed for that purpose by the Minister of Justice by order.

The Chamber may, after a member has had an opportunity of stating his case before it, revoke the approval given to him to be a principal to law apprentices if the member has been convicted by a Disciplinary Tribunal and in view of the conviction the Chamber is of the opinion that he is not fit to serve as a principal to law apprentices.

An appeal will lie to the Supreme Court against a refusal to give the necessary approval to a member to be a principal to law apprentices or a revocation of such approval.

The period of law apprenticeship is two years, unless the law apprentice qualified abroad as an advocate and practised abroad as an advocate or served in a judicial function for at least two years, or served abroad for at least two years in a judicial function for which only a person with legal education is qualified, in which case the period of law apprenticeship will be one year or such shorter period, not less than six months, as the Chamber may fix, while if he practised or served as above for less than two years, the period of law apprenticeship will be such period, less than two years, but not less than one year, as the Chamber may determine.

If the period of law apprenticeship is one year or more the person serving it must serve at least six months thereof in the office of a private advocate or in the office of the State Attorney or of a District Attorney.

During the last six months of his period of law apprenticeship a law apprentice may represent clients of his principal in the Magistrates' Court if his principal is present in Court or if the Court permits him to continue to represent them in the absence of his principal.

At the end of the period of law apprenticeship the candidate for membership of the Chamber must undergo examinations of the Chamber in practical subjects, but if he qualified abroad as an advocate, or served in a judicial function for at least five years, or served abroad for at least five years in a judicial function for which only a person with legal education is qualified, and he commenced his law apprenticeship within ten years of his immigration to this country he will be exempt from the said examinations. The examining committee will be composed of three members, namely, a Judge, as chairman, one advocate who is a member of the Legal Service and another advocate. The members will be selected from a panel of examiners drawn up by the Minister of Justice.

During the period of his law apprenticeship and until a final decision is taken regarding his acceptance as a member of the Chamber the candidate will be subject to the control of the Chamber and its disciplinary jurisdiction.

The fifth chapter of the law deals with membership of the Chamber.

A person who is qualified to be an advocate, who is a resident of Israel, and who is twenty three years of age, will become an advocate upon his acceptance as a member of the Chamber.

The Chamber may, after an opportunity has been given to a candidate for membership of the Chamber to state his case, refuse to accept him as a member of the Chamber despite his being qualified therefor, if (1) the candidate has been convicted of a criminal offence which in the circumstances involves moral turpitude, and the Chamber is of the opinion that in view of the conviction he is not fit to be an advocate; (2) other facts have come to light, either as a result of a judgment of a Disciplinary Tribunal or an objection lodged to the acceptance of the candidate as a member of the Chamber, or otherwise, and the Chamber is of the opinion that, in view of those facts, the candidate is not fit to be an advocate; (3) the candidate engages in any of the occupations in which an advocate is forbidden to engage, namely, auditing, commercial business, save to the extent permitted by rules made by the National Council with the approval of the Minister of Justice, any other business prescribed by such rules as a business which is not befitting the profession of advocacy. If the Chamber decides not to accept a candidate as a member of the Chamber it must inform him in writing of the reasons for its refusal and the candidate may appeal to the Supreme Court against the refusal.

If the Chamber decides to accept a candidate as a member of the Chamber, or the Supreme Court sets aside its refusal to accept him as a member, the Chamber must register him in the register of members of the Chamber and give him a certificate of membership, and from the date of his registration he may practise the profession of advocacy.

A District Disciplinary Tribunal may cancel the registration of a member of the Chamber if it is proved to it that the registration was obtained by fraud. An appeal from its decision will lie to the Supreme Court.

The membership of a member of the Chamber will terminate in any of the following cases: (1) he has notified the Chamber in writing of his withdrawal from the Chamber; (2) he has ceased to be a resident of Israel; the date of his ceasing to be a resident of Israel will be fixed by the Chamber subject to an appeal to the Supreme Court; (3) he has been declared bankrupt; (4) he has been sentenced by a Disciplinary Tribunal to expulsion from the Chamber and the sentence has been carried out.

The membership of a member of the Chamber will be suspended if he has been declared by a judgment as legally incompetent by reason of mental illness—so long as the judgment is not set aside, or if the Chamber has decided, subject to an appeal to the Supreme Court, on the basis of a certificate of a District Psychiatrist, that he is incapable by reason of mental illness of looking after his own affairs—so long as the decision is not set aside, or if he has been ordered to be suspended by a Disciplinary Tribunal—for the period of suspension.

A person who has withdrawn from the Chamber, or whose membership has terminated for some other reason and that reason no longer exists, may apply for renewal of his membership of the the Chamber, and provisions similar to those applicable to an application for acceptance as a member of the Chamber will apply to the application for renewal of membership, save that the Chamber may not refuse renewal of membership except by reason of a conviction or facts which came into existence after the termination of his membership. A person who has been sentenced to expulsion from the Chamber may not apply for renewal of his membership until after the expiration of ten years from his expulsion, and the Chamber may, in its discretion, agree to the renewal of his membership or refuse it.

Special provisions are made for members of the Chamber who become Judges or do not practise as advocates.

The sixth chapter deals with professional etiquette and disciplinary jurisdiction, defining in detail the powers and procedure of the Disciplinary Tribunals.

With regard to professional etiquette it is provided that an advocate must preserve the honour of the profession of advocacy and refrain from doing anything liable to affect it. In the performance of his duties he must act for the good of his client faithfully and devotedly and assist the Court in doing justice. He must not advertise himself as practising the profession of advocacy. The cases and manner in which he may, or is obliged to, indicate his name and profession will be prescribed by rules made by the National Council of the Chamber with the approval of the Minister of Justice. An advocate may not, by himself or through any other person, solicit any person to give him professional work. He must indicate his profession by use of the title 'advocate', or the corresponding title in other languages to be fixed by rules, but by no other title. He may not practise his profession in partnership with any person who is not an advocate, or share his net or gross income with any such person in consideration for the services, assistance, or other benefit, to his business from that person. An advocate may not employ in his office, without permission from the Chamber, a person who has been suspended, during the period of suspension, or a person who has been expelled from the Chamber.

The law defines the acts or omissions which constitute disciplinary offences and provides that an advocate is answerable before the Disciplinary Tribunals of the Chamber for a disciplinary offence even if it is committed abroad.

The penalties which a District Disciplinary Tribunal may impose upon a person convicted of a disciplinary offence are (1) a warning (2) a reprimand (3) suspension for a period not exceeding five years (4) expulsion from the Chamber.

A District Disciplinary Tribunal may also, upon the application of an accuser, impose one of those penalties upon an advocate convicted in an ordinary court or a court-martial by a final judgment of a criminal offence if it finds that in the circumstances of the case the offence involves moral turpitude.

Both the accused and the accuser may appeal to the National Disciplinary Tribunal against a judgment of a District Disciplinary Tribunal, and so may the Attorney General even where he was the accuser. The accused may appeal to the Supreme Court against a conviction by the National Disciplinary Tribunal.

The seventh chapter of the law deals with advocate's fees, including minimum and maximum tariffs of fees.

The National Council of the Chamber is empowered to fix a minimum tariff of fees for the services of an advocate, and when a minimum tariff of fees for any particular service has been fixed, an advocate may not agree to, or receive, a lower fee than the minimum, save with permission of the District Committee given in any particular matter or class of matters, but an advocate may give his services free of charge if he gives the District Committee a reasoned notice thereof.

Where the Minister of Justice has prescribed by regulations particular classes of services for which a maximum tariff of fees is to be fixed, the National Council of the Chamber must fix the tariff, and when it has fixed the maximum tariff of fees for any particular service, an advocate may not agree to, or receive, a higher fee, save with permission given by the District Committee in a particular matter.

Both the minimum and maximum tariffs of fees require the approval of the Minister of Justice.

An advocate may not agree to, or receive, for his services in a criminal case a fee which depends upon the results of the case. Where an advocate has agreed to, or received, a fee depending upon the results of a case other than a criminal case and it appears to the Chamber that the fee is excessive it may, upon the application of his client, fix the appropriate fee.

An advocate may not agree to, or receive, from his client any payment which includes both his fee and the expenses he disbursed, without distinguishing between his fee and the expenses and without giving details of the expenses.

If an advocate agrees to, or receives, a fee contrary to the above, he will be guilty of a disciplinary offence, although in certain cases he will not be disentitled to a proper fee for his services, and where a person has paid a fee in excess of that due from him he may demand the refund of the excess notwithstanding any agreement.

In order to ensure payment of his fees and the reimbursement of the expenses disbursed by him, an advocate may retain moneys of his client which he has obtained with the consent of his client by reason of his services to his client, save for moneys given to him on deposit or as a trustee, and so long as he is a trustee thereof otherwise than only for the benefit of his client, and save for moneys constituting maintenance for a wife or children, and he may also retain property and documents of his client which he has obtained by reason of his services, provided that he files a claim for his fee or his expenses within three months of the date when it became known to him that his client disputes his right to that fee or those expenses.

An advocate is forbidden without his client's consent to disclose in any legal proceeding, or any enquiry or search, anything or any document passing between him and his client connected with the professional services rendered by the advocate to his client.

The budget of the Chamber will be fixed by the National Council, and it may by decision of the National Council, impose upon its members membership dues and fees to finance its activities.

Notaries for Foreign Documents

Notaries for foreign documents are licensed under the Notaries for Foreign Documents Law, 5710–1950, of the 18th May, 1950, by the Minister of Justice on the recommendation of a committee composed of the Attorney General to the Government, as chairman, and four other members appointed by the Minister of Justice from among the members of the Chamber of Advocates upon the recommendation of the National Council of the Chamber of Advocates. Applicants for a licence must be registered in the register of members of the Chamber of Advocates and have served or engaged, continuously or intermittently, for at least ten years, at least two of which were in this country, in one of the following functions: (1) advocacy (2) a Judge to whom the Judges Law, 5713–1953 applies (see p. 204); (3) a judicial or legal function approved under section 2 of the Judges Law, 5713–1953; (4) a judicial, legal or notarial function abroad, for which only a person with a legal education is qualified.

Notaries for foreign documents are authorised to do the following acts: (1) to attest signatures on documents signed before them (2) to certify the correctness of copies of documents, provided that the document and the copy are produced to them (3) to certify the correctness of the translation of documents into languages with which they are fully conversant, whether the translation has been made by them or by some other person (4) to receive and attest declarations on oath, declarations on affirmation and all other declarations (5) to certify that a particular person is alive, provided that such certification may not be given unless that person appeared before the notary on the day on which the certification was given (6) to certify the correctness of an inventory drawn up by him or by someone else in his presence (7) to certify that a person who signed before him a document for a corporation was authorised to sign the document for the corporation, provided that the authority of the signatory so to sign has been proved to the notary by the registers kept in

accordance with any enactment, either by a public official
or otherwise, or by means of other documents which afford
evidence thereof (8) to certify that a person who signed before
him a document on behalf of another person was authorised to
sign that document on behalf of that other person, provided that
the authority of the signatory so to sign is proved to the notary
by means of documents which afford evidence thereof. The above
attestations and certifications will only be valid for use abroad,
including use in any legation of a foreign state in Israel.

In addition, a notary for foreign documents may draw up any
document, and do any other act in connection with documents,
where the drawing up of the document or the doing of the act by a
notary public is required for use abroad including use in any legation of a foreign state in Israel.

The Minister of Justice, upon the recommendation of the Recommendations Committee, may, in certain specified cases take a-
gainst notaries disciplinary action similar to that which may be
taken against an advocate under the Chamber of Advocates Law,
5721–1961, (see pp. 240–1). The notary may appeal to the
Supreme Court against such a recommendation.

The fees which a notary may take for his services and the cases
in which there is an exemption from fees are prescribed by the
Minister of Justice by regulations.

Notaries Public

In addition, there are Notaries Public who are State officials
attached to the Courts. They act under the Ottoman Notary Public Law (of 1913), and their main functions are to draw up the
documents specified in the Law, to certify translations and signatures on documents, to register protests of bills for non-payment and to send notarial notices. Documents drawn up by Notaries Public, under the Law, need no further proof, and when
they are submitted to the Courts and Government Departments
there is no need to prove their contents, although when a Notary
Public does not draw up a document but merely certifies the signature thereon, his certification proves only the date and signature
but not the contents. Certain documents drawn up by a Notary

Public, such as acknowledgments of debt, may be executed as if they were a judgment of a Court.

FUTURE LEGISLATION

FROM THE foregoing summary, it can be seen that, quite apart from the law applicable in matters of personal status, the law of Israel is still far from homogeneous in its composition and that in order fully to understand it, it is necessary to have a knowledge of three systems of law—the Mohammedan, the French and the English systems of law, and the four languages in which that law, or the law upon which it was modelled, was originally written— namely, Turkish, Arabic, French and English, and also a fifth language, namely, Hebrew, in which the laws of Israel are now being written.

During the period of the Mandatory regime all legislation was published in each of three official languages, English, Arabic and Hebrew, and, under section 34 of the Interpretation Ordinance, 1945, in the case of any discrepancy between the English text and the Arabic or Hebrew text, the English text prevailed. Hebrew is the language of the Israel legislation, and official translations in Arabic and English, prepared in the Ministry of Justice, are published. Section 32 of the new Hebrew version of the Interpretation Ordinance, 1945, provides that, where there is any discrepancy between the Hebrew text of any enactment and the official translation thereof into a foreign language, the Hebrew text shall prevail, and that, where there is any discrepancy between the English text and any other text of any enactment passed before the establishment of the State and not published in a new Hebrew version under section 16 of the Law and Administration Ordinance, 5708 - 1948, the English text shall prevail. The said section 16, as enacted by Section 1 of the Law and Administration Ordinance Amendment (No 10) Law, 5724–1964, of the 2nd April, 1964, empowers the Minister of Justice to publish in *Reshumot* a draft of a new Hebrew version of any law, including any Order in Council, which obtained in Palestine on the eve of the establishment of the

State and is still in force in Israel and such version embodies all the changes resulting from the establishment of the State and its authorities and all the changes made in that law by legislation after the establishment of the State. The Minister of Justice establishes Advisory Committees composed of five members, one of whom, the chairman, is a Judge recommended by the President of the Supreme Court, the second is the Attorney General or his representative, the third is a member of the Chamber of Advocates recommended by that Chamber, the fourth is a jurist recommended by the Law Faculty of the Hebrew University, Jerusalem, and the fifth is a person recommended by the Minister charged with the implementation of the law in question. That Committee examines the draft version and submits to the Constitution, Law and Justice Committee of the Knesset its proposals as to the corrections which, in its opinion, should be made in order that the draft version should be in conformity with the original law and include the said changes. The Constitution, Law and Justice Committee then fixes the final text of the new Hebrew version in the light of the proposals of the Advisory Committee, and when it has done so, the new Hebrew version must be published in *Reshumot* under the hand of the Minister of Justice within the time fixed by the Constitution, Law and Justice Committee. When the new Hebrew version has been so published it will come into force on the date of its publication or the date fixed by the said Committee, and it will constitute the binding version of the law, and no other version of the law will thereafter have any effect, and no plea that the Hebrew version deviates from the original law will be entertained.

Similar provisions are made by the said section 16 for the preparation, publication, and binding effect, of a consolidated version of any law enacted in Israel, including any new Hebrew version.

The first Palestine Ordinance to be published in a new Hebrew version under the said section 16 was the Interpretation Ordinance, 1945, which was published in *Reshumot* on the 1st January, 1954, and since then twelve other Ordinances have been published in a new Hebrew version. They are: the Bills of Exchange Ordinance, the Customs Ordinance, the Intoxicating Liquors(Manufacture and Sale) Ordinance, the Methylated Spirits Ordinance, the Banderolles Ordinance, the Matches Excise Ordinance, the Playing Cards Excise Ordinance, the Tobacco Ordinance, the Income Tax Ordinance, the Road Transport Ordinance,the Municipal Corporations Ordinance, and the Local Councils Ordinance. In addition, the following laws have been published in a consolidated version: the Knesset Elections Law, the State Comptroller Law, Traffic Offences-Trial of Soldiers Law, Disabled (Gratuities and Rehabilitation) Law, Security Service Law, Reserve Service (Gratuities) Law, Cooperative Houses Law.

It will be the task of the legislature of Israel to replace the heterogeneous body of Israel law by a homogeneous body of law written in one language—Hebrew—and suited to the needs of a modern, progressive state. What will be the basis of such law is not yet known, despite the fact that more than one thousand laws have been enacted since the establishment of the State. Whatever it may be, the legislature of Israel has a truly formidable task ahead of it.

BIBLIOGRAPHY

There are many books written in Hebrew on a large variety of branches of Israel law, such as Civil Procedure, Criminal Procedure, Evidence, Criminal Law, Civil Wrongs, Contracts, Legal Drafting, Taxation, Bills of Exchange, Companies, Cooperative Societies, Arbitration, Land Law, Labour Legislation, Local Government, the Knesset, Road Transport and Personal Status, but there are few books written in English, or any other European language, on any branch of Israel law. Nearly all the literature on Israel law in any of those languages is confined to articles in foreign legal periodicals, collections of essays and reports to international conferences, and a few articles in Israel periodicals and publications such as the annual Public Administration in Israel and Abroad, monographs published by the Institute for Legislative Research and Comparative Law of the Law Faculty of the Hebrew University of Jerusalem, and the annual survey of Israel legislation written by the author of this book and published annually since 1950 in the Israel Year Book.

A comprehensive Israel Bibliography in European Languages compiled by Dr. Ernst Livneh and containing over 300 entries was published in 1963 by the said Institute under the auspices of the International Association of Legal Science, and a supplement thereto containing about 90 entries was published in 1965. Since then the first number of the English language Israel Law Review, published under the auspices of the Law Faculty of the Hebrew University of Jerusalem, appeared in January, 1966 and thereafter has appeared regularly once every three months, and, among others, the following books have appeared:

The Israeli Criminal Procedure Law, 5725—1965, being Volume 13 of the American Series of Foreign Penal Codes edited by G.O.N. Mueller.

Studies in Israel Private Law by Prof. G. Tedeschi. (1966)
Evasion and Avoidance of Income Tax by Dr. A. Lapidoth. (1966)
Government in Israel by Dr. Y. Freudenheim. (1967)
Knesset : The Parliament of Israel by A. Zidon. (1967)

INDEX

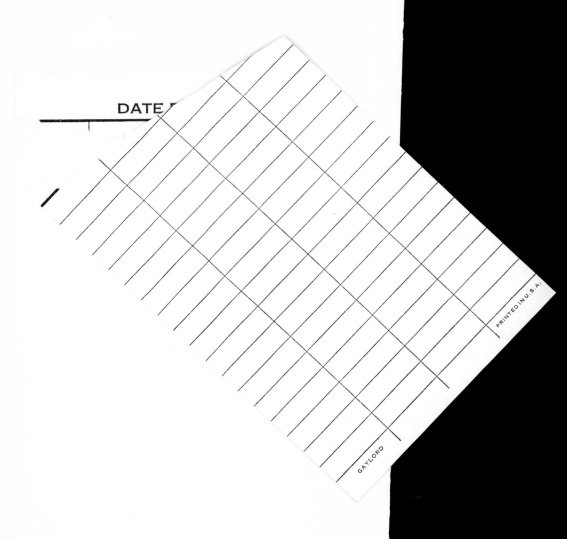